Ready or Not

KAY S. HYMOWITZ

Ready or Not

What Happens

When We Treat

Children as

Small Adults

ENCOUNTER BOOKS
SAN FRANCISCO

ENCOUNTER BOOKS

First paperback edition published in 2000 by Encounter Books, an activity of Encounter for Culture and Education, Inc., a nonprofit tax exempt corporation.
First published in 1999 by The Free Press.

Encounter Books website address: www.encounterbooks.com

Cover design by Nick Collier

Manufactured in the United States and printed on acid-free paper.

The paper used in this publication meets the minimum requirements of ANSI/NISO Z39.48-1992 (R 1997) (Permanence of Paper).

Library of Congress Cataloging-in-Publication Data

Hymowitz, Kay S., 1948–
    Ready or not : what happens when we treat children as small adults / Kay S. Hymowitz.
        p. cm.
    Includes bibliographical references and index.
    ISBN 1-893554-20-1
    1. Children—United States-Social conditions. 2. Children and adults—United States. 3. Child rearing—United States. I. Title.
HQ792.U5H86 2000
305.23'0973-dc21   00-32764
                                                                        CIP

To Danny and Nora: *Ready*

and Anna: *Not Yet*

Contents

Empty
Nests

"The twentieth-century," predicted Ellen Key, an early twentieth-century advocate for children, "will be the century of the child."[1] At the time Key was writing, there was reason for such a hope. Building on a long-standing American concern with children, progressive reformers set out to "discover" childhood. They rid the nation of child labor and ensured educational opportunities through much of the teenage years. They instituted a separate justice system intended to protect mischievous or "delinquent" adolescents from overly harsh penalties and adult jails. Yet as the century draws to a close, Key's optimism, one shared by many people of her time, can't help but hold a special poignancy for America. For it appears that the century has discovered childhood only to lose it.

Few Americans are unaware of the profound transformation over the last thirty years in the way children look and act. Indeed, these changes seem connected to some of our most troubling and prominent social problems. Children are committing so many more serious crimes of the sort once thought beyond their capacity that some legal experts are recommending abandoning the juvenile court that was designed to protect them and simply trying them in adult court.[2] Nor are these crimes limited to poor and older adolescents. The city of

Indianapolis was forced to expand its gun search policy into its elementary schools after an eight-year-old pointed a gun at a classmate for "teasing him about his ears."[3] And in a crime that left the nation reeling, two gun-wielding youths from well-to-do, two-parent homes killed twelve of their classmates and a teacher in Littleton, Colorado in April 1999.[4]

Sexual intercourse, once considered a pleasure reserved for adults, has become commonplace among kids and has led to dramatic increases in the rates of out-of-wedlock childbirth, welfare dependency, fatherlessness, and abortion. Even though the percentage of teens having sex has decreased somewhat in recent years, sexual activity has trickled down to ever-younger ages.[5] Experts say they are unsurprised by the sexual sophistication of twelve-year-olds. In 1993 the schools in New Haven, Connecticut, began distributing condoms to fifth graders.[6] And according to the *New York Times* health columnist Jane Brody, experts believe parents should begin teaching girls "how and why to say 'no' and what to do should they say 'yes'" at *nine* years old, an age that would shock almost any culture.[7]

Signs of the waning of childhood are also evident in the ordinary day-to-day rhythms and symbols of children's lives. Infants now have "lapware" computers with educational programs and work out at baby gyms. It's not uncommon to hear about soccer teams for three-year-olds and tackle football teams complete with shoulder pads and helmets for seven-year-olds.[8] Indeed, by elementary school many children are on the fast track: some educators have damned recess as "a waste of time" and have markedly increased the homework loads even of first graders.[9] No information is off-limits for children today. Third graders recite jokes told by David Letterman the previous night—and their napping and irritability in class suggest that they heard them firsthand.[10] Nor is the media their only source: kindergartners might be studying the Holocaust or AIDS in school.[11] Marketing expert Faith Popcorn predicts that in the next millennium "we're going to see health clubs for kids, kids as experts on things like the Internet, and new businesses like Kinko's for Kids, to provide professional-quality project presentations."[12]

Perhaps the most noticeable changes, occurring largely during the last decade alone, are among kids between eight and twelve, known to marketers as "tweens." Bruce Friend, vice president of worldwide research and planning for the children's television network Nickelodeon, reports that in the last ten years, kids between ten and twelve have started to act and dress more like yesterdays's twelve-to-fourteen-year-olds. By eleven, Friend says, kids in focus groups say they no longer think of themselves as children. The Nickelodeon-Yankelovich Youth Monitor Survey found that by the time they are twelve, children describe themselves as "flirtatious, sexy, trendy, cool."[13] The cosmetics and fashion industries have introduced lip gloss, "hair mascara," body paint, and scented body oils (with names like Vanilla Vibe and Follow Me Boy) for the ten-year-old sophisticate. By contrast, the toy industry has nothing to celebrate in the twilight of childhood marked by the arrival of the tween; whereas a generation ago the industry could count on those between birth and fourteen as their target market, today that market has diminished to those between birth and ten.[14]

What is it about our contemporary social environment that has made childhood an endangered species? The psychologist David Elkind believes "the hurried child" is the offspring of stressed-out, overambitious parents responding to an increasingly competitive society. Citing the rapidity with which divorce and family breakdown spiraled upward through the seventies, Marie Winn argues that children are "without childhood" because there is now an "end of secrecy"; their parents are no longer protecting them from what was once considered adult, especially sexual, information. Social critic Neil Postman shares Winn's view that the end of secrecy is key to the "disappearance of childhood," but he believes the culprit is television. Because they possess more information, Postman argues, parents have power over children, just as political leaders have power over their subjects. When literacy was a prerequisite for knowledge, children could be kept in the dark. But television, Postman says, is "a total disclosure medium"; it makes formerly taboo knowledge available to the youngest children and puts them on an equal footing with their elders.[15]

While acknowledging the impact of these social realities—the de-

cline of traditional domestic arrangements, the demands of a merito-
cratic society, the growing presence of a hypersexualized, violent media—this book will point to another cause of childhood's present
state. The disappearance of childhood is, to a far greater extent than
previously understood, a result of conscious human design. It is directly related to the ideas and actions of those who help shape our
understanding of children—psychologists, psychiatrists, educators,
child advocates, lawmakers, advertisers, marketers, and storytellers
both in print and on the screen. Very rarely have any of them openly
rejected the idea of childhood, of course. What they have done is far
more subtle. They have helped to advance the idea of children as capable, rational, and autonomous, as beings endowed with all the qualities necessary for their entrance into the adult world—qualities such
as talents, interests, values, conscience, and a conscious sense of themselves. In this view, children need little shaping by adults; they are essentially "finished," and childhood has lost its traditional purpose as
the time set aside for shaping raw human material into a culturally
competent adult.

The idea that Americans think of children as already complete
may seem counterintuitive. Don't we believe that people are products
of their environment? Don't we worry about children growing up in
poverty for precisely that reason? Well, yes and no. Americans do
take it as a given that children need certain fundamentals to thrive—
things like food and shelter, love and stimulation. They assume that
in the absence of these things children do poorly in school, take drugs,
get pregnant, or commit crimes. What they don't believe, what they
no longer articulate, is the idea that children must be inducted by
their elders into a preexisting society, into a web of meaning—in
short, into a culture. Instead, it is up to kids to create the world for
themselves. As Patricia Hersch writes in her book *A Tribe Apart,*
which chronicles the lives of high schoolers in Reston, Virginia,
"Everything is up for debate, from the meaning of calculus to the
meaning of life itself."[16] In contemporary America, cultural authorities portray children as solitary and autonomous observers, investigat-
ing and judging the world entirely on their own terms. Adults are reduced to personal trainers or mere companions for the child in his or

her solitary development. They may have a role in instructing children in some skills and in delivering some unfamiliar information to them, but they have no role in either socializing them or investing the information with meaning and value. Their job is to "empower" children, build their self-esteem, and lovingly wait for the complete individual to sprout into being from inside its bodily husk.

The belief that the child should develop independently of the prevailing culture and even in opposition to it is what I call anticulturalism, and it is at the root of what has gone wrong with childhood in America. Anticulturalism is the dominant ideology among child development experts, and it has filtered into the courts, into the schools, into the parenting magazines, into Hollywood, and into our kitchens and family rooms. It is no mere abstraction. The era of anticulturalism is producing a new kind of American personality, one that should give us great pause.

One dominant theory about moral development offers a good overview of what anticulturalism is all about. In most cultures, it is axiomatic that adults civilize children by teaching them the rules of morality and insisting that they restrain their antisocial impulses. But for Carol Gilligan, the most influential American expert on moral development today, adults are the problem; the kids are okay. Gilligan's theory evolved as she studied the students at the Laurel School, a private school in Cleveland. From her observations she concluded that preadolescent girls are more moral than either their older counterparts or their elders. They are "genuine," she claims, and they "speak of their thoughts and feelings about relationships in direct ways."[17] This authenticity is a sign of their "wisdom and generosity" and a product of insights that "constitute the core of moral wisdom."[18] The real problem for children occurs when adults interfere with these abundant natural gifts. Though the girls at the Laurel School might strike some as cliquish and cruel, Gilligan is convinced that her subjects have undergone not too little of the civilizing process but too much. As they mature, the innately moral self of these girls is drowned out by the "foreign voice-overs of adults," "the disembodied lines from parents and teachers." Attempts to make them do such things as complete their homework, wait their turn, and share with their classmates result in "psychological foot-binding." The once lively, honest girls lose their natural and authentic "voice" and succumb to doubt, self-abnegation, and "silence."[19] Here is the anticultural myth resplendent: children are naturally moral creatures who are ruined by the adults who attempt to civilize them.

A new crop of books, supposedly more realistic about children's need for real guidance from adults, likewise reveal the persistent hold of anticultural thinking. Robert Coles' bestselling *The Moral Intelligence of Children* at first appears to avoid the anticultural trap, as the author asserts that parents and teachers are not offering enough moral guidance for children. But his claim about "how 'character' develops in the young" is at odds with Coles' conclusion that children are not simply moral, but "morally intelligent." He ponders children's observations as if they were the koans of Zen masters. He cites "the stillness of bodies, the rapt attention" and the "moral vitality" of children during his classroom discussions with them. A treasured anecdote, repeated by Coles in a number of television interviews, demonstrates the wisdom of his nine-year-old son, who tells him to slow down because he might cause an accident when he is racing the injured boy to the hospital. "My son had become my moral instructor," Coles marvels.[20] In the anticultural United States, the child is often father to the man.

It may make sense to suggest, as Gilligan and Coles do, that human beings have an innate capacity for moral behavior. After all, we could not have developed a civilization without some natural orientation toward group feeling and harmony. But it makes equal sense to conclude from history, not to mention children's treatment of their siblings, that there is also a darker side to human nature. Until the middle of the twentieth century, it was considered an obvious fact that children are prone to cruelty, aggression, and boundless egotism and that a major purpose of their upbringing is to restrain and redirect those impulses. Though his contemporaries held back, Freud went so far as to add sexual perversion and patricidal wishes to the gallery of childhood evils.

One sees abundant proof of the existence of this darker side in newspaper headlines and school playgrounds, but rarely is it visible in the tracts of American experts. After perusing books on moral development, the political scientist James Q. Wilson expressed surprise that he could not find one reference to self-restraint.[21] He needn't have been surprised, for in the experts' view, America's children have no urges worth restraining. Children's nature has been whitewashed. The word *impulse* has been erased from expert tracts, and *instinct,* which once evoked our animalistic legacy, has been sanitized into constructive drives such as the "language instinct." Even sociobiologists, who seek the sources of human behavior in our distant animal past, seem more inclined to explore the biological tendency toward altruism and empathy than the aggression we usually associate with the life of the beast.

According to the social historian Peter Stearns, while nineteenth-century advice manuals worried about children's cruelty *toward* animals, by the middle of the twentieth century experts were more likely to fret about their fear *of* animals.[22] Anne MacLeod, in a comparison of nineteenth- and late-twentieth-century children's literature, has found something similar: Nineteenth-century books contain child characters who frequently misbehave or demonstrate cruelty, such stories dramatizing for children the dangers of their self-centeredness. But by the mid–twentieth century, child heroes seem to have no personal lessons to learn and never require punishment. Judy Blume's highly popular novels, for instance, portray many egotistic children "without comment and certainly without criticism."[23]

Parents, though they have plenty of reason to dispute this sunny thinking, seem to share this strain of expert optimism about their children. One study found that American mothers tend to see their children's positive characteristics as "inborn and stable over time" while their less positive ones are viewed as "transitory and extrinsically caused."[24] A common complaint among educators is the tendency of today's parents to insist, "It wasn't my kid; it must have been the other one," when confronted with evidence of the child's misbehavior. In fact, Americans cling to the idea—and the hope—of children's overall mental and emotional competence. In the middle decades of the century, the Swiss psychologist Jean Piaget was confronted so often by experts and parents who wondered whether children could be propelled faster through what he believed to be slowly unfolding developmental stages that he dubbed it "the American Question." It appears to remain so. Thirty years later, David Elkind lectured across the country about the myth of what he called the "Superkid"—to no avail. On the subject of children's competence, he found, Americans will not be moved.[25]

This sturdy optimism about children's natures should not be confused with romantic and Victorian pieties about childhood innocence. True, the romantic legacy shows signs of life in American culture. Writers like Coles and Jonathan Kozol sometimes recall this tradition at its most bathetic. "This is not God's kingdom," says a Christlike twelve-year-old in Kozol's *Amazing Grace: The Lives of Children and the Conscience of a Nation* as he gestures toward his devastated South Bronx neighborhood. "A kingdom is a place of glory. This is a place of pain."[26] A ten-year-old leukemia victim described by Coles ("light shone in his eyes") still manages a prayer for his doctors and nurses.[27] And politicians on both sides of the aisle are also prone to imagine children as Blakean figures of social protest against a selfish and immoral age.

The contemporary competent and self-sufficient child, however, is less the offspring of the romantic tradition than the progeny of unique modern forces, among them science and technology. The child of the computer age is efficient and orderly rather than pure and innocent. The changing view of infancy over the past few decades provides the most dramatic example of this shift. Unlike the behaviorists, who dominated the world of psychology for many decades and who believed that the infant brain was a blank slate upon which parents could write, cognitive scientists, who rose to prominence in the late 1960s with a version of that brain that continues to predominate, view infants as wondrously practical and constructive. "Babies are learning machines," *Newsweek* announced in 1997.[28] Ceaselessly, automatically learning, children are unperturbed by emotions and irrational needs. They want only information and input. It is little wonder that in just a few years they will display a natural gift for morality.

By adding hip sophistication to the list of child talents, the market has also helped to flesh out the picture of child competence. Sophisticated kids with a knowing smirk on their face are a common motif on the screen and in glossy magazines. These kids are frequently accom-panied by clueless adults, most of them men. The following text of a 1994 ad for *Time* runs above a picture of a worried-looking middle-aged man and a teenager with a "can you believe he's so stupid?" ex-pression: "These days when a father says, 'Son, I think it's time we have a little talk about sex,' the reply is apt to be 'OK, Dad, what did you want to know?'" Though stirring up trouble between the genera-tions has been a media ploy since at least the 1930s, television has insis-tently summoned children to consider themselves autonomous indi-viduals who have little to learn from their elders. Especially over the past twenty-five years, as women have moved into the workforce in large numbers, the divorce rate has soared, and "home alone" chil-dren have come to make more and more decisions about family pur-chases as well as their own, this image of hip sophistication has topped all others; cuteness, reports one media watcher, is "now considered passé."[29] Kids are more in charge, and marketers, knowing an un-tapped market when they see one, are not ones to protest. "Power to the people! The Little People that is!" cries an article about advertis-ing to children in the *New York Times*.[30]

The idea that children are autonomous, independent individuals discovering their own reality is an understandable outcome of the evolution of American political thought. Individual autonomy, the right to live life as we want, to think and judge for ourselves, to make our own decisions, has always been a central dogma in the nation's civic religion. Indeed, self-determination is the founding principle of this country. But children muddy this sacred principle. How can we who value self-determination so highly tell people, even little people, how to think and what to do? "Children are the Achilles heel of lib-eral ideology," one legal scholar has wisely observed.[31] At some point, most American parents are confronted with a child who upon being told she cannot see a desired movie or go to a certain friend's house cries, "It's a free country!" These words signal the child's discovery that something is amiss, or "not fair," in his social standing. This is a dilemma among parents as well, as Robert Bellah and his cowriters reveal in *Habits of the Heart,* an analysis of late-twentieth-century American beliefs about individualism. "For highly individuated Americans," they write, "there is something anomalous about the relations between parents and children, for the biologically normal dependence of children on adults is perceived as morally abnormal."[32]

When you add to this moral quandary the giddy chaos of a young, driving, ever-changing immigrant country, you end up with conditions unfriendly toward the conventional arrangement between adults and children. Under ordinary circumstances, children are strangers in a strange land and parents act as their experienced guides into the sacred knowledge of their culture, its language and emotions, its beliefs and rituals. For immigrants, the situation is often painfully reversed: it is the children who quickly come to understand the customs and language of their country, and the parents, tied to old-world ways and slower to absorb a new language, must learn from them. Native-born American parents, however, have not been spared this generational confusion. In a society infatuated with progress and all things new, parents often hesitate before asserting familiar rules; instead, they turn to their children for cues about what the seductive and unpredictable future holds.

But if in deeming the child an autonomous, self-determining individual Americans are holding fast to some of their own ideals, they are turning their backs on other universally understood truths. Even in the most primitive societies, people have believed that the transformation of children into socialized individuals who understand the requirements of their culture is an intensive process lasting years and requiring the active and sustained intervention of mother, father, grandparents, older siblings, and other relatives. During the seventeenth and eighteenth centuries, in response to technological and social changes, Western cultures began to lengthen and intensify this process, increasing the number of years children were kept out of the workforce, separated from the adult world, and given more parental devotion.

In America, these Western notions took on their own distinct coloring. By the early 1800s, ministers, intellectuals, and other cultural representatives began the process of framing what I'll be calling a "republican childhood," one in keeping with the ideals of the new country. Republican childhood had one central purpose: to vigorously prepare the young for freedom. In order to shape "self-governing" individuals, its architects rejected what until that time was an almost universal acceptance of corporal punishment and urged parents to appeal to their children's hearts and powers of reason. They encouraged them to awaken their children's minds and stir their interests by giving them time to play freely and by supplying the now recognizably middle-class home with toys and books. Yet republican childhood was still a serious business. Parents had to teach their children to balance personal ambition with a concern for the public good, respect for the law with critical independence, fidelity with entrepreneurial drive. No one believed that the transmission of these complex and highly contradictory cultural values would come naturally. Republican theorists saw it as a mammoth human undertaking, the psychic equivalent of digging a huge, multileveled, interconnected subway system. They believed that successful completion of this project required fifteen or twenty years, the hour-by-hour attentions of a mother, the emotional and financial support of a father, and the respectful attention of an entire society.

Today we cast a dubious eye on the domestic arrangements that supported republican childhood, which, we now understand, are peculiar to the modern Western world and have so often been stifling for women. But that should not prevent us from appreciating many of the goals and methods of this republican tradition, both of which remain highly relevant to us today. For all its problems—and there were many—republican childhood was based on a number of seemingly paradoxical truths that anticulturalism ignores: that adults must mold children into free individuals, that children do not naturally know how to shape their lives according to their own vision, and that both democratic government and free enterprise impose especially strong demands on us as citizens *and* as parents.

Under the reign of anticulturalism, the sense of adult purpose that was inspired by these truths is largely lost. Doubtless this is partly a practical matter. Many Americans simply feel they don't have the time to satisfy the demands of traditional parenting. Financial pressures have led many women out of the home and into the workforce. In 1960, close to 70 percent of American children had the day in, day out attention of stay-at-home mothers. By contrast, today only about 30 percent of kids under eighteen, including only a little over 35 percent of preschoolers, have mothers at home all day. Of course, middle-class women have also moved into the workplace in huge numbers. Regardless of family income, kids are spending less time with their parents and home life has become what the psychologist Kenneth Gergen has called "less a nesting place than a pit stop."[33] "By 8:30 A.M.," writes Patricia Hersch of suburban Reston, Virginia, "neighborhoods stand still and silent—hollow monuments to family life."[34] In the wealthy county of Westchester, New York, some children go to "homework clubs" that are open from 3 to 8 P.M., where working parents hire surrogates to watch their kids, help them with homework, supervise their violin practice, and occasionally feed them dinner.[35] Other kids are not so fortunate. It has been estimated that some seven million children are in "self-care" after school.[36] Between 1970 and 1990, white children lost an average of ten hours a week of parental time and black children, twelve.[37] In a 1996 study of twenty thousand teenagers, Laurence Steinberg concluded that disengaged parents were the primary reason the schools were seeing a greater number of troubled and indifferent students.[38]

Economic and work pressures may make some of this parenting drain unavoidable, but a good deal of it is related to the anticultural ideas we will explore throughout the following pages. Surrounded by putatively competent and autonomously developing children, parents—in fact, all adults—find themselves lacking a clear job description in their relationship with children. In her 1961 classic, *The Death and Life of Great American Cities,* Jane Jacobs evokes the casually assumed role of adults of a previous era. "When Mr. Lacey, the locksmith, bawls out one of my sons for running into the street, and then later reports the transgression to my husband as he passes the locksmith shop, my son gets more than an overt lesson in safety and obedience. He also gets, indirectly, the lesson that Mr. Lacey, with whom we have no ties other than street propinquity, feels responsible for him to a degree."[39] Mr. Lacey would appear to have gone the way of the iceman: A survey published by Public Agenda found that only 39 percent of adults would be comfortable reprimanding kids who are misbehaving in a public area, and only 33 percent would be comfortable telling neighbors if their child was getting into trouble.[40]

Parents too show signs of withdrawing from their role as guides for the inexperienced. According to the same study by Public Agenda, parents feel "tentative and uncertain in matters of discipline and authority."[41] Evelyn Bassoff, a Colorado therapist, reports that when she asks the women in her mothers' groups what happens when they discipline their daughters, they give answers such as "I feel mean," "I feel guilty," "I feel like an old fuddy-duddy," and "I quake all over; it's almost like having dry heaves inside."[42] Wealthy parents trying to avoid encounters that might bring on such feelings have been known to hire tutors to do homework with their kids.[43] Educators around the country report witnessing this anxious confusion. "I'm hearing statements like, 'What can I do? I can't make him read,'" the director of a New York City middle school told me. "And the child is in fifth grade. What does it mean that an adult feels he cannot make a ten-year-old do something?" A rural New York principal concurs: "I used to say to a kid behaving rudely, 'Young man, would you speak that way at home?' and he would hang his head and say, 'No.' Now I ask a kid and he looks surprised and says, 'Yeah.'"[44]

This youthful incivility points to the disturbingly ironic consequences of anticulturalism. Many people today believe that traditional American childhood, which is now misleadingly imagined as an endless repetition of a *Father Knows Best* episode rather than an arrangement founded on republican ideals, was as stifling and oppressive to children as it was to mothers. The 1998 movie *Pleasantville,* for instance, depicts a domestic scene of smiling faces and punctual family dinners that belies the small-mindedness and emotional shallowness that gripped the movie's families. But whatever the considerable limitations of American life in the 1950s, it is impossible to conclude that the waning of childhood that has come about because of anticulturalism has added to individual freedom. Quite the opposite. For one thing, because children are not the moral competents psychologist

Carol Gilligan has promised us, the adult failure to insist on informal cultural constraints and expectations has made them into prisoners of their own untamed impulses—and all too often of the law. Although juvenile crime rates have dropped from their peak in the past several years, ever-younger children are in jail in record numbers for having committed crimes much more serious than was the case twenty years ago.[45] Defense lawyers wonder at the change in their clients. "The kids I represented ten, fifteen years ago were so different," says a California attorney interviewed by Edward Humes in *No Matter How Loud I Shout*. "They were still kids. They knew right from wrong more or less ... Now ... they seem like they are brain-dead. You can't reach them."[46] Even on college campuses, according to the National Center for the Study of Campus Violence, crime has increased in amount and severity: "Harassment becomes assault," says the director of the center. "Instead of pilfering, you get grand theft auto."[47]

But though the rise in juvenile incivility and crime may be the most glaring result of anticulturalism, other more subtle consequences are in their own way just as disturbing—and as threatening to individual freedom. The stark lesson children receive from their earliest days— that they are supposed to be fully rational and self-sufficient—has carried with it a radical "downsizing" of their emotional lives.[48] Conventional wisdom has it that people today are beneficiaries of the march of emotional progress which began in the 1960s. Where once Americans were forced to repress their emotions, they now have permission to express themselves more freely and openly. This version of history ignores how much value we now place on rationality and independence at the expense of other human emotions. Simply put, the self-sufficient child cannot afford to need others very much.

To get a fuller picture of this downsizing, consider the change in the quality of the American child's home life. Compared to children of the past and in other cultures, our own kids live a remarkably isolated and fragmented existence with fewer strong and reliable attachments. Starting in infancy, they watch people come and go from their lives at nickelodeon speed. A study by the National Institute of Child Health and Development found that babies cared for by people other than their parents will typically see those caretakers change twice in their first year of life; one-third of these infants will watch three or more nurturers come and go.[49] In *The Time Bind,* a study of how employees at a Fortune 500 company balance work and family, Arlie Hochschild writes that "real people—neighbors, relatives, friends, baby sitters, teachers in after-school programs, and parents with flexible work schedules—have disappeared, while MTV, the 'new neighbor' for the latchkey child, remains only a press of a button away."[50] Almost half of all American children will spend part of their childhood living apart from a father or mother, which in turn often means not only half as much contact with grandparents, aunts, uncles, and cousins but the distracted attention of their own custodial parent.[51] Children in joint custody move from mother's house to father's every week or month, turning them into rootless migrants without a sense of place or coherent relationships. Five-year-old frequent fliers traveling alone between mother in California and father in Pennsylvania have become a common sight to airline personnel. According to writer Barbara Whitehead, "even infants are transported between households in cars or taxis, with frozen breast milk and ear infection medication tucked into their diaper bags."[52] They also have fewer siblings—as of 1994, the mean number of children under eighteen in households with children was 1.4, compared with 2.4 in 1962—and are less likely to know their neighbors or to see their grandparents regularly, though for the first time in history chances are that the elderly are likely to survive throughout their grandchildren's youthful years.[53]

There are even chillier signs of this emotional downsizing. The relationship between adults and children has been infected by the legalistic ethos that so dominates our society. Work Family Directions, a Boston company, has published a booklet titled *I Can Take Care of Myself* that recommends a pseudolegal agreement between parents and their "self-care" children about what is expected of each of them.[54] Adults working with children are warned by superiors worried about lawsuits against showing too much affection toward their young charges. "Teach but don't touch," a lawyer for the National Education Association told the membership in 1995. "If you hug a child, even a child who is hurt or crying, I will break your arms and legs . . .

If kids need help in the bathroom, take an aide with you, or let them go on the floor."[55] Trained as if they were preparing to enter the opposing counsel's meeting room, camp counselors have become "less relaxed around children," according to one camp consultant, even though youngsters "come to camp with more emotional baggage than they did just five years ago."[56] The prohibition against touching a child affects caretakers, who hold themselves back from comforting or showing affection toward their charges, fearing a misinterpreted pat or hug. Though based on a reasonable concern about accusations of physical and sexual abuse, such a prohibition, when set in the wider context of today's child's lean-and-mean emotional life, seems a sign of something larger: Americans simply do not want their children overly involved with them. In other cultures parents cite things like becoming a good spouse and parent, good citizenship, or kindness and sensitivity as their chief goals for their children. What do Americans want for their children? In every study, one stark answer predominates: independence.[57] Hochschild found that latchkey kids were more often than not the children of professional or managerial workers who wanted their kids to be self-sufficient. Evidently, it's never too early. "Of a three-month-old child in nine hour daycare," she writes, "a father assured me, 'I want him to be independent.'"[58]

As children grasp that life in their culture demands that they quickly shed signs of their vulnerability, neediness, or bewilderment, they adopt the "cool" persona of the child sophisticate modeled in the stories they read and the images they see. Hollywood has been particularly ingenuous in helping to shape American children's acceptance of their subsistence diet in the emotions. Television and movies tutor children from the time they are tots in what the historian Peter Stearns has called the "emotional style" of "American cool."[59] As neophytes in the subject, they watch the wisecracking, eye-rolling hipsters on *Sesame Street* and *Rugrats,* move on to the novice level with *The Simpsons,* and then proceed to graduate work with David Letterman and *Saturday Night Live.* Bombarded with these models, children adopt a knowing posture that adults frequently mistake for true sophistication. Actually, children are simply responding to the drumbeat of a message: intense emotions and passionate commitments are out (as the dearth of convincing love stories also suggests). Skeptical nonchalance and cool irony are in.

The combination of the relentless and early presence of media images in children's lives and the emptying of the familial nest also portends a loss of individual freedom. For all its problems, the private, sheltering nuclear family that supported republican childhood not only nurtured deep emotional bonds but also protected the vulnerable young from both the market and the crowd. Until the fifties, the child's often weepy entrance into the public world generally came in kindergarten. Today's hardened five-year-old has been around the block a few times. As of 1997, children were spending two hours a day more in preschool and school programs than they did in the early 1980s. In that same period they lost ten hours a week for playtime.[60] And as parents and the home lose some of their hold on their imaginations, senses, and emotions, children naturally turn elsewhere for spiritual and psychic sustenance. They find it in the media and its indomitable infantry, the peer group. Typically, American parents, unlike those from more traditional societies, have shied away from using siblings and peers to socialize their children, precisely because they have been troubled by the bullying and conformity that went along with this approach.[61] But today peer groups are more powerful. They are replacing simple friendships and are invading earlier grades, where they oversee dress and behavior more cruelly and exactingly than adults ever did.[62]

The shrinking of inner life is reinforced by the influence of science on childhood. Science has drawn a picture of a child as an efficient learning machine that needs information and input rather than meaning and values. Play, for instance, was once thought of as a means of exercising and freeing the imagination but is now increasingly described as a way to facilitate achievement. Quasi-scientific thinking has also encouraged Americans to think in terms of transmitting skills rather than knowledge to the young. Young children are supposed to listen to classical music, we are now informed, not because it enriches the spirit by connecting us to a meaningful tradition or by expanding a shared vocabulary of human feeling, but because it advances spatial and temporal reasoning. Families should eat together not because mealtime allows them to partake in the timeless rituals of civilized manners and communal sharing, but because children who listen to mealtime conversation do better on vocabulary and reading tests.[63] "How Love Boosts Brainpower" is the title of a 1997 article in *Parents*.[64] Machine-like, the child is revved up, tuned up, fueled up—and cut off from the web of human meaning.

"Our society," the late Christopher Lasch wrote, "far from fostering private life at the expense of public life, has made deep and lasting friendships, love affairs, and lasting marriages increasingly difficult to achieve."[65] The myth of anticulturalism should make it easy to see why. Treating children as autonomous, self-sufficient loners inevitably corrodes their capacity for both strong, trusting connections and for independent individuality. Anticulturalism may have promised freedom—the competent child could be freed from unnecessary cultural constraint—but it has not delivered. Its celebration of childhood independence has instead helped to shrink individual possibility.

But the waning of childhood does not merely mean a loss for individuals. It also raises questions about the future of democracy. As liberal philosophers have well understood, there is no way around the paradox that a certain amount of childhood constraint is fundamental to democracy. Freedom is meaningful only when individuals possess the ability to direct their lives and the life of their nation in a deliberate fashion. To achieve this sort of self-governance, individuals must be self-aware, self-controlled, forward-looking, and deliberative, all qualities that must be learned over time and under the proper conditions. In their exaltation of the child's individual autonomy and self-determining choice, Americans run the risk of destroying those conditions and of weakening the self-restraint and sociability which have historically been such a vital counterpoint to the extremes of American individualism.

Social critics like Lasch and Robert Putnam have alerted us to a breakdown in civil society. According to Putnam, Americans are demonstrating less interest in joining organizations, ranging from bowling leagues to parent–teacher associations. "Every year over the last decade or two," he wrote in his essay "Bowling Alone," "millions have withdrawn from the affairs of their communities."[66] In *One Na-*

tion After All Alan Wolfe describes a similar retreat: "American suburban communities do seem to be chilly places. Devoid of people during the day, they are filled with people sitting behind television or computer screens in the evenings, too self-preoccupied to live a Tocquevillian life of civic engagement."[67]

Throughout the following chapters I will discuss the origins of such a nation. Taught to seek meaning and value only from inside, today's children can't help but absorb the American fantasy of a pure freedom transcending the limits of custom, the constraints of community, and even the burdens of love. They are citizens not so much of a society as of their own undernourished imaginations.

....

Chapter 1

The Nature Assumption

When my children were toddlers, I, like many parents, used to show them a book with pictures of a mother pig and her piglet, a mother cow and her calf. Understandably obsessed with "big" and "little," they seemed to love these pictures. But the illustrations also served to reassure them that childhood and the tie between mother and child are immutable facts of nature. Mommies and babies are on the farm, in the woods, in the trees, in the jungle, under the water. Everywhere.

Childhood *is* a fact of nature: the young of mammals have to depend on their mothers for survival. Yet scholars have also come to understand that different societies have different notions about how long the young should remain dependent and how they should be treated. Childhood, as current academic argot would have it, is "culturally constructed." In some societies, twelve-year-old girls are being prepared for their weddings; in others, children are still leaving their laundry around well into their teens—and that's if you're lucky. Some seven-year-olds spend their days herding cows, planting corn, or working in factories, while elsewhere on the globe they are corralled into buildings and seated at desks in rows while they copy the notations an adult makes on a blackboard.

The bazaar of human childhoods is an interesting, if sometimes distressing, curiosity, but it would be a serious mistake to dismiss it as arbitrary. Humans "construct" childhood not to indulge their whims or, as it sometimes seems, to drive women crazy. Human beings fashion the childhood their culture needs. Childhood prepares the individual for life inside his or her specific culture, for living according to its expectations and grasping its values. Compare a tribal or premodern culture whose children need only learn ancestral methods of hunting, weaving, marrying, and worshipping with a modern democratic society whose children must learn to find work that conforms to their own inclinations, to choose their own spouses and leaders, and simultaneously to adapt to rapidly changing conditions. The former is fairly straightforward: children can learn a great deal of what they need to know through simple imitation and unembellished verbal commands. The latter is an enormous project requiring years and years of technical training and psychological preparation. "Give me other mothers and I will give you another world," St. Augustine wrote, and although they might want to change *mothers* to a more current term like *childrearers,* modern anthropologists have found this statement to be true from Samoa to Kabul to Boston.

Professors and philosophers have not been the only ones to grasp this concept. In the earliest days of the republic Americans intuited that families—especially, but by no means only, mothers—provided the essential breeding ground for the democratic, adaptable, creative, energetic, entrepreneurial, self-regulating individual the new country needed. Deliberately and with a sense of optimism, they concocted a recipe for this personality, which remained, despite some tinkering, part of the American creed for well over a century. Somewhere around the middle of the twentieth century, however, Americans began to lose sight of the recipe for some of these qualities. In fact, they began to lose sight of the meaning of childhood altogether. They began to forget the nearly universal idea that childhood is the time to mold individuals out of raw human material and to believe instead that the child, far from needing shaping, is already a complete individual. Though only a few radicals said it quite this way, childhood seemed passé.

Even so, Americans continue to have rather distinct ideas about how to treat children. Consider our approach to the infant. While almost universally babies sleep with their mothers throughout infancy and sometimes well into childhood, Americans insist upon putting their babies in their own crib in their own room. While babies in many cultures are strapped to their mother's back and spoken to, if at all, in a calm, soft voice with little facial expression and minimum eye contact, American parents put their babies in infant seats and high chairs and chatter, laugh, and frown with them as they would with their best friend at lunch. They frequently use their baby's name: "How big is Megan?" "Where is Megan's mouth?" In many cultures, it is common to tease an older infant by holding food or a pacifier just out of reach, but this is relatively uncommon among Americans. While mothers in other cultures hold their babies for most of the day, American parents "childproof" their homes so that their young can move around and explore. In general, American babies—and their older siblings—are held and touched less than their counterparts in most other cultures.[1]

Cultural psychologists, scholars who combine the disciplines of anthropology and psychology, see in these American customs of infancy the seeds of a specifically American way of construing experience. In all of these instances, parents send their babies an unspoken message: *You are an independent and autonomous individual.* Compare this outlook to that of the Gusii tribe of central Africa: In order to discourage independent emotional expression in their children, Gusii mothers deliberately turn away from their infant's excited laughter. Anthropologists have found that by six months the placid babies rarely initiate any sounds and respond only to commands.[2] Or compare it to a culture much closer to home. Italian parents often make their infant's own drives yield to the larger needs of the family. Unlike American parents, who defer to the rhythms of their babies, Italians think little of waking a sleeping child if someone wants to play with him or of making him wait to eat until the family dinnertime or of holding him on their lap when he wants to move around. Sociality more than individuality is their goal.³ American parents are teaching their children to be self-directed and private individuals. We are not born that way.

Americans in the early days of the republic grasped instinctively that their new form of government required a new sort of personality. A young democracy called for self-regulating and independent citizens, and a mobile capitalist economy demanded self-starting, industrious workers. Children preparing for such a life could not remain mere passive subjects within an old-world patriarchal family. Unlike European children, who were taught to say "Yes, Papa" from an early age, these children were going to enjoy a more egalitarian and companionable relationship with their parents. They, after all, had to grow up to be "vigilant" toward authority, to use Jefferson's term. Later in the century Walt Whitman chided a visitor who wondered whether American children were duly respectful toward their parents and leaders. "Allons, comrade! Your old world has been soaked in reverentiality. We are laying here in America the basements and foundations of a new era."⁴

To lay these basements and foundations, Americans had to break with both their European and Puritan past. It's hard for us to imagine how thoroughly children of the old regime were taught to curb their own desires and ignore their own thoughts. The diaries of Heroard, the doctor of Louis Dauphin, who in 1610 became King Louis XIII of France, offer a startling picture of the extreme lengths to which people went in order to squeeze the child dry of individual urges: If the dauphin showed pleasure in a certain food, he would be denied it. If he disliked a food, it was served to him repeatedly. In order to impress upon him his powerlessness, he, the future king, was taught to serve his father at meals. At age two, he began to be subjected to a regime of whippings, first by his nurse and then, as he grew older, by the soldiers of the guard. He was whipped if he failed to demonstrate adequate affection for his parents. He was whipped even after he became king at age nine.⁵ Children, whether they were kings or servants, were to obey parents with the same unquestioning fear with which parents were to obey God. Though they were more solicitous toward their infants than others had been before them, the Puritans transported a similar set of ideas to the new continent. "Children should not know if it could be kept from them, that they have a will of their own," the pastor John Robinson pronounced. "Neither should these words be heard from them, save by way of consent, 'I will' or 'I will not.'"[6] Children should "have never known or felt their own wills till they were one and twenty years of age," agreed Benjamin Rush, writing late in the eighteenth century.[7]

Americans today might view these methods as ruinous to children's self-esteem, but that misses the point. Individuals were not supposed to *have* a self, esteemed or not—at least, they were not supposed to have a self independent of the exacting requirements of their family and community. Children were not being trained to choose an independent career as a doctor, scientist, or tennis coach. They were being prepared to become drones in the family economy. In New England, boys were quickly put to work in the fields herding cattle or planting corn while girls worked in the house weaving, spinning, and caring for younger siblings. "Surplus" children were sent off to neighbors to become domestics or apprentices. Indeed, boys as young as seven were often "bound out," that is, given over to a "master" who, in return for food, shelter, and some scattershot training in reading, could expect a hardworking servant. Wages were given to the child's father. In the Middle Atlantic and Southern colonies, more than half of the population was made up of indentured servants, most of whom were under the age of nineteen. Few children had anything more than the most rudimentary schooling. Why would they? They had no independent economic future to prepare for. They had only to work at the manual jobs allotted to them.

But as the idea of republican childhood began to emerge around the turn of the nineteenth century, American ministers, intellectuals, and moralists took another look at this period of life, emboldened by the egalitarian spirit of their new country and inspired by the philosophy of John Locke and Jean-Jacques Rousseau.[8] A free country, they believed, called for a new kind of childhood. The most noticeable change came with the common school movement, starting in the 1820s. Under the leadership of a Massachussetts reformer named Horace Mann, Americans gradually moved children out of the fields, craftsmen's shops, and kitchens and into the classroom.

But reformers went further than promoting schools as the proper place for children to spend their days. Far from despising the child's "I will," as the Puritans had, they began not only to look more benevolently at the child's "I" but to draw it out, massage it, and elaborate upon it. As cultural psychologists would put it, they set out to build in the American child a private and autonomous self that could engage actively in both civic and economic life. The most obvious shift in the new childrearing involved methods of discipline. Parents of the old school thought little of whippings and beatings; now parents were told to use them only as a last resort. Reasoning and love should replace brute force. "Affectionate persuasion addressed to the understanding, the conscience, and the heart is the grand instrument to be employed in family government," wrote Herman Humphrey in his *Domestic Education*.[9] In the schools, too, corporal punishment was to be thought of as "a relic of barbarism," in Mann's words.[10]

It would be naive to conclude that just because children were subjected to pleas and cajolery, instead of the other side of the whip, they were free to make their own choices. The point of the new "gentle" methods of discipline was not to empower children in any contemporary sense. Mothers were still expected to control their children through their "affectionate persuasion," through appeals to the child's "heart," or, failing that, through threats to withdraw love and approval, a punishment that children know can be tearfully harsh. But it would be equally foolish to assume that these new disciplinary methods didn't amount to much or that their subtle coerciveness made them equivalent to old-regime brutality.[11] Rather, the very fact that parents rejected the language and gestures of their absolute authority and relied instead on reason and persuasion meant that they were changing the way their children would come to understand themselves. The parents wielding these new methods had absorbed Locke's lesson that the child who lives in quaking fear of authority cannot become free. Fear deprives its subjects of the experience of self-sovereignty, as any victim of childhood abuse can attest. On the other hand, the new discipline, dubbed by one historian "the gentle revolution,"[12] gave children the tools with which to experience themselves as rational and free beings and prepared them to become autonomous moral and economic actors. "As the fitting apprenticeship for despotism consists in being trained to despotism," wrote Mann about the new theories of discipline which he prescribed for schools as well, "so the fitting apprenticeship for self-government consists in being trained to self-government."[13] Training for self-government was the point of it all.

Seen in this light, the ideals of republican childhood represented a profound moral achievement and, like the Revolutionary War itself, a giant step forward for freedom. This achievement is also evident in the other ways in which the republican theorists sought to enliven and enrich the child's inner life. Some child experts were particularly interested in ways to draw out the child's mind and perceptions. In her 1831 *Mother's Book*, Lydia Child exhorted parents to encourage their children to explore and to be active, observant thinkers. "All the faculties of a child's mind should be cultivated," she wrote, advising parents to encourage "habits of attention and activity of mind."[14] Her contemporary Bronson Alcott, father of the author Louisa May Alcott, went further: "The *child* must be *treated* as a *free, self-guiding, self-controlling being,*" he announced.[15] Mann also sought to bring to the schools respect for the child as an "active, voluntary agent" rather than "a passive recipient." The future citizen, Mann wrote, "must do more than admit or welcome; he must reach out, and grasp, and bring home."[16]

This new respect for the child's individuality is evident in Americans' changing attitude toward babies. The old world barely noticed infants. People forgot their ages and their names; they casually transferred the names of recently dead babies to newborns. Many European infants were sent away to wet nurses and were often bound inside tight, dirty swaddling clothes for hours on end. Beginning with the Puritans, however, Americans had shown more solicitude toward their babies by avoiding swaddling and endorsing maternal breast-feeding.[17] By the nineteenth century, 95 percent of infants were breast-fed by their mothers until they were between two and four years old.[18] In fact, parents began to demonstrate a new affection and sensitivity toward their youngest children, forging a pattern that continues to this day. Parents now made a point of referring to their infant by their first name, which was now far less likely to be the name of a parent or dead sibling. They began celebrating their children's birthdays. They avoided the habit of quieting fussy babies by using the sedative laudanum, and they were warned against overfeeding because it promoted lethargy. The republican theorists saw babies as Americans-in-training, and for this they had to be active and alert. In 1830 Jacob Abbott wrote in praise of a mother who allowed her infant to tear the pages of a book. "It is not mischief," Abbott reassured his readers. "A piece of paper is something new and curious to him."[19] It is no surprise that the fertility rate fell steadily throughout the nineteenth century; raising an active, individualized child, as parents today know, is labor intensive.[20]

The republican experts also sought to bring some air to the individual feelings so darkly confined by the Puritans. They were setting out to evoke what the philosopher Charles Taylor called "a new form of inwardness in which we come to think of ourselves as beings with inner depths."[21] Never in all of history could children hope for so much attention to their feelings, their thoughts—and their pleasure. Though their recommendations seem monkish by current standards, experts encouraged parents to awaken their children's senses and to indulge—at least occasionally—their playfulness. "Every effort should be made to make home the most desirable place," wrote John Abbott in 1833, "to gather around it associations of delight."[22] Critics have described recommendations like these as part of the nineteenth century's "cult of domesticity," designed to keep women confined to the home. Seen from the child's perspective, it's not so simple. A "delightful" home offered children enriched sensual memories and more Proustian moments of comfort and well-being. Mirrors, framed pictures, and upholstered furniture began to appear in the homes of the growing middle class. The piano—and the ability to play it—became a primary symbol of middle-class gentility. Parents could delight their children with the manufactured toys and games they found in mail-order catalogues. A burgeoning mass market also promoted the rise of the children's novel. By the beginning of the Civil War, three hundred juvenile books were being published yearly. Many of them were novels and poems appealing to children's fantasy and pleasure, in contrast to the severe Bible tales and instructional literature of the Calvinist past. As the century wore on, children even came to be valued as creatures endowed with spontaneous perceptions and a sense of wonder. Children like these could not be workers; no, they needed space and time to play freely, to dream, and to imagine.

Thus, romantic and republican notions had a tremendous practical impact. They taught children that independent imagination and self-directed activity were highly valued in the world to which they had to adapt. In fact, many children learned this lesson at a young age; sentiments of freedom are a common theme in nineteenth-century memoirs. Jane Addams recalled "games and crusades which lasted week after week, and even summer after summer" during her childhood on the Illinois prairie.[23] In a study of these memoirs, Anne Scott MacLeod found many examples of girls who hunted, fished, ran, and explored, living up to the general expectation that they enjoy a "season of freedom."[24] (The gap between this girlhood independence and the confined motherhood of their later years undoubtedley sowed the seeds of later nineteenth-century feminism.) In *A New England Girlhood,* Lucy Larcom "clung to the child's inalienable privilege of running half wild." "Our tether was a long one," she wrote, "and, when grown a little older, we occasionally asked to have it lengthened, a maternal 'I don't care' amounted to almost unlimited liberty." Larcom shook her head in sorrow at the English children she read about who had to be "so prim and methodical," who were never allowed to "romp and run wild." "[We had] a vague idea," she concluded with some cause, "that this freedom of ours was the natural inheritance of republican children only."[25]

But republican childhood also had a rigorous side, one that is more in line with the conventional view of the period.[26] As much as republican child theorists wanted to promote the cause of freedom, they also feared it. They saw danger in human "passions" and were set on teaching their young moderation and self-control. And with one foot in the Puritan and old-world past, they found the conditions of social and geographic mobility in this new country far more troubling than we do today. Detached from his roots and far from the watchful eyes of kin and neighbors, the wanderer had always been an ambiguous figure. Now everyone was a potential wanderer. Under such fragmented conditions, how could you ensure that children would grow up to adhere to a common set of values, a coherent culture?

These anxieties were the source of a number of contradictions. For one thing, most of the childrearing tracts of the early nineteenth century, though filled with talk about "affectionate persuasion," nevertheless harped on the theme of obedience. Republican theorists took it for granted that parents had absolute authority over their children and that children should be conscious of it even if they were never to bear the scars from a whip. But if the means of imposing that authority had changed from the past, so had its goal. Parents were to use their power not to crush the child's will but to prepare the child to become the independent moral actor demanded by a free society. Knowing that republican government depended on individual virtue, they set out to construct in their child's heart and mind an internal moral compass they thought of as "character."

This project could be so grim and full of anxiety that it belied the republican's own avowed trust in the virtue of moderation. Children were subjected to frequent stern lectures, overheated exhortations, and tiresome maxims about duty, morals, and integrity. Experts recognized the need to counterbalance the potential for egotism contained in many of their own precepts. As citizens of a republic, children could not merely devote themselves to their own private happiness. They had to grow up believing in duty if they were to be trusted to seek the common good later in life. Even the permissive (by their standards) Lydia Child instructed parents to teach children "to abhor what is selfish and always prefer another's comfort and pleasure to their own." Child suggests, as an example, that parents force their children to give to others the largest slice of their apple.[27]

There are any number of provisos that need to accompany this picture of republican childrearing. It's difficult to know how many children enjoyed the full benefit of these new approaches with their elaborated and expansive "I." We certainly know of many who did not. Most glaring were slave children, whose laborious childhoods ironically and tragically freed their owners to pursue the time-consuming tenets of enlightened childrearing for their own young. And many white American children continued to live under the harsh Calvinist regime endured by their own parents and suffered frequent whippings in their parents' pursuit of absolute obedience. John D. Rockefeller's mother would strap him to an apple tree and beat him with a birch switch. ("I'm doing this in love," she would say.)[28] In school, his teachers would hold a slate threateningly over the head of a misbehaving student. And even the gentlest parents sometimes resorted to corporal punishment. They found themselves pitted against stubborn children who were willing to endure long evenings alone and dinnerless rather than say they were sorry or who, like Alcott's two little daughters, seemed inclined to kill each other. Alcott mournfully admitted that he spanked Louisa, though he found the practice "barbarous." Harsh Puritan nostrums about the will may have been overthrown, but children's actual willfulness was not so easily disposed of. Nor were traditional responses to it.[29]

Farm children and impoverished city children also benefited little from the new dispensation. Forced to work brutally long hours, they had no time for the romps in the woods remembered by some memoirists. Hamlin Garland recalled working ten hours at the plow. The naturalist John Muir went him one better: during haying he was in the fields for seventeen hours straight.[30] Young boys served as drummers and messengers on Civil War battlefields.[31] At four or five, girls spent innumerable hours "quilling," that is, winding thread on spools, sweeping, sewing, cooking for farmhands. It was immigrant children, not their mothers, who were their family's second wage earner. A study of working-class families in Massachussetts in the 1870s found that children as young as ten were providing a quarter of the family budget.[32] Child labor continued among immigrants into the twentieth century. Between 1880 and 1910, manufacturers were still reporting that about one-quarter of their workforce was under sixteen.[33] The lives of children in isolated farmsteads, in factories, and in mines were often unimaginably dreary and spirit deadening; contemplating such an existence brings to mind a quip by the psychologist William Kessen in response to complaints about the tedium of American schools: "Is school, even in its most awful forms, more boring than cutting wet sod?"[34]

And there are other cautions. In many fundamentalist families, austere self-denial remained a cornerstone virtue. Play and material pleasures were not available to children in these families. "I am so glad my son has told me what he wants for Christmas," Rockefeller's wife, a pious and humorless woman, said in a way that reminds us of the fate of poor Louis Dauphin, "so now it can be denied him."[35] Parents like these also had a profound hatred for idleness and often subjected their children to crushing moral pressure to do their "duty."

Even among those parents who had relaxed their guard against pleasures and "delight," one arena of selfhood continued to come under strict discipline: the body. Masturbation, or "self-abuse" as it was called at the time, epitomized the fear of lack of self-restraint and became an anxious preoccupation among parents for well over a century. As late as the 1930s, catalogues aimed at parents advertised thigh spreaders to keep children from pleasuring themselves by rubbing their legs together. The same catalogues even offered aluminum mittens and cuffs to hold the elbow stiff in order to prevent children from sucking their thumbs.[36]

Even under the best of circumstances, there were high costs attached to the new childrearing, especially for women. Secluded from the public sphere and deprived of a meaningful civic role, women found themselves steaming in a hothouse of overrefined maternal emotion. For children also there was the danger of overheated, suppressed intimacies, or as Christopher Lasch called it in his own ambivalent critique *Haven in a Heartless World,* "the emotional overloading of the parent-child connection."[37] Ironically, both women's frustration and their children's inevitable self-importance contained the seeds of the unraveling of republican childrearing.

Even taking into account all these cautions, there can be no question that Americans were succeeding in inventing a new childhood, which though overbearing by our own standards was nevertheless in keeping with democratic and individualistic ideals. Foreign visitors who arrived on American shores during this time were struck—and frequently appalled—by the feisty independence of its children. Their complaints will sound familiar; one sometimes hears them from foreigners today. These children, one visitor harrumphed, had decided to apply the Declaration of Independence to themselves.

British naval officer and author Captain Frederick Marryat wrote of an encounter he observed in 1839 that involved a three-year-old named Johnny who was called by his mother to come in out of the cold. "I won't!" the little imp answered. "Come my sweet, I've something for you," his mother implored. "I won't!" Johnny insisted. After more pleading, Johnny's mother finally turned for help from her husband, who took the masculine approach and simply ordered the child inside—still to no avail. "I won't!" the child repeated. The father turned, smiling, to the horrified captain. "A sturdy Republican, sir!" he exclaimed. Johnny's father was surely more lenient than many of his contemporaries—perhaps too lenient for some even today—and though he horrified the good captain, his view of his son's behavior captures the revolutionary American attitude toward children.[38]

More subtle-minded travelers saw the point of it all. The English reformer Harriet Martineau, who spent the years between 1834 and 1836 traveling in the United States, was one of the few foreigners to note the virtues of the sturdy republican child:

> For my own part, I delight in the American children; in those who are not overlaid with religious instruction. There are instances, as there are everywhere, of spoiled, pert, and selfish children. Parents' hearts are pierced there, as everywhere. But the independence and fearlessness of children were a perpetual charm in my eyes. To go no deeper, it is a constant amusement to see how the speculations of young minds issue, when they take their own way of thinking, and naturally say all they think. Some admirable specimens of active little minds were laid open to me at a juvenile hall in Baltimore . . . If I had at home gone in among eighty or a hundred little people between the ages of eight and sixteen, I should have extracted little more than "Yes, ma'am," and "No, ma'am." At Baltimore, a dozen boys and girls at a time crowded round me questioning, discussing, speculating, revealing in a way which enchanted me.[39]

Like Alexis de Tocqueville, who traveled in the United States around the same time, Martineau had happened upon what remains a defining quality of the American personality. Released from old-world manners that codified the inequality of adult and child, prodded to observe and refine their inner voices and to unleash their vitality, children burst upon experience curious, questioning, noticing. If these children could at times be accused of disobedience and egotism, they also exuded an "independence and fearlessness"—though held in check by a set of common moral assumptions—well suited to the new world. The foundations and basements of a new era and a new national personality were in place.

This history may surprise readers who have been assured that it was only recently that we have been liberated from the long, oppressive reign of seen-but-not-heard childhood. Doubtless, the liberties granted to children today can make the past, with its talk of obedience and character training, look like boot camp. Still, there can be no question that by the mid-nineteenth century Americans had developed a childrearing blueprint which, while it varied greatly in practice and fell far short of our own sentiments on these matters, embraced the goals of freedom and individuality in ways both distinctive and original.

Though the main tenets of republican childhood held sway for more than a century, there were some early signs of strain. The most significant came in the early decades of the twentieth century as scientific experts overthrew the theologians, moralists, and philosophers who had been the bearers of republican childrearing wisdom. In their writings these experts betrayed a deep suspicion about parents' influence over children, an approach far different from the morally uplifting exhortations that permeated the republican tracts. Progressive reformers ruminated over "the unchecked tyranny or unchecked indulgence of the private home."[40] "We are saying to the father and the mother," wrote Justice Julian Mack, one of the founders of the first juvenile court, "that they have not the wisdom, or the ability, or the willingness, properly to train the child. The State is going to step into the home."[41] Expert-guided, scientifically calibrated feeding schedules and behavioral personality training began to replace the republican approach of character formation through affectionate persuasion. The most extreme expression of these views came from the behaviorist John Watson, who warned that "mother love is a dangerous instrument." "Never hug and kiss [your children] . . . Shake hands with them in the morning," he advised. Watson even wondered "whether there should be individual homes for children—or even whether children should know their own parents."[42]

As mistrustful of parents as they were, scientific experts of the first decades of the century never questioned childhood's purpose or adults' role in shaping the young. But around the middle of the century, both of these came under attack. Americans lost sight entirely of the two central understandings of nineteenth-century childrearing: first, that children's individuality must be shaped and "constructed" and, second, that the egotism inherent in American individualism must be countered by grounding in a common culture. What emerged in their place was anticulturalism. Unlike republican philosophers who wanted parents to actively shape the raw human material which is a child into an individual, anticulturalists viewed the child as an already complete, finished individual lacking only some skills and information. Not only would these complete individuals require no shaping by parents and other representatives of the culture into which they were born, but they would develop best outside of, or even in opposition to, that culture. The republican child who was supposed to be reared in an atmosphere of bounded freedom evolved into the anticultural child who required no rearing at all.

The first distant strains of anticulturalism could be heard in the mid-1950s as a number of commentators began to explore the quandary of the American adolescent. A relatively new social type, the adolescent was an understandable subject of concern. Up until the early twentieth century, most young people in their mid and later teens went to work in the fields and factories or as apprentices in training for specialized skills. Progressive reformers set out to change that. Believing that the teen years are a time for continued education and alarmed at the harsh conditions in the urban factories that employed many lower-class and immigrant children, they redefined the adolescent as a still vulnerable individual who could benefit from a prolonged republican childhood. Throughout the early decades of what they pronounced the "century of the child," experts worked tirelessly—and successfully—to pass state, and eventually federal, child labor legislation and compulsory education laws, both of which would effectively remove youths under seventeen from the workplace and collect them into a new institution we now take for granted: high school. For the first time, the adolescent was to be thought of as a student and a child.[43] Indeed, adolescents were called "youngsters" up until World War II, when the more familiar term "teen-ager" came into widespread use.[44]

Midcentury sociologists quickly grasped the potential problems that accompanied this new appendix to childhood and that we have come to associate with the term *teenager.* They warned of an increasingly powerful, segregated youth culture with its own language, dress, music, and, they feared, values.[45] But other critics went much further and questioned the entire enterprise. They argued that it was absurd to expect full-grown men to disguise themselves as boys. Whereas sixteen-year-old Samoans might be running a household (probably including children of their own), foraging for food, and helping govern a village, sixteen-year-old Americans were told to clean up their rooms, do their homework, and shun sex. For the first time, the years of socialization we call childhood seemed restrictive and demeaning. Children, at least children in their teens, did not *enjoy* the wonder years so much as *suffer* them.[46]

Of course, many recognized that a complex society like America requires years of job training before a child can become a card-carrying adult. But few seemed to grasp the possibility that lengthening childhood into the mid and late teens might expand rather than foreshorten individual freedom. Adolescence provides what the psychologist Erik Erikson called a "psychological moratorium"; it allows individuals to "explore their identity," or to "find themselves," as we commonly put it, before they are forced to make the consequential choices of adulthood.[47] Far from a mere holding cell, adolescence allows individuals to practice love and work, as if they were full-grown, without making a final commitment to marriage or career. It is no coincidence that adolescence was invented at a time of increasing social mobility. As the number of choices available to individuals expanded, so too did the time allotted to make them.[48] From this perspective, adolescence is hardly a state of arbitrary confinement. It is a time to form a more mature understanding of one's future role as citizen, worker, spouse, and parent and to acquire the mastery and self-awareness for graduation into adulthood that would not have been possible at a younger age. Anyone who has watched a moderately well-adjusted child mature from fifteen, say, to twenty knows what I mean.

By the late 1960s and 1970s, however, these notions got lost in the noisy protest against adolescence. The entire idea that childhood represents a time of freedom seemed increasingly suspect to many critics. For them, young people shared some of the qualities of oppressed minorities who were becoming the center of social concern. Tracts with titles like "The Student as Nigger" appeared on campuses; New York City high school students began wearing armbands emblazoned with the words FREE THE NEW YORK 275,000! The adolescent in the view of many vocal social critics seemed a completed individual who needed neither protection, shaping, nor even education and who suffered under the domination of his elders.

The juvenile court, which had been founded in part to give troubled youth a chance for more lenient treatment than they would otherwise receive in adult court, was a special source of outrage. It was damned as a subtle means of "social control," not an entirely unmerited charge given the hubris and elitism of some of its founders and advocates. But critics questioned not only the workings of the court but also the very meaning of adolescence that had inspired it. One measure of this social control was, according to one critic, a "regressive and nostalgic" view of childhood. The architects of the court "implicitly assumed the 'natural' dependence of adolescents and created a court to impose sanctions on premature independence."[49] Laws relating to teens, wrote one legal scholar in this heated vein, were "strongly reminiscent of those that were found in runaway apprentice and servant laws and fugitive slave laws."[50] To paraphrase Rousseau, everywhere, it seemed, adolescents were in chains.

This mistrust of youth's dependence on adults did not stop with the critique of adolescence. It trickled down until it saturated much of the contemporary discussion about childhood. The bible for this doctrine, published in English in 1962, was *Centuries of Childhood* by the French historian Philippe Ariès. Ariès' ideas merit careful consideration not just because *Centuries of Childhood* is a landmark book and not just because it was the first and most scholarly to examine modern childhood—though it is both—but because it did so in a way that solidified the cause of anticulturalism.

Ariès' book highlights the notion long grasped by philosophers: rather than a mere biological fact, childhood varies from culture to culture. Where Ariès differed from philosophers was in his flat announcement that in the Middle Ages, the period of his own scholarly expertise, "the idea of childhood did not exist."[51] Compared with our own precious darlings, children of the Middle Ages, we have seen, were commonly treated with casual indifference. No one imagined they might have what psychologists today call "developmental needs." Children played and worked alongside adults. They took part in the same games, and they heard the same stories, no matter how ribald or gory. The little red schoolhouse did not exist simply because no children would have attended it. By the time they were seven or so, they were laboring as apprentices, farmhands, and servants.

Much of Ariès' book chronicles the very early signs of the shift towards the modern, protective childrearing described earlier in this chapter. However, while many historians have seen in this shift a victory for the young, Ariès was an iconoclast. He demonstrated a clear preference for the distant past. He saw the growing influence of the nuclear family and the school as a threat to the freedom and individuality of the young. Instead of the casual socialization they received as they wandered the marketplace and village square, children were forced to be "quarantined" within the family.[52] Under these conditions, he believed, children were more closely monitored and more harshly disciplined. Celebrating "medieval unruliness," with its vagabonds, beggars, and outlaws and its "gay indifference" toward the young, Ariès' book is a treatise in favor of the casual sociability of the Middle Ages and its putatively relaxed control over children.[53]

Ariès' widely accepted notion that casual socialization translates into more freedom for children is a highly important, though subtle, example of anticultural thinking. Resting on the presumption that the free individual is a fact of nature, it ignores that childhood is the time when individuals are given the specific materials with which to "construct" their identity, including their identity as free individuals. The casual treatment of medieval children could not possibly do that. It reflected not a respect for children's autonomy but an utter indifference toward individual experience.

This indifference began with the medieval infant's body. Medieval infants were wrapped so tightly in swaddling clothes that they sometimes developed abscesses and deformed legs. With all but their face bound in dirty swaddling, they could not move their body. Older babies may have had their arms freed, but they were still were given no opportunity to crawl, an activity much despised because it reminded adults of animals.[54] Medieval toddlers were probably similarly confined. Though we have little information about the details of early childrearing in the Middle Ages,[55] anthropologists studying premodern societies often find not the existential paradise imagined by Ariès but children under strict surveillance, constantly being told what to do and what not to do by parents and older siblings, who often punctuate their commands with a quick swat, kick, or caning. Margaret Mead also set up a strawman-land of exotic freedom; she wrongfully described Samoan adolescents as living a life of utopian sexual freedom but was nevertheless observant enough to note that this freedom did not extend to younger children. Samoan toddlers were forever hearing "Keep still!" and "Keep your mouth shut!" from the older children watching over them, even when they were "as quiet as a row of intimidated mice." Toilet training was often reinforced by blows, as was much of their restlessness and mischief.[56]

Most important, medieval parents had no notion of bodily privacy. People of the time thought nothing of fondling and kissing young children's genitals. The ladies-in-waiting of Louis XIII, for instance, masturbated him, kissed his genitals and urged him to touch theirs, threatened to cut off his penis and nipples, showed him pornographic books, had sexual intercourse in front of him—all before he was seven years old.[57] Parents of the Middle Ages could not imagine, nor could they communicate to children, that the body was ground zero of the private self. Yet as victims of abuse well know, children who are repeatedley fondled or neglected or ordered to shut up are not in the best position to grow up to experience themselves as autonomous and free individuals. On the contrary, they tend to have enormous problems taking control of their life.

The contrast between medieval and republican childhood could hardly be more striking. Republican theorists urged parents to awaken babies to their own identity, urged them to throw away the swaddling clothes and to call them by name. Like the enlightened European child theorists of the eighteenth century who inspired them, they abhorred the fondling and sexual games practiced with young children under the old regime. Similarly, they warned against hitting and caning and the thoughtless obedience that came along with them. Republican theorists were seeking to instill in American children a sense of themselves as autonomous and free beings whereas medieval people very likely wanted the opposite.

That Ariès did not grasp this was due in part to his disdain for the bourgeois family and in part to an anticultural misunderstanding. For him, childhood was a form of control; the absence of childhood, as he thought was the case in the Middle Ages, meant freedom. Thus, freedom is not a human invention requiring human planning. Rather, it is nature's default position, the condition individuals fall into if society does not interfere in the form of a supervised childhood. In fact, Ariès' assertion that in the Middle Ages "the idea of childhood did not exist" and that this resulted in greater individual freedom encouraged the mischievous idea, seized upon by many of his American readers, that childhood itself is entirely artificial and that modern childhood in particular is like a prison.

The most extreme version of these anticultural views came from liberationist thinkers of the late sixties and seventies, particularly the feminist Shulamith Firestone and child liberationists Richard Farson and John Holt. Their vision was as pure an expression of anticultural thinking as one can find. They believed children to be naturally capable, fully conscious, and intentional, so much so that they should be able to choose with whom they want to live, how to spend their money, how they want to be educated, who should be their political leaders, and what their religious and ethical belief system should be. They should even have the "right to sexual freedom."[58] For the anti-culturalist, children's sexual desires are always natural and benign, and they, being competent, lucid creatures, should be able to act on them. In the name of "childhood innocence," as one article in *Feminist Review* put it, "adults repress children's own expressions of sexuality, deny them control over their own bodies and 'protect' them from knowledge."[59]

These liberationists believed that society was bent on seeking out and eliminating the individual child's naturally authentic and competent self. In fact, they considered childhood nothing more than a ruse dreamed up by a malevolent society to oppress the competent young by forcing them to obey meaningless rules and customs. "In most cases society has arbitrarily assigned goals that children are expected to achieve," wrote an activist. "Norms of appropriate behavior, dress and language have also been established. The child is expected to act, think, feel, and behave in a prescribed manner."[60] In short, liberationists appeared to reject the universally held notion that socialization, the social molding of raw human material, is inevitable and necessary.

Though from today's vantage point these views may sound overheated, it's important to grasp their roots in American thinking. The tension between the democratic ideal of equality and the inequality built into family relations had long been recognized by liberal philosophers like Locke and John Stuart Mill. Aware of this tension, Americans sought to reinvent the traditional patriarchal family in a new mold. Already in the 1820s, Tocqueville had noted the "influence of democracy on the family" so pronounced that "a species of equality prevails around the [American] domestic hearth."[61] But while liberal philosophers and the architects of republican childhood who followed in their footsteps accepted the paradox that children's lack of freedom provided a preparation period for the freedom they would exercise as adults, many social critics of the 1960s and 1970s could not. Dedicated to a pure vision of individual freedom and demanding that America live up to its own democratic ideals, they likened the child's predicament to that of other oppressed minorities. Teachers and parents began to look like suspect authorities like the police, the army, and the president, and none of them was going to be exempt from suspicious scrutiny. "The family's vital role in authoritarianism is entirely repugnant to the free soul in our age," one children's rights advocate announced.[62]

Social critics of the time understood very clearly that they were re-belling against the tradition I've been calling republican childhood. For them, mothers' "affectionate persuasion" and "the gentle revolu-tion" were not a moral triumph but a nefarious scheme to disguise the absolute power of adults; at least children under the belt knew what was happening to them. Parental love was a "force of violence" bent on "destroying most of [children's] potentialities," in the words of the psychiatrist R. D. Laing.[63] Of course, no one directly addressed the question of how children would learn without guidance to become self-directing, self-aware adults. So troubled were critics by the gross inequality between adults and children that they viewed all attempts at influencing children's development as equally sinister. Startling new information about child abuse, which had began to appear in medical journals in the late 1950s and which became a fixture of head-lines and personal memoirs beginning in the late 1960s, confirmed their suspicions. It came to seem that the privacy of the American home and the high expectations placed on parents did not ensure the generous environment for children they promised. Rather, these con-ditions provided numerous opportunities for mischief and for unen-durable frustrations that increased the chance that parents would abuse their children. Critics ignored the massive historical and cross-cultural record of whippings, abandonments, fondlings, and mar-riages forced on ten-year-olds that republican childhood made unten-able, if not impossible. Evading the much greater risk of children in foster placements and in broken families, child abuse experts and so-cial critics misleadingly cautioned that children were more in danger in their home than anywhere else, as if their parents were out to get them.[64] Firestone summed it all up in a crude restatement of Ariès: "Childhood is hell."[65]

For obvious reasons, feminists were especially prone to adopt this new loathing for traditional American childhood and to accept the underlying anticultural assumptions that went along with it. As feminists added men to the list of authorities under suspicion, some began to look at children as comrades in suffering at the hands of an oppressive patriarchy. Ignoring the republican theorists' genuine concern for children and the efforts needed to shape the free individual, they spied only a plot to keep women confined to their separate sphere. Dependency, and even protectiveness, were both regarded as benign disguises for those who really only wanted to assert power. "Women and children share a similar victim status in that both groups are dependent upon another group of people from whom rapists, or abusers, are drawn," pronounced one feminist tract. "Just as women have traditionally been dependent on men, children are dependent upon adults for economic support, for social identity, for protection."[66] Protectiveness was viewed as "an ideology of control" and children as victims of "structural oppression."[67] Again the problem of how children might be prepared for freedom without some version of republican childhood went unaddressed. For these more radical thinkers, the belief that childhood was nothing but a prison, that women were similarly confined victims, and that men were tyrannical or even brutal sentinels was enough to end the discussion.

A similar attack on schools reflected the same impatience with republican ideals. It wasn't just that Horace Mann's dream of a democratic institution that would inspire children to, in Lasch's words, "the fullest use of their powers" hadn't been achieved. It was that those intentions were not what they seemed to begin with. Using terms like *social control, indoctrinating obedience* and *enforcing conformity,* some critics failed to distinguish necessary socialization from soul-killing authoritarianism.[68] "The only people in our society who are incarcerated against their will," wrote Farson, "are criminals, the mentally ill, and children in school."[69] School was nothing but a "blackboard penitentiary."[70]

While many of these liberationists took extreme positions, their general skepticism about childhood as a necessary period of preparation began to seep into mainstream thinking, especially among legal activists. Nearly always citing Ariès, child advocates working within the system recommended that government help children achieve earlier independence, for the child, according to one prominent psychologist, is in a state of "social captivity and legal status as a non-person."[71] In several articles published in the mid-1970s, Hillary Rodham deplored children's political powerlessness and called for a redefinition of childhood in the eyes of the law. "The legal status of infancy, or minority," she wrote, "should be abolished and the presumption of incompetency reversed"; when it comes to "decisions about motherhood and abortion, schooling, cosmetic surgery, treatment of venereal disease, . . . employment" and other matters that will "significantly affect the child's future, . . . a competent child should be permitted to assert his or her own interests."[72] Around the same time, Harvard law professor Lawrence Tribe proposed turning childhood into "a semi-suspect classification,"[73] a phrase that perfectly captured the new ambivalence toward childhood, while the chairman of the American Bar Association's section on Rights and Responsibilities proposed finally that "all legal distinctions between children and adults be abolished."[74]

A quarter century later, few Americans consciously believe that childhood is "suspect" or that children should vote or that the government should force parents, as Rodham would have it, to let children who so desire hold after-school jobs or get nose jobs. And yet these ideas continue to have considerable relevance today. Ariès has achieved a saintly status among academics in law, political theory, sociology, history, and women's studies. Armed with the discovery that childhood is a product of cultural prejudice—one even occasionally comes across the word *children* in quotation marks!—Ariès' disciples continue to equate the socialization of children with the "power" of the dominant over the weak.[75] In this vein they have questioned everything from child labor laws to playgrounds (both considered insidious inventions of the Progressives),[76] and have lent support to teenage motherhood and even incest.[77] To cite one remarkable example, Maria Tatar concludes in her analysis of fairy tales that they are really an attempt to "coerce the child into docile behavior." And she goes further, stating "that the entire project of childrearing including the telling of tales is invested in a microphysics of power and is therefore never really in the best interests of the child."[78] In short, Tatar proposes that it could be harmful to read to your child because doing so is an attempt at control. Notice the anticultural assumptions at work: if you don't socialize your child by doing things like reading to her, some fundamental or natural self will emerge. How ironic that postmodernists like Tatar insist that the autonomous self is a fiction, a passive medium through which the voices of gender, class, race, and ethnicity recite their ideologies. They themselves seem to secretly hold on to a dream of pre-social identity, of the self liberated from culture. If only parents would stop trying to exercise power over their children by reading them fairy tales and taking them to playgrounds!

Nor is this gnawing at the idea of a long, protected childhood limited to the academic left. Conservative politicians and policymakers also show signs of forgetting the purpose of republican childhood. Several have condemned adolescence as just so much coddling. Newt Gingrich has called high school "subsidized dating," and Thomas Sowell has announced it is time to "abolish adolescence."[79] Conservatives have also joined liberals in attacking the juvenile court, the separate justice system for those under seventeen.[80] Over the last decade there has been a 70 percent increase in the number of children tried as adults in state courts, a development largely promoted by conservatives. In Illinois alone, transfers to adult court rose from 334 in 1992 to 2,718 in 1994.[81] Although the Supreme Court has ruled it unconstitutional to execute an individual who was under sixteen when he committed a crime, a number of conservative politicians have urged its application to fourteen-year-olds. In 1996 Governor Gary E. Johnson of New Mexico proposed allowing executions for thirteen-year-olds, and one Texas state legislator has even suggested eleven as the age of full responsibility.[82]

But anticulturalism is far more prevalent and insidious than these extreme examples suggest. Even as American parents continue to place their babies' cribs in separate rooms from their own, to talk with them, to eschew playpens, and to childproof their homes in order to give their babies maximum freedom to explore,[83] the fact remains that Americans have accepted the idea that children already own the materials out of which to build their individuality and autonomy and that adults, or "society," must beware of disturbing them. This anticultural fallacy undermines adult commitment to preparing children for life in a democracy. It argues against teaching the next generation the just claims of the community and the need to limit their own egotism. But that is only half the story. While anticulturalism champions autonomous individuals, it also deprives them of the nourishment to stand alone. By reducing culture to indifferent, arbitrary information to which the individual may or may not feel committed, it depletes the sources of a full-bodied individuality. Anticulturalism denies the next generation a rich language for building their inner lives and imagining their experience. The following chapters will bring to light some of the many hidden examples of anticultural thinking and the sad results for American children.

Chapter 2

Baby
Geniuses

The anticultural fallacy does not imply that Americans don't pay enough attention to children or don't recognize them as different from adults. In fact, Americans can be obsessed with children, and it is an obsession that begins with infants. Governor Zell Miller of Georgia demonstrated his own concern by proposing in 1998 that the state pay to provide each newborn child with a cassette tape of music by Bach or Mozart. Why this particular gift for his infant constituents? Because "listening to music at a very early age affects spatial and temporal reasoning" and encourages "those trillions of brain connections to develop."[1] Miller is on the same wavelength as Sera, an architect and thirty-three-year-old mother of two whose childrearing practices were described in the *New Yorker*. Sera designed an intricate, comprehensive menu of activities intended to stimulate visual, motor, or auditory skills in her children. Following the menu, the nanny would, for instance, show Sera's fifteen-month-old daughter and newborn son prints of Matisse paper cutouts on the nursery walls in order to focus their eyes. She would make sure classical music played in the house whenever the babies were awake. Still

Sera worried: "Sometimes I wake up at night and have an anxiety attack—that I've forgotten about this or that part of my child's brain."[2] Americans are concerned about children all right, but, as these examples suggest, sometimes that concern takes a peculiar form.

In a landmark essay entitled "The Child and Other Cultural Inventions," Harvard psychologist William Kessen noted how the major theorists in child psychology "have gathered an assembly of vastly different children." It seems that in some respects theorists express as much about their personalities and their era as they do about facts of human nature. "Charles Darwin observed son Doddy," he wrote, "and found emotions, James Mark Baldwin observed daughter Polly and found thoughts, Sigmund Freud observed Anna and found wish-fulfillment, John Watson observed Billy and found unconditioned responses, Jean Piaget observed Jacqueline and found adaptive assimilation, B. F. Skinner observed Debra and found a baby in a box."[3] And contemporary scientists, to pursue Kessen's point, have observed infants and found little scientists with computerized brains. It is this vision that has inspired Sera and Governor Miller.

This new portrait of the baby tells us something about our age. It lends a great deal of support to the myth of anticulturalism—that is, that children develop on their own and do not need to be shaped by culture. And as a result, it helps to alter the relationship between adults and children. Whereas adults have most commonly been understood as nurturers and representatives of cultural knowledge like manners, values, and morals, their primary job today has been reduced to communicating information or, in the case of babies, providing stimulation. The consequences of this view are disquieting indeed.

According to biologists, helplessness is one of the distinguishing traits of human infancy. The human brain grows slowly. It remains in an unfinished state far longer than is the case with other animals—so long that Adolf Portmann has called infancy "a special extra-uterine first year."[4] Compared to other primates, Stephen Jay Gould has written, "human babies are born as embryos. During their first year, human babies share the growth patterns of primate and mammalian fetuses, not of other primate babies."[5] Unlike animals whose innate instincts will carry them a long way toward survival, humans have to

learn how to master their specific enviromments. And those environments are highly varied. The infant brain must be capable of understanding and adapting to life in an African tribal village or in a mansion in Beverly Hills, California. It is precisely because humans are
born so helpless and incomplete that human cultures could be so
heterogeneous.

This picture of infant helplessness has become increasingly difficult to reconcile with what Americans have been hearing from psychologists over the last thirty years. Before then, people had sub-
scribed to William James' turn-of-the-century idea that the infant
exists in a hazy netherworld of "booming, buzzing confusion." But in
the middle of the century, scientists began to introduce a new and remarkably lucid baby. The first sign of change came as the theories of
Swiss scientist Jean Piaget reached American campuses and laboratories. Unlike the behavioral psychologists who had dominated the field
of psychology since the 1920s, Piaget believed that children do not
merely passively register the events around them but actively interpret them. By thinking about past experience, they engage in "accom-
modation"; that is, they modify their understanding of past events
and reason their way into novel action. An eighteen-month-old experimenting with actions like pressing, pulling, and sliding can figure
out how to open the latch of a supposedly childproof cabinet, as many
a staggered parent can attest. Every action—sucking a thumb, finger-
ing a blanket, dropping pieces of bread from the high chair—is
loaded with cognitive potential that children seize upon and ponder.
Piaget's children are rather like dedicated scientists working in their
home laboratory. One of Piaget's followers compared his toddler
watching the pieces of bread he throws over the side of his high chair
to Galileo dropping balls from the tower of Pisa.[6]

Piaget performed much of his reseach by jotting down observations of his own three children. His followers often moved the research site into the laboratory, where they continued simple experiments like hiding toys from babies or flashing pictures at them. But by
the late sixties what had been the desultory, naked-eye-and-notebook
field of infant research was transformed into a high-tech industry.
Scientists began to use video cameras, machines to measure heart

rates and electrogalvanic responses, electronic pacifiers to measure sucking patterns, and computers to quantify changes. Most recently, brain imaging technology has given us remarkable photographs of babies' neurons and neurotransmitters working at top speed in response to every bit of stimulation they receive.

Advances in technology allowed scientists to peer into the infant brain and discover talents even Piaget had doubted. Piaget had believed that babies do not have a sense of "object constancy," that is, an understanding that objects continue to exist even when hidden from view. Newer studies led some researchers to conclude that babies do understand object constancy, their increased heart and sucking rates indicating surprise when an object is missing from where they expect it.[7] In one study, babies who were shown a gallery of photos could even discriminate the sex of other babies, a feat impossible for adults![8] Discoveries concerning newborns were especially dazzling. While Piaget believed the infant began to imitate in the latter half of the first year of life, now there were studies proving they can match facial expressions soon after birth. From studies using videotapes, some researchers even suggested that babies could be prodded to stick out their tongues after a mere hour on this earth.[9] Other researchers announced that babies can recognize their name and discriminate between two colors as early as two weeks of age.[10] And by one month, they can distinguish between sounds as similar as "pah" and "bah."[11]

So fast and furious were the discoveries resulting from these new technologies that by the mid-seventies scientists were ready to overthrow entirely the traditional picture of the helpless infant. The new baby was crowned the "competent infant." In the preface to a huge volume of research by that name published in 1973, the editors shake their heads in wonder at the "embarrassing . . . false pronouncements" of earlier experts about a "completely helpless [infant], at the mercy of his environment." Light years beyond this earlier version, the competent infant is innately equipped with all sorts of behaviors that scientists had once assumed either had to be learned or appeared only at a later developmental stage. In language that has become boilerplate in the field, they announced "that from his earliest days every infant is an active, perceiving, learning and information-organizing individual."[12]

The "competent infant" and the "information-organizing individual" were only the beginning. It began to seem as if babies could not only recognize their own name but were ready to compete on *Jeopardy.* One developmental psychologist at the University of Pittsburgh discovered that babies at five months could "compute the results of simple arithmetic problems."[13] Other researchers found that *within minutes after birth* infants could pick out their mother's face from a gallery of photos.[14] They could even recognize a story that was read to them while they were still in the womb.[15] In 1989 the competent infant progressed to *The Rational Infant,* the title of a book by the developmentalist T. G. R. Bower, who refers to the human baby as "the most powerful learning system in creation." In one chapter, "The Logical Infant," Bower describes how infants "can detect contingent relations . . . The baby will then seek for information to specify the initial hypothesis, to change its value from *neither true nor false* to *true* or *false.* Having worked out an hypothesis that fits the information given, the baby will seek information that would contradict the hypothesis under test."[16] More recently, Alison Gopnik and Andrew Meltzoff have formulated what's known as "the theory theory," that is, a theory that babies form "a succession of theories about people and the world" which they then test by experimenting. "We can't help but be struck," they conclude, "by how similar [infant] behavior is to the behavior we normally associate with scientists."[17]

Regardless of what seemed at times a portrait increasingly at odds with everyday experience, the competent infant was enthusiastically greeted when he ventured outside ivied walls and hospital laboratories. In fact, almost immediately upon the first discoveries of infant eye-tracking, he was introduced to the general American public with the cheers and backslapping usually reserved for a returning war hero. "Baby, You're Incredible!" crowed the title of one early article.[18] Another, entitled "Babies: They're a Lot Smarter Than They Look," informed its readers that "the new baby learns much the same way an adult learns from the very first day of his life."[19] And the hoopla continued. "Your child is a genius," begins a 1985 self-help book entitled *Your Child Is Smarter Than You Think,* which goes on to explain that "his or her capacity for learning is virtually limitless."[20] In 1995 the linguist Stephen Pinker announced with the same breathless enthusiasm, "The three-year-old is a grammatical genius."[21]

The baby given to us by science who now strides across the pages of advice books and popular parenting magazines is "a genius," busily constructive, happily striving, and reveling in his "appetite for learning," his "joy of learning." Sturdy and unflappable, he never seems to become overstimulated, nor does he ever long for quiet. His job is taking in data and he is a workaholic. "As you get to know your new baby," write the authors of the 1994 *Discovery Play: Loving and Learning with Your Baby,* a volume dedicated to "nurturing a philosophy of learning in babies and preschoolers," "you'll soon discover she is learning all the time. What you may view as everyday routine, she sees as a great adventure . . . your infant cannot wait to explore new situations and problems."[22] Though few laymen fully realized it, Americans had traded in the old-fashioned infant known throughout history and across cultures for a shiny, new—and completely unfamiliar—model.

Can all these claims about the infant's capabilities be true? Doubtless, infants are capable of a great deal more than they were given credit for in the days when they were imagined to neither see nor hear nor feel. And doubtless, also, they are learning much of the time. Nevertheless, there are several reasons, aside from common sense, to balk at accepting the baby as a warm-blooded smart machine and to consider his image to be as much the product of a scientific culture as of science itself. One anthropologist has observed that lab settings themselves limit the universality of scientific findings; for example, in many cultures mothers would not allow their babies to be separated from them and placed on a plastic seat.[23] Moreover, the myriad articles and books testifying to the subject of infant competence leave out just how much this competence depends on the right props and coaching. Consider just one of the competent infant's many gifts—the ability to reach for an object as early as a few days after birth, far before the long-accepted five months or so once recorded in textbooks. In order for infants to reach at this age, it turns out, researchers must support the newborn's head so that its excessive weight does not interfere by pulling on the spinal column. In other words, the baby has to be propped up in a sitting position. "In my own laboratory," one researcher has acknowledged, "we allow two hours to obtain a five-minute video recording of one infant reaching. Most of the time is spent ensuring that the baby is in the optimal condition to display the behavior, if he (or she) is going to."[24] Another researcher was surprised to find babies performing their tasks brilliantly, in this case imitating an adult sticking out his tongue—until he found out that mothers were practicing with their babies before bringing them to the lab.[25]

Though most child developmentalists are likely to pronounce themselves "interactionists," (i.e., they recognize the interplay between the child and the environment), the fact is that the environment of many of their experiments is as strangely bleak as a Beckett play, a minimalist stage set featuring objects like balls and boxes and physical events like falling and thumping. Human beings appear only to make boxes vanish, to pull faces for imitating, to bang drums for counting. But there is every reason to believe that babies rely constantly on gestures and signs, many of them minute and unconscious, from their elders about what to make of the strange things they are encountering. When faced with unknown situations, a frequent occurrence with newcomers to the world, babies will frequently look at a caregiver's face for a sign that they are safe. Kenneth Kaye in *The Mental and Social Life of Babies: How Parents Create Persons* draws attention to another ordinary scenario:

> I am holding a 3-month-old in my lap. She stares at the toy about 6 inches in front of her on the table. Her fingers scrabble on the table surface, then she extends her arm toward the toy but, with her fist closed, knocks it a few inches away. I reach for it and move it back to where it was. I have no lesson plan, in fact, I act without really thinking. I don't care very much whether the baby succeeds. I enjoy watching her clumsy failures, but I cannot do so when the toy is out of her reach. So I move it back. Yet in doing so, I have demonstrated the correct way to reach and grasp the

rattle. Adults perform dozens of demonstrations like that for infants every day without realizing it.[26]

And not only is it likely that older experienced members of a society model a behavior like reaching; they also interpret the baby's gestures in ways that are then communicated to him. The Russian psychologist Lev Vygotsky described how from unsuccessful attempts to reach for an object and the adult's tendency to help him out, the young baby comes to understand the gesture of pointing.[27] A failed reach is given significance by others. Furthermore, by focusing attention on a specific object, older members of the society communicate to the child a sense of the object's meaningfulness. Kaye notes a study which suggests that when given a choice between an object used by an adult and a nearly identical copy of that object, an infant will prefer the first. When it comes to learning language, the same rule holds. As Jerome Bruner notes, "the child is not learning what to say, but how, where, to whom, and under what circumstances."[28] Yet children can only learn all this from experienced members of their culture.

In order to produce the competent infant, research scientists have also had to edit out irrational behaviors, such as crying or sleeping, that might confuse this picture. Brain researchers have to work hard to get babies to attend to the computer screen if that's what they need to do. They program the computer to stop recording noise during distracted periods and to repeat images missed by the child.[29] Infant studies are performed only under optimum conditions. Researchers ask mothers to make sure their babies are well fed, rested, dry, and healthy before bringing them to the lab. They measure only the most Pollyannaish behaviors—surprise, curiosity, and concentration—and ignore fear and misery. Not surprisingly, the 50 percent or higher drop-out rates among babies for any lab study rival that of many inner-city high schools. As one skeptic has pointed out, you would never guess from perusing contemporary research that infants under three months, who spend an average of between 95 and 180 minutes a day crying and fussing, are active and alert as little as 25 percent of the day.[30] In actuality, as many parents might attest after rocking and walking their colicky newborn for hours every night for three months, the infant usually seems more like a crying machine, rather than an information-processing machine, whose competence lies mostly in disrupting parental meals and sleep.

It's worth noting as well that the picture of the competent, rational infant that emerges from the research lab is something entirely new in the history of the world. Earlier in the nation's history, as we saw in the last chapter, Americans had come to prefer to keep their babies active and alert. But they were also deeply aware, often due to painful personal experience, of the fragility of the newborn. They shared the presumption of people from most cultures that overstimulation can be harmful. In 1888 when Alice H. Putnam, superintendent of the Chicago Froebel Association, ventured the revolutionary idea that mothers might hang a bright but simple object over their baby's cradle, she was wary; anything too baroque or colorful might tire the brain, for, she warned ominously, "the seeds of most of the insanities are sown at or before this time."[31] And though Piaget may have helped introduce a picture of the young child as an active and curious explorer, he, unlike his American followers, nevertheless believed that infants were subject to all sorts of primitive misconceptions.

That the lucid, rational child is more the artificial dream of a technological age than a natural fact becomes especially clear when one considers the substance of popular advice books of the past half century. These works tend not to draw too heavily on the sort of laboratory research that inspired the honorific "competent infant," but they have nevertheless added to his impressive resumé and advanced his career into the toddler years and even middle childhood. One need only examine the works of the most popular experts: Benjamin Spock, T. Berry Brazelton, and Penelope Leach (who, though English, has an enormous following in the United States). All of them evoke a lucid, independent, and self-regulating baby.

The picture that emerges, especially from Dr. Spock, might bring a bitter laugh from many exhausted and frustrated parents in the trenches. Babies "want to fit into the family's way of doing things, with only a minimum of guidance from you," Dr. Spock announces cheerily.[32] The words *peaceful, quietly friendly, fond,* and *gentle,* noted one critical reader of Spock, litter his discussion. "Three-quarters of the things that we think we must impose on children as unpleasant duties," Spock notes, "are things they enjoy learning to do themselves." Children only misbehave if they are "bossed and disciplined too much."[33] Though anthropologists have found that cultures universally have "a more or less standard pattern and time for weaning,"[34] Spock's baby has no need for prodding from outsiders. "Take it easy and follow your baby's lead," Spock advises on this subject; he also claims that most babies willingly give up their pacifiers by three or four months, a fact that would surprise the many parents who have three-year-olds who go into fits of despair at the mere threat of several minutes without their "binkies."[35] If we leave them to their own devices, our youngest children will also eat sensibly. The unspoiled child, Penelope Leach announces, will try new foods easily and will ultimately choose a balanced diet: "Trust him to know best."[36] As for the older baby, Spock adds breezily, "Each child herself wants to eat at sensible hours and later to learn good table manners."[37]

Advice about toilet training offers a fascinating minihistory of the emergence of this miraculously independent and self-regulating baby. Though Americans had long shown an unusual interest in children's perceptions and emotions, no one imagined that children might have feelings about how they should be escorted from diapers to the privy. Until the middle of the century, children were toilet trained much as dogs were; parents gave as much thought to their youngster's experience of learning bowel control as they did to Fido's. In an age when mothers not only had to wash diapers but to sew and mend them— keep in mind that at seven diapers per day a mother would have laundered five thousand diapers by the time her child turned two—expedience in the service of health was the main concern, especially when the threat of cholera loomed large. Luther Emmett Holt, the famous pediatrician-author whose stern advice cast a pall over Spock's own childhood, recommended beginning bowel training as early as two or three *months*.[38] His instructions, which if enacted today would bring a visit from child welfare authorities, were nevertheless cautious compared to those of Frederic Bartlett, written in 1932: "If you can, start training your infant to have a bowel movement in the chamber each morning at the age of one month. Fix a definite time . . . place the chamber on your lap . . . and hold the infant over it . . . Insert about two inches into the rectum a tapered soap stick, keep it there from three to five minutes . . . If you keep this up with regularity, a daily bowel movement will probably result."[39]

In one of those cultural transformations that has as much to do with technological as moral progress, this approach began to lose favor by the 1940s. As washing machines and ready-made diapers became more affordable and mothers were freed from the tyranny of washing by hand and sewing, experts could now encourage parents to delay toilet training to the middle of the second year without being laughed out of print. Instead of mothers' drudgery and public health, they began to focus attention on the child's own psyche. Rebelling against what they viewed as the bourgeois obsession with cleanliness and the "mechanized body,"[40] Freudians like Erik Erikson and Selma Fraiberg warned of a litany of neuroses—compulsions, homosexuality, excessive greed, stinginess—awaiting the rigidly trained child. They took parents on a tour of the child's unconscious mind, noting all the primitive fears and pleasures associated with the bathroom. In a popular work entitled *The Magic Years,* Fraiberg devoted more than ten pages to the subtleties of bowel training in which she described the child's view of the flushing toilet as a "vitreous monster with its yawning jaws."[41]

Today's competent and sensible toddler has escaped this primitive Freudian fantasyland. Parents are no longer needed to help their youngsters negotiate the terrors of the bathroom. In fact, now the danger is neither disease, the young child's impulses, nor unconscious fears but rather the parents' meddling in the child's natural ability to regulate herself. Spock, following the research of T. Berry Brazelton, describes a child who essentially trains himself: "Children should become trained of their own free will . . . No pressure to sit down on the seat if the child has any disinclination. No detention on the seat— even for a second—when the child wants to get up."[42] A more recently popular book, *What to Expect: The Toddler Years,* responds to the question of when to begin toilet training with what has become conventional wisdom: "Look no further than your toddler for the answer. Only your child can tell you."[43]

And so many children have. In 1957, when parents still had some say in the matter, 92 percent of children were toilet trained by eighteen months. Today only 4 percent of children are trained by age two, and only 60 percent have completely given up diapers by thirty-six months. Some four-year-olds are now pushing the envelope, leading the diaper industry to introduce a new breed of giant-sized products.[44] Popular experts explain all this with vague assertions that children give up their diapers "when they are ready." But this ignores the vast majority of peoples throughout history whose children are trained before age two. Instead of acknowledging the universal truth that children are incomplete creatures looking for signs from their culture of what is expected of them, the current view implies that our youngsters are so self-aware and so reasonable that they choose to become civilized in their own way, at their own pace. They don't need any guidance on these matters at all.

Like the research scientist, popular experts airbrush irrational behaviors that might ruin the picture of their competent, independent child. Willfulness has faded into archaic history. Egotism and selfishness—gone, just like that. Even aggression, jealousy, cruelty, if they appear at all, show up only fleetingly. Instead of stubborn tendencies of human nature, they are merely symptoms of some temporary madness known as a "stage."[45] The spin on the toddler temper tantrum offers a perfect example of the lengths to which experts are willing to go to maintain their portrait of the sensible child. This is Leach's admittedly no-holds-barred description:

> He may rush around the room, wild and screaming . . . anything moveable that happens to be in his path will be knocked flying . . . he may bang into solid walls and heavy furniture. He may fling himself on the floor, writhing, kicking and screaming as if he were fighting with demons. He may scream and scream until he makes himself sick. He may scream and turn blue in the face.[46]

What do we make of this sort of Neanderthal display? Leach sees it as a result of contradictory feelings. On the one hand, the toddler continues to want to cling to his mother. On the other, he is asserting his "desire to be independent, to shake off the absolute control adults have and to become a person in his own right."[47] T. Berry Brazelton, in his often sensible *Toddlers and Parents* agrees. The tantrum's writhing, kicking, and screaming reflects the child's natural assertion of his right to independence.[48]

Pause for a moment and consider how great a leap is contained in this view. The architects of republican childhood believed that adults had to shape an independent, rational, and self-regulating individual; today's experts appear to be convinced that children naturally evolve to such a state. Moreover, earlier theorists fretted that their recommendations might have the effect of spurring children's egotism and selfishness. They believed adults had to find ways to counteract those traits. Such concerns are entirely absent in the current literature. In fact, our own experts have come full circle and interpret what might once have seemed evidence of the young child's willfulness and egotism as a good augury, that is, as evidence of a secure, independent-minded, and motivated child. "Your toddler is rapidly developing a sense of being a separate, independent person with personal rights, preferences and ploys. His 'willfulness,'" Leach writes (using condemning quotation marks), "is a sign that he is growing up and that he feels secure enough at present to try to manage things for himself."[49]

Likewise, in a survey of research on the effects of day care, Allison Clarke-Stewart concedes that in some studies day care children appear to be more rebellious and irritable than their stay-at-home counterparts. But, she reasons, this is a *good* thing, because it means that day care kids are "developmentally advanced" (which is a coy way of saying smart) and also more independent, which makes them more easily annoyed at infringements on their freedom. Children in day care "think for themselves . . . and are not willing to comply with adults' arbitrary rules."[50] Note the word *arbitrary;* although most parents find that most of the battles they have with their toddlers are over issues like going to bed at a reasonable hour or wearing a snowsuit in the winter, the term implies that parents are being capricious or even power mongering when they demand these things. In this interpretation, the ideal child is not only smart and independent but gives life to these qualities by being defiant. According to the tenets of anticulturalism, the child who is in opposition to the world is more completely herself.

The point here is not that tantrum-throwing toddlers deserve the belt or harsh lectures about their sinfulness or that our experts are overly "permissive." Spock in particular has been accused of the latter, but the charge is unmerited. In *Dr. Spock's Baby and Child Care*, he usually advises parents to remove the child and wait out the storm, and he frequently calls on parents to be "firm" and to refuse to allow their children to become tyrants of the household. This is consistent with American childbearing at its best, balancing the need to contain children's egotism with a respect for self-assertion. However, by depicting a child so serenely self-regulating, so reasonable, so honestly and earnestly independent, experts can't help but paralyze parents.

Take the common approach to teaching manners, one of the universal tasks of socialization. Manners serve a profound social function: they offer a ritualized means of transcending our latent egotism. Saying *please* or *thank you* allows us to recognize the efforts others take on our behalf. True, Americans have long been suspicious about overly refined manners, which they associate with old-world hypocrisy and formality, and they pride themselves on their informal naturalness. But experts seem to have forgotten altogether the purpose of manners. They simply do not recognize the egotism that manners are supposed to transcend as a significant part of the child's makeup. For them, the real problem is society's demands on children's good nature, what Carol Gilligan refers to as "the tyranny of the nice and the kind."[51] The authors of *What to Expect* warn us, "Children who are nagged about their manners or are punished for not saying 'thank you' or for not using a fork . . . won't feel positive about manners and are likely to ignore them completely when out from under the eye of the enforcing parent."[52] At any rate, not to worry. According to Spock, "Good manners come naturally,"[53] an opinion that confirms what the alert reader has begun to suspect, namely, that the world's premier pediatrician, a man whose name has been synonymous with childbearing wisdom and experience, *never, ever spent a day with a child.*

Among more theoretical academic thinkers on social development, the same dewy thinking holds sway. Current theories about how children develop a conscience, or a sense of guilt, are a perfect example.

Earlier explanations of the emotion recognized its source in a struggle between one's ideals and one's actual desires or actions. We feel guilty when we fail to live up to our standards of good behavior, or even when we think bad thoughts. Good behavior comes about only after a struggle. Not many people today would accept Freud's theory that children develop a conscience out of their fear of their parents' anger over their incestuous wishes as well as out of love and identification with them, but it captures the once common assumption that good behavior, far from coming easily, is born in conflict. People were said to wrestle with their consciences, because they were so commonly tempted to do wrong. Guilt was the engine behind moral behavior.

This is far from the current view. Today psychologists believe that children suffer no ambivalence or conflict. They *want* to be good and they *will* be good—with maybe just a gentle nudge or two. To understand the contemporary take on guilt, it's necessary to grasp psychology's interest in the emotion that is considered guilt's closest cousin—empathy. Spurred by the research of sociobiologists who have discovered evidence of food sharing and mutual concern among primates, psychologists have made empathy the subject of numerous books and papers. Their conclusions will probably come as no surprise, given all the other childhood virtues: empathy comes naturally to children. According to some theorists, empathy is so fundamental to human nature that it makes its first appearance in the hospital nursery. When newborns fuss at the sound of another baby's cry, William Damon, author of *The Moral Child: Nurturing Children's Natural Moral Growth,* tells us, they are demonstrating the "spontaneous tendency to identify with another's discomfort . . . Here we see, in the primitive world of the crib, one human sharing another's burdens."[54] Empathy theorists point to other examples of the supposed spontaneous empathy of children, examples of behavior familiar to parents: the eighteen-month-old who brings his mother to comfort a crying playmate, the three-year-old whose eyes fill with tears at the sight of an injured dog. It's important to understand that experts go much further than merely concluding that human beings are naturally empathic, just as they are, say, naturally fearful or naturally curious. Empathy is both automatic and total; it is "largely involuntary if one pays attention to the victim," according to Martin Hoffman, of New York University, the most frequently cited empathy theorist.[55]

So what does empathy have to do with guilt? In Hoffman's view, children feel guilty when they experience what he calls "empathic distress"; that is, they identify with the pain they may have caused others. As they get older and their awareness of others expands, so does their capacity for guilt. This "true interpersonal guilt," which Hoffman defines as "the bad feeling one has about oneself because one is aware of harming someone" is quite different from older models of the emotion.[56] Closely allied with sympathy and imagination—the guilty child has projected herself into the painful experience of another— guilt confirms not the child's ongoing struggle against her own egotism but her noble and fine nature. This empathy version drains guilt of hot, red-faced shame, and the individual is transformed from the hero of Greek tragedy to the heroine of a sentimental novel. Hoffman believes parents have a minimal role to play in helping children develop their innate capacity for guilt. Since empathy is total and automatic, parents need only occasionally point out any pain their child might have inadvertently caused and can let nature do the rest. What all this implies may be appealing, but it is highly questionable. The implication is that doing the right thing requires no learning, that children who are doing good are merely expressing their true self.

Science has always had a lot of advice for parents, but that does not mean that it has been friendly to them. As we saw in chapter 1, since the beginning of the century experts and scientifically influenced advocates have often looked with suspicion on parents, regarding them as inefficient and overemotional in their dealings with their children. But by giving us a portrait of the child as competent information processor, science today goes much further. It reduces parenting to an exercise in ambivalence and absurdity and leads us further from the stable ground of republican childhood and into the marshes of anticulturalism. After all, how does one rear children who don't need rearing?

Yes, parents have to provide nourishment and love, but that's about it. They have no positive role to play in shaping their children's individual urges or in helping them contain their egotism. And they certainly don't have any knowledge worth passing down. Penelope Leach advises against almost all attempts to guide a child's behavior. "Rules are very useful in keeping a small child safe," she writes, adding illogically, "but they really don't play much part in teaching him how to behave."[57] It often appears that because they are experienced and authoritative members of society, adults pose a risk to their children. Experts repeatedly warn adults of the dangers of their authority, or, as it is sometimes termed, their "power." So deep is the fear of adult authority that it even infects some of the experts who have recently taken to arguing for more parental discipline. William Damon's book *Greater Expectations,* for instance, takes as its starting point today's "diminution of expectations and standards" and explicitly sets out to rebuke dithering adults, but in the end his recommendations for discipline are so complex, so filled with hesitation and caution, so *worried,* that he exacerbates the very anxiety he sets out to mollify. Don't threaten, he tells us; don't assert power, don't sanction too much, use only "minimally sufficient" external incentives, don't communicate too much emotion—or too little—and on and on.[58] Even parents of newborns have to worry. They must beware of interfering with the private, solitary adventure that is mental development. In the chapter entitled "The Second Month" in *What to Expect the First Year* is the warning "Make sure your baby, not you, is in the lead." Adult guidance, the authors contend, "deprives a baby of a sense of control, turns off the interest in the subject."[59]

It's important to distinguish the healthy wariness toward raw parental power that Americans have demonstrated since the invention of republican childhood from the paralyzing ambivalence we see at work in passages like these. Though they did not come up with a solution to satisfy contemporary tastes, republican writers struggled with the question of how parental authority should be modified in order to prepare children for a free adulthood. Many of our current experts' suggestions—such as giving children reasons for our requests of them or allowing small negotiations over them—when applied in moderation to older children are fine means of promoting independent minds capable of carrying on that tradition. But in other ways, these specialists communicate that exercising parental authority should make us tremble in fear. They counsel parents, particularly those with toddlers, to engage in almost any charade that hides the fact that they are in charge: bargaining, negotiating, playacting, bribing. Leach tells parents they will need not only patience and good humor but "talent as an actor too." She provides this example: "Are you in a hurry to get home? If you swoop the toddler into his stroller when he wanted to walk, all hell will break loose. Act as if you had all the time in the world, offer to be a horse and pull him home and you will get there as fast as your legs will take the two of you."[60] If your child refuses to get out of the stroller, counsel the authors of *What to Expect,* you might "suggest, perhaps, that the dog get in the stroller or pretend to get in it yourself . . . Give orders pretending you're a dog or a lion, Big Bird, Mickey Mouse."[61]

There is one important exception to this anxiety of parental influence. Adults do have one indispensible role to play: supplying their infants with stimulation. Recent brain research has asserted that babies are dependent on adults to help them "grow their brains." The advice literature that stems from these discoveries would turn parents into personal cognitive trainers for the infant cerebellum. *How to Have a Smarter Baby* recommends a fifteen-minute-a-day program to exercise your baby's senses so as to "increase his concentration span." Training should begin *before* birth: "fetal learning" requires placing headphones on the mother's belly so that the fetus can hear a tape of personal messages and a bit of classical music introduced by its title. The tape should be played at least once, but hopefully four times, through the evening when the fetus is most alert.[62] Matchbox Toys came out with a pediatrician-tested Babycise Shared Development System, which includes a videotape with five ten-minute exercise segments, two baby barbells, and an exercise mat, among other accessories, to stimulate baby's large motor skills.[63] In other cultures mothers are advised to keep their infants soothed and comforted; they speak softly to their fragile offspring and hold them close. American mothers, on the other hand, are counseled to keep their babies in a perpetual state of industrious activity. "Don't make a move, at least when you're around your baby, without talking about it," the authors of *What to Expect* advise the parents of two-month-olds. "Think of yourself as a reporter, your baby as an intriguing interviewee."[64]

In some respects, this busy industriousness and dedication to self-improvement is in the American tradition. As we saw, nineteenth-century parents often expressed a strong displeasure with their children's idleness. But whereas in the past, advice givers were well aware of the dangers of egotism that lurked in the creed of competitive individualism, today nothing is to get in the way of "building baby's brain."[65] The Japanese also provide a pointed contrast to current American thinking. In Japan the baby is believed to be born an isolated creature. The mother's job is to entice him out of the void and tether him tightly to her and eventually to the wider community.[66] Americans go to the other extreme—the child's individual development trumps all else. The author of *Your Child Is Smarter Than You Think* instructs parents about the learning opportunities in every room in the house, which is baby's "first school"; for example, in the kitchen, activities like folding laundry and unloading the dishwasher can teach classification and sorting skills.[67] In this case, tasks which family members do for one another as members of a larger, mutually caring unit are transformed into an exercise for the self-improvement of the autonomous young intellect-in-training. For the solitary learner, social embeddedness and emotional connections bow down before the god of individual achievement.

In fact, the apparent dedication to the child's individual development that is so much a part of anticultural thinking actually disguises a tendency to downsize his social—and emotional—life. The role of the child as a rational, autonomous information processor swallows up others. The ascent of the infant toy nicely illustrates this process. If you look at the toys inside their cribs and strollers, it would appear that contemporary American infants are truly blessed when it comes to their opportunities for play. Until the late 1960s, when crib mobiles first came on the market, no one imagined that the infant *required* toys.[68] Today, thirty years later, mobiles are only a subsistence diet in a groaning board of baby learning accessories. A cornucopia of toys, usually with the imprimatur of expert consultants, crowds the toy warehouse aisles: musical mobiles, toy bars, crib bumpers, mirrors, crib panels with flipping pictures, cradle gyms, activity cubes, stroller play centers, "infant stimulation sets" with high-contrast rattles, stuffed animals, ball and mirror, elaborate bath works. When they are not playing with their toys, today's lucky infants can go to baby playgrounds like Gymboree or Discovery Zone.

Yet it turns out that all this colorful plush and plastic is not exactly for the pleasure of "His Majesty, the Baby," to use Freud's felicitous title. Infant play is quite unlike that recommended by republican theorists, who after overthrowing harsh Calvinist strictures against pleasure came to endorse play for older children as an outlet for free imagination. Those children who had not been too severely enlisted in their parents' war against idleness had unheard-of amounts of freedom for imaginative play with siblings and neighboring children. But today's experts have reverted to a view of play more in keeping with the Calvinist ideals that republican and romantic thinkers had overthrown. Today play, even for infants, has one purpose: achievement. What the solitary information-organizer needs is not amusement or sensual pleasure but input. Toy manufacturers couldn't hope for better promotional material than the many advice books which define toys as necessities for baby's cognitive work. "Toys are learning tools, ways of providing stimulation to your child," instructs *Your Child Is Smarter Than You Think*.[69] A company called Bright Starts even encloses a paperback copy of *How to Have a Smarter Baby* along with its line of infant toys.

The collaboration between learning experts and the toy industry is nothing new, nor is the notion of achievement play. After World War I, experts were known to lecture at department stores about the importance of "graded" toys. "Toys that teach" were common in the twenties and thirties; the products developed by Playskool Toys, founded in 1928, were actually inspired by IQ test materials. But achievement play has been defined down from the six-year-old sitting at an imitation school desk banging out the alphabet at a miniature typewriter to the infant lying in her crib gurgling at a teddy bear. Toy ads of the 1950s, according to several researchers, were likely to show children having fun within a social group, usually the family. Today ads show children, including babies, alone with the toy, which is increasingly touted as fostering learning. The language of developmentalists is used to exalt everything from stacking blocks to rubber balls to stuffed animals. "I develop speech skills," promises the caption above a picture of a furry white talking bear in one catalogue. One company sells an "infant development toy" known to earlier generations as a rattle. Another, called Early Learning, makes a series of rattles "designed to build manipulative skills and prompt experimentation." There are toys promising to improve everything from eye–hand coordination to spatial relationships.

This kind of technical rationalism infects a good deal of anticultural thinking in its more scientific guises. Rational self-sufficiency is the defining quality of the information-processing infant. In this guise, he does not need others so much as need what they can do for him.

This is true even with respect to mothers. Under the reign of anticulturalism the task of mothering is drained of much of its conventional feeling and given a mechanical cast. The theorists of the nineteenth century swooned over the mother as "the angel in the house," the quietly self-sacrificing and all-loving saint. It was a vision that easily slipped into condescension and sentimentality. But the techno-mom that science has concocted poses another kind of problem: it turns mother love into a technical device for individual advancement. In a 1997 issue devoted to babies, *Newsweek* quickly passes over the health and emotional benefits of breast-feeding to get to the real point: breast-feeding may "make a baby smarter."[70] Judith Rich Harris' controversial 1998 book, *The Nurture Assumption,* employs similar language; parents, she writes, "are an aspect of the environment, like light and pattern, that a baby's brain needs to develop normally."[71] Actor Rob Reiner's "I Am Your Child" campaign website, which includes a list of "brain facts," declares, "Your love for your child is, of course, the key to the powerful connection between the two of you. But it is the *expression* of your love that affects the way her brain forms connections [emphasis in the original]." Note that the value of "cooing, singing, talking, and reading" is coldly utilitarian; it wires the brain.[72]

The up-to-date mother–infant relationship, then, is a far cry from anything that has ever been imagined before. Mother is a reporter interviewing her baby, a personal trainer working out his brain. She should not engage in "motherese," the high-pitched baby talk practiced universally. No, recommends *Growing Up Smart and Happy,* mothers should talk to their babies the way they would to adults. The book idealizes "one ingenious mother [who] solved the problem of intellectual stimulation for her baby *and* herself by occasionally reading the newspaper aloud to the baby while she offered the bottle."[73] A woman reading the newspaper to her suckling is another remarkable late-twentieth-century twist on mother and child.

The discovery of the self-sufficient information processor who does not need a mother in any recognizably human sense came at a particularly opportune time in American social history. As women moved into the workforce in massive numbers and as the divorce rate skyrocketed, those in the lab and the academy were able to assure Americans that our youngest children could not only take these developments but, given their insatiable need for stimulation, even benefit from them. Arguably, given the American affection for the new and modern, a better, smarter baby might have seemed an irresistible sign of American ingenuity and know-how and earned an enthusiastic reception at many points in our history. But the fact is that the theory of the competent infant clinched the changes in the American family over the past thirty years. In the middle years of the century, attachment theory, a psychoanalytically influenced countervoice to the dominant behaviorism of the time, exerted the greatest influence on the popular imagination about the needs of infants. It stressed both the primal importance of the mother–child connection and the baby's emotional well-being. In a study of parenting magazines, Kathryn T. Young found that from the mid-1950s until the early 1970s, mothers were viewed as central to the infant's well-being.[74]

These days many feminists argue that attachment theory was never really hard science so much as a mythology formulated to keep women out of the workplace.[75] Without question, attachment theory fit hand in glove with the mother-at-home, father-at-work arrangement that had dominated middle-class American society since the nineteenth century. But it is equally true that the competent infant is a welcome theory for its own time. It is no accident that by the mid-seventies, just as women started going to work in great numbers, the popular image of the baby began to transform from helpless neediness into competent information processing and, at the same time, the mother–infant relationship and attachment theory faded from the headlines. To be sure, experts still encouraged mothers to be affectionate and nurturing—and some still fretted about babies deprived of too much maternal attention—but Young found that articles in the magazines made fewer references to the mother–infant relationship and that when they did, they pronounced mother's continuous presence to be no longer "vitally" important. The infant's emotional and social welfare began to seem a simpler matter, one that adults could take for granted with hugs, kisses, and quality time. It was cognitive development that merited anxious attention.

Yet as we have seen, when cognitive development becomes the dominant task of infancy, it alters the relationship between adult and child. Brain building, a technical and emotionally neutral job, does not necessarily require the presence of a parent. One can just as easily instruct a baby sitter on how to provide stimulation for one's baby (as Sera, whom we met in the opening of this chapter, did) or trust a professional to do it in a good day care center. The new brain research, cautions one article, "challenges deeply held beliefs—that infants will thrive intellectually if they are simply given lots of love and that purposeful efforts to influence babies' cognitive development are harmful."[76] An explosive growth in toddler classes over the last decades—with many parents insisting that their children be allowed to enroll even if they have not reached the recommended age—is part of the same phenomenon.[77] Day care advocates are also well aware of the implications of the baby information processor; they frequently cite brain research to support their proposals. "Head Start may be too little, too late," cautions one article in this vein[78]; day care is the logical place to start brain building.

Nothing better symbolizes the way the image of the information processor threatens the best tradition of republican childhood and its promise of a rich individualism than the day care center. Unthinkable a generation ago, day care centers are commonplace and likely to become more so. Thirty percent of the preschool children of working mothers are now in institutionalized day care. The number rose sharply this decade: 23 percent just between 1991 and 1993. While the number of youngsters in day care went up, the percentage of those children cared for by nonmaternal relatives declined by 5 percent.[79] It's a good guess that these numbers will continue to fall since boomer grandmothers will likely be less inclined to take over the child care for their working adult children than their own nonworking mothers were.

It is doubtless the case that the large majority of children who attend day care centers will grow up "normal." They will do their homework, pass their courses, and graduate from school. They will make friends, marry, and have children of their own. And it is possible that they will get the stimulation they need for building better brains. But it is also without question that children who spend the bulk of their time in an institution are going to learn a fundamentally different way of constructing an inner life than those who spend most of their days with an adoring parent. The architects of republican childhood had a vision of shaping an American personality, one that was simultaneously intensely individual and resolutely public-spirited. Such a child is unlikely to be the product of eight or ten hours a day in a center. Babies in day care centers are by definition in an impersonal environment organized to meet the needs of a large group rather than those of individuals. And regardless of their quality, day care centers are institutions whose atmosphere is determined by regulations, budgets, staffing, contracts, and formal rules. In centers, babies sleep in rows of cribs, they are fed in rows of high chairs, they are tied together in wagons for outings to the park. Observers have found that even the better caretakers sometimes forget their charges' names and refer to them as "little girl" or "little boy."[80] Forced to rely on their peers for much of their identity, day care kids are on the road to becoming conformists.

Moreover, children in day care centers for many hours a day will have to learn to downsize their emotional expectations. The anthropologist Margaret Mead, although she was hardly a champion of the American middle-class home, recognized that the Samoan children

she studied who were reared communally demonstrated less emotional intensity than their Western counterparts.[81] Day care personnel
and observers often note the tendency of harried and guilty parents to
detach themselves from their children over time. Parents, usually
mothers, often cry when they first leave their children in a day care
center. But according to Eleanor Reynolds, who has observed day care
centers for over twenty years, that changes as they tell themselves,
"My baby seems fine; he hardly notices when I leave; she doesn't need
me all the time; he really loves his new caretaker."[82] There is no way
that this emotional downsizing can be addressed by what advocates
call "quality day care." Day care workers are being paid to watch over
their charges, who, after all, come and go; they cannot possibly be expected to devote their strong affections to them. Furthermore, there is
an enormous rate of turnover among day care personnel. It is not surprising that some studies find children in day care to be more aggressive and less attentive to adult instruction than their stay-at-home
counterparts.[83] They are not fully attached and identified with the
specific adults who are with them during much of their day.

"There is no such thing as a baby," the English psychoanalyst
D. W. Winnicott once announced. "There is a baby and someone
else."[84] Winnicott was referring, of course, to the obvious physical
helplessness of the infant but also to something more existential.
Young children simply have no way to translate the world into meaningful terms without "someone else." The picture of infant and toddler competence vastly understates just how dependent babies are on
adults, not to learn in any technical sense but to render the world
meaningful.

Young children do not merely need information punctuated by
kisses. They need to bring order to their chaotic perceptions and to
know how to interpret them. They rely on experienced representatives of their culture to explain and bring order to the unfamiliar objects and events around them and to give them the language and the
mental structures with which to do so. When I used to ask my

preschool children, "What did you do in school today?" they, like most kids, often didn't answer. If I asked, "What songs did you sing?" or "What toys did you play with?" they were more likely to respond. By asking these specific questions, I wasn't merely giving them attention in a generic sense. I was introducing what some psychologists call "schema" to order their experience. I was calling attention to the ways they should construct meaning out of flux. In time, with repetition, they would learn to internalize these and many other schema. These would allow them to become autonomous observers and thinkers, though in a specific cultural format.

Recent studies have begun to flesh out the way young children depend on adults to help them interpret their experiences. In one, preschoolers were first told a story and then later given misleading information about it in two separate interviews, one with an adult and another with a seven-year-old child. Two days later they were questioned. The researchers found that the preschoolers frequently incorporated the misinformation from the adults and, though less so, that from the other children.[85]

Young children's reliance on adult perception became obvious during several notorious trials in the 1980s involving day care workers. In all of these cases, children accused their teachers of the most bizarre acts: licking peanut butter off their genitals, forcing them to drink urine and eat feces, pushing a sword up their rectum, killing a horse with a baseball bat, eating a human head. Many parents and onlookers concluded that children couldn't possibly make up these horrors, that they must be true. "Believe the children," became the mantra surrounding these cases. And so people did, despite the fact that some of the accusations depicted acts that were just about physically impossible and despite the fact that many of the accused had worked successfully with children for years.[86]

What happened here was that social workers, parents, lawyers, and judges were duped by a particular form of the anticultural fallacy. They assumed that very young children already have a firm grip on an independent reality. When they questioned their young witnesses—and questioned and questioned again—they failed to realize how much the children were depending on them, as experienced members of their culture, to guide them into understanding the world around them. Transcripts show that in several cases interviewers asked children to show them where a teacher had touched them by pointing to a doll. If the children poked the doll in the eye or knee, interviewers often continued to ask, "Where else?" But if the children touched the doll's vagina or anus, or otherwise confirmed what the interviewer already believed, they would receive praise—"Wow! That's great!" or "You're so smart!"—and even the promise of rewards. Some interviewers even told children that they themselves had been abused when they were little and that one feels better after admitting to such an experience. In time, children began to truly believe the fantastic stories.[87] After all, adults considered them true.

"I just don't believe that we have this incredible power to influence children," said an exasperated Kee MacFarlane, lead investigator in the infamous McMartin preschool case in California, in response to a reporter's questions about her interviewing methods.[88] Given the lone information processor science considers the child to be, the mistake made by MacFarlane and all of those who "believed the children" was an understandable one. They have learned from science that children interrogate the world on their own: their explorations are supposed to be self-directed, their theories self-discovered, their sense of reality autonomously constructed.[89] Thus, whether or not babies are in day care centers or at home with mommy, and whether she is reading the newspaper or singing a lullaby, our *understanding* of what children need and what it is we adults owe them has shifted dramatically, not only from the best tradition of American childrearing but from childrearing as it has been universally understood.

Anthropologists find that children are recognizably American or Indian or French, that is, that they interpret the world in ways typical of their culture, by the time they are five years old—and possibly even as early as several months.[90] For the most part, science has no way of accounting for how this transformation occurs. This means that science is silent about what is perhaps the most important thing we have to teach our children: how they should view the world. According to anticultural scientists, we do not impart to our children an intricate web of relationships, behavior, and inherited values which give life meaning; rather, we are technicians, tuning up our advanced, self-directing intelligence machines. Our baby geniuses do not need "someone else" to show them how to enter their world. They merely need information and input for their own achievement. Whether this information has any meaning, whether it can be converted into value-laden, ordered knowledge, is irrelevant. Parents reading the newspaper to their suckling newborns, taking them to the gym, dropping them off at "school," showing them flash cards, treating them as interviewees, playing them Mozart sonatas, or showing them Matisse drawings—these are images which suggest how science, far from clarifying the mysteries of child nature, merely reinvents childrearing in its own image. The important question is whether the child's mind can efficiently manipulate symbols. The actual content of those symbols is immaterial.

We have already seen that anticulturalism tends to diminish the depth of children's emotional bond to their caretakers. This suggests that it also shrinks their devotion toward the wider world. By placing the individual child outside of culture, the myth of anticulturalism deprives him of the meaning and richness that culture should bestow. Inextricably bound to practical benefits like intellectual advancement, culture becomes a grab bag from which parents choose the activities they think most useful for their own individual children. Games like pat-a-cake and peekaboo are meaningful not because one's mother and grandmother played them or simply for the unrivaled joy of a laughing infant but because these activities offer "interactive forms of stimulation." Stripped from their cultural context, Matisse drawings or Mozart sonatas are no longer food for the soul but data for the computerized brain. By draining the content of culture of any significance and by usurping the terms of childrearing—the most culturally loaded task there is—science *becomes* culture. Such is the sterile worldview we are passing down to the next generation.

....

Chapter 3

Anticultural
Education

Sol Stern and his wife felt extremely
fortunate to have their two sons enrolled at P.S. 87, a New York City
public elementary school. *Parents* magazine had called it one of the
country's ten best—public or private—and indeed many middle-
class families in Manhattan viewed it as one of the few attractive
schools in a public system so ineffective that it had driven many of
their peers to the suburbs. And the Sterns were pleased with the
school—at least for a few years. Gradually they began to realize that
in English class the children were spending much of their time writing freely in journals without much supervision from teachers. They
were not learning grammar or spelling, leaving some fourth graders
unable to compose a correct sentence. In math, things were not
much better. Teachers believed that their students needed to understand math within the context of real-life problems and that memo-
rizing mutiplication tables or practicing addition and subtraction
problems could not help them in that project. In third grade, the
Sterns' older son spent many months on a multidisciplinary project

building a Japanese garden. Day after day, when he came home from school and his parents asked him what he had done in math class that day, he answered, "We measured the garden." Over time, the Sterns saw that the school was not going to do much of what they had assumed schools were supposed to do. The parents began teaching their boys by using workbooks at home; during fourth and fifth grades, the boys stayed home twenty to thirty days a year. In their "modified" home schooling, the Sterns found that a two-to-three-hour study session at home accomplished more than weeks in the school classroom.[1]

Bad as it was, the Sterns' school experience is not all that unusual. Educators have been extolling the general methods used by the teachers at P.S. 87, and children have been languishing for many decades. Touting labels like *discovery learning, constructivism, lifelong learning,* or *child-centered curriculum,* educationists have prided themselves on the notion that they are teaching "children, not subjects" and that children are making meaning for themselves. During the years that these ideas have been at the core of educational thinking, parents have rebelled, counter movements like back-to-basics have sprung up, politicians have railed, newspapers and magazines have run exposés—to no avail. Not only have these ideas triumphed in education circles, but they have expanded into ever new and more extreme forms.

Anticulturalism helps explain why the basic ideas of the child-centered curriculum have been so tenacious in the face of failure and why genuine education reform in the United States has been so difficult to accomplish. To reduce it to its essence, educators don't know what kids are like. Like the psychologists we saw in the previous chapter, they begin by assuming the existence of a rational, organized, and self-directed youngster; "the child of five, six, or seven is is many ways an extremely competent individual," writes psychologist Howard Gardner, a highly influential education theorist.[2] Throughout history, human beings have imagined education as a process whereby a teacher, experienced in the ways of a culture, passes that culture on to the ignorant and inexperienced young. That approach, now damned as the "control model," is evidently no longer necessary.

Today's kids can figure everything out for themselves. Call it anticultural education.

Reform-minded educators are fond of repeating a story that with minor variations goes like this: "Traditional" American education was invented at the turn of the century when schools were modeled on the factory. Children sat rigidly and miserably in rows, where they memorized and spewed out a meaningless series of facts. This mass-produced education continued pretty much in this fashion throughout the century. But in recent decades, reformers explain, it's become clear that this archaic model has outlived its usefulness. Research is proving that children are, and therefore should be treated as, "active learners" and "problem solvers." Instead of sitting still and being quiet in artifical rows, they should move easily around the room to work centers, where they work on projects of their own devising either alone or in groups and "construct" their own knowledge. These new methods, as one enthusiast puts it, "are the educational equivalents of the polio vaccine and penicillin."[3]

There is some truth to this story. Accounts of school life from the early decades of this century often paint a grim picture. The philosopher Sidney Hook recalled being under the control of "martinet" teachers who gave orders: "Take pencils!" "Write!" "Pencils down!"[4] And there can be no question that, as the philosopher Alfred North Whitehead said, "education is not a process of packing articles in a trunk," whereby the child simply loads unexamined information into his brain.[5] Such an approach cannot teach children to reason and question independently, one of the central goals of education in a democratic society.

Still, there is a good deal of melodrama in the reformer's narrative. After all, child-centered learning arrived on the American scene a century ago. Certainly, today's classrooms are more likely to resemble those encountered by the Stern children than that endured by Sidney Hook. Further, good and bad educational practices can't be divided neatly into categories marked "traditional/bad" and "new/good."

Anyone who can recall a poem from his youth knows that memorization can often enrich and expand the imagination. And traditional education is not simply drill and rote memorization; it includes compare–contrast essays which require factual knowledge *and* thinking.

But another important flaw in the reformer's story is the assumption that we can rely on science to lead us into the pedagogical sunlight. Science, particularly cognitive science, is merely reinforcing a mythological vision of children that had already taken hold through progressive ideas. The child that emerges from cognitive theories, much like the machinelike learner we saw in the previous chapter, learns automatically, untiringly, and happily; it is only when something external (i.e., cultural) interferes with this natural process that children are "turned off."

Two good examples of how these ideas manifest themselves in the classroom are the controversial whole language approach to reading instruction and "learner-centered math." These approaches suggest that children will come to read and do math naturally if they are placed in a language- or number-rich environment. Although not strictly the discovery of cognitive scientists, these approaches repeat the cognitivist idea of the child's innate learning structures. For example, misguidedly adapting Noam Chomsky's theory that children are innately equipped to learn spoken language, whole language theorists argue that children are also naturally disposed toward literacy. This belief has propelled them to reject the universal approach to reading instruction since the time of the Greeks—teaching children the correspondence between sound and written symbols. Dispensing with lessons that isolate skills like recognizing spelling patterns or word families, whole language proponents believe that children should learn with minimal guidance from teachers by being exposed repeatedly to written texts and encouraged to decipher meaning from context. As a result, kids who learn through the whole language approach "think everything is trial and error," according to one special education tutor. "When I tell them there are rules that govern our language, they are stunned."[6]

Instead of directly teaching children the rules and concepts of math and written language, many educators influenced by cognitive science propose that teachers help children understand the "thinking strategies" required to figure them out for themselves. Metacognition, as it is sometimes called, focuses children's attention on what's going on, or what needs to go on, in their brains in order to attack the problem at hand. Even very young children are taught to monitor their thinking processes. Children in a whole language classroom will be encouraged to guess at meanings by thinking about the picture on the page or by inferring an unknown word after gathering the meaning of the rest of the sentence. Metacognitive strategies can be used across the curriculum: children can keep journals to examine the thought processes they use when writing, they can keep logs of their hypotheses and evidence and compare them with their classmates when they are doing science projects, and so on.[7] Children learn not by acquiring knowledge but by "adding better rules to their production systems."[8] Demonstrating this process of thinking, they "become mathematical problem solvers" and learn to "communicate mathematically," a goal that is judged more important than learning to come up with correct answers.[9]

Though statements implying that teachers shouldn't worry so much about correct answers drive education critics into a frenzy, it's important to acknowledge that a true understanding of math is more than simply wielding arithmetic facts and concepts in the predictable series of questions children encounter in most standardized tests and that a genuine comprehension of a written text requires more than decoding print. But educators go much further than this and argue that it isn't even *necessary* to teach children math concepts or how to decode print, claiming that a child's innate drive to learn is so powerful that the traditional curriculum can be entirely discarded.

Whether preschoolers or undergraduates, students can choose the topics that they want to study, because when they do so, according to this rationale, they are able to follow their natural inclinations, just as the expert's child we saw in the previous chapter naturally chooses a healthy diet. "Since the children choose activities that interest them," states an orientation pamphlet for a Honolulu preschool in typically circular language, "they are meeting their own needs."[10] The new Standards for the English Arts, published by the International Reading Association and the National Council of Teachers of English, says that "children's perspectives, interests, and needs [should] shape classroom discussion, writing projects, and curriculum choices."[11] High schools offer a menu of choices, following the logic that a student can then "build a program around his or her needs."[12]

In true anticultural fashion, educators insist that the only thing that prevents children from learning is adults—or, more generally, culture. Left to themselves, children will be carried along by what anticultural educators call "intrinsic motivation." Unlike extrinsic motivation, such as clearly laid out assignments, grades, and rewards like gold stars offered by the teacher, intrinsic motivation comes entirely from inside the child. Teresa Amabile, an oft-quoted expert on the subject, believes that elementary school children should be "largely responsible for monitoring their own work . . . The teacher will give them goals to accomplish in particular areas within a given time period . . . but the children will have autonomy in deciding exactly how to accomplish those goals and they will have responsibility for keeping track of their progress toward the goals."[13] Harvard psychologist Howard Gardner, best known for his theory of multiple intelligences, has initiated a similarly optimistic project, entitled the Arts PROPEL program, for middle and high school students that uses student portfolios, an increasingly popular way to judge performance, in place of tests. "The student is asked to bring about change in herself," Gardner writes, "rather than to wait for change to be imposed from the outside . . . and to accept the possibility that assessment may be the burden not of the teacher primarily but of the learner herself."[14] Similarly, the children in my older daughter's fourth grade classroom some years ago each chose the books they wanted to read, instead of all reading the same book. When I objected that my daughter, a highly competent reader, was choosing books from the Babysitter's Club series—popular but poorly written texts characterized by simplistic sentence structure, second grade vocabulary, and banal plots—her teacher promised that because my daughter was in charge of her learning, she would be more motivated to choose more challenging texts on her own in the future. In other words, she would come to Shakespeare or Wordsworth naturally—that is, as long as adults did not interfere.

"Alternative assessments" of the sort recommended by Gardner go far beyond rethinking the multiple choice standardized tests criticized by many thoughtful education critics. They reflect the anticultural assumption that children should be held not to any external cultural expectations but only to the expectations created by their own needs. Some experts recommend only the kind of tests that would, as the education writer Edward Fiske puts it, allow students without time restraints and without any "secret agendas" (which presumably means adult expectations) to "show off in whatever way comes most naturally to them."[15] In a number of particularly innovative schools, parent–teacher conferences have been replaced with conferences where students "set their own educational goals and then assess how well they have done." Other schools have replaced report cards with a kind of pedagogic growth chart. Four Baltimore middle schools under the auspices of researchers at Johns Hopkins University are experimenting with "improvement scores," under which each student begins the year with a baseline score and improvement is then evaluated monthly.[16]

What is most striking about all of these ideas is not only the amazing strengths that educators ascribe to children but the complete denial of their less obliging side. These qualities—the restlessness, impulsiveness, resistance to hard concentration, and preference for the easy way out—which have an enormous bearing on learning (and which parents see on an hourly basis), do not make an appearance in today's utopian education texts. Anticultural educators assure us of a child self-aware and ceaselessly driven to learn.

Yes, it's true that some lucky individuals fall in passionate love with a subject that sets in motion a life of hard, devoted work for which they need little incentive or reward. Einstein remembered a triggering moment in his lifelong interest in science when at four or five his father showed him a compass.[17] But any parent who has succumbed to buying a pet for a pleading child knows the reality: most children's interests are as fleeting as rings on the surface of a pond. Children's shelves provide an archeological field site of yesterday's fierce obsessions—baseball cards, Barbie dolls, soccer trophies, dinosaur replicas—obsessions which have as much resonance to maturing individuals as their baby rattle. As for children being natural readers and mathematicians, some recent research suggests that human beings *are* born with a rudimentary sense of number and geometry. But nowhere is there evidence that there is anything natural—or immediately pleasurable—about complex skills like advanced algebra. If there were, children throughout history would have sat in corners calculating pi rather than playing tag or clobbering their siblings over the head.[18]

This denial about children's antisocial tendencies and the optimism about their natural drive to learn have very deep roots in pedagogic thinking, deeper really than the influence of cognitive science. Their origins lie a hundred years ago in the philosophy of John Dewey, the godfather of American pedagogy. Dewey believed that children possess an innate drive to understand and control their environment, an important notion that would probably not meet with much disagreement anywhere in America today. However, he didn't stop there. He pronounced the child endowed with four "impulses," a word he used interchangeably with "instinct" and "interest" in the following contexts: communicating, inquiring, creating or constructing, and striving toward artistic expression.[19] These "natural drives" were thought to be strong enough to guide the curriculum. Dewey's child, like that of today's scientifically oriented experts, is a wondrously constructive learner with no sign of a darker side. According to Dewey, the child's energies are no threat to education; in fact, they are the source of genuine learning. Dewey's very use of the word *impulse,* a word which commonly contains a hint of animal energy, is striking in this context. One need only compare the impulse toward artistic expression in Dewey's child with the impulses of the child imagined by his contemporary in Vienna, which were more along the lines of incest and murder, to get the flavor of Dewey's optimism.

Still, this optimism was contained within a broad and serious vision of democratic goals. By nurturing the child's natural impulses, Dewey believed, the schools could liberate the "free and powerful character" needed in a democratic society. And, though Dewey was often maddeningly vague and inconsistent, he appeared to understand children's impulses to be just that: inchoate drives in need of careful guidance and structuring. The success of the "hands-on" activities in his experimental Lab School—where, for instance, children raised wheat which they then used for baking bread—depended on their being one step in a highly structured curriculum designed to lead children toward more traditional disciplines. Teachers encouraged children's inquiries into science, providing a foundation for later, more abstract study of biology and chemistry. Profoundly sensitive to the personal initiative and adaptability needed to thrive in modern America, Dewey nevertheless made a point of distinguishing between indulging a child's interests and directing them toward social ends.[20]

These subtleties have been entirely lost on today's educators.[21] They do not conceive of shaping the child's energies toward broad social ends or democratic goals; they simply let children learn what their impulses tell them to learn. In some "shopping mall" high schools, students choose from four hundred available courses.[22] Though it would be impossible for younger children to move from class to class on their own, many reformers recommend that they work within classrooms on their own projects or on those of other kids or that they help the teacher decide what the class should study. Educators from High/Scope, the organization that founded one of the most highly respected Head Start programs in the country, recommend that "teachers share decision-making with children about what will be learned and how they will learn it."[23] The author of *Schools That Work* praises classrooms that allow "choices whenever possible" and provides the example of a science teacher in Amesville, Ohio, who began the year by asking, "What would you guys like to study?" The answer provided by one fourth grade class given such a choice was "reproduction."[24] In a wittier world this answer would serve as a reminder of the more forgotten side of children's impulses.

All of this suggests that contemporary educators, like the advice givers we saw in chapter 2, are unconcerned with the child's potential egotism. In fact, in their own way they endorse it wholeheartedley. Underlying their theories is the radical sentiment that it is unnecessary for teachers to introduce children to an independently existing, knowable universe outside themselves. They even believe such instruction can be downright destructive. Whole language proponents, for instance, discourage any activity that might imply that written language is a man-made, rule-bound code with a long history and rich traditions. For them, language is not an external thing that can be studied and modeled but an interior process that must develop. Likewise, advocates of learner-centered math argue that children "invent their own ways of adding and subtracting."[25] "Children don't get ideas," one constructivist asserts. "They make ideas."[26]

It should be plain by now that anticultural education requires a dramatically changed relationship between teacher and student. Traditionally, educators have considered it their mission to introduce knowledge valued in their culture to its newcomers. When they required students to take specific courses or to undertake specific homework projects and when they gave children gold stars, prizes, or high grades, they were dramatizing cultural values for the young who don't yet understand them and who often fail to find their demands immediately pleasurable. But the anticulturalist does not believe in passing down knowledge to the young. A study from the research group Public Agenda found that only 7 percent of education professors think teachers should be "conveyors of knowledge who enlighten students with what they know." Ninety-two percent believe teachers should only "enable students to learn on their own."[27] In the current argot, teachers are not even supposed to be teachers. They are "facilitators," "managers of instruction," or "coaches." Seymour Papert, author of *The Children's Machine,* views teachers as "co-learners";[28] in some schools, students even grade them in "reverse report cards."[29]

It might seem curious that teachers would accept this new role, since they have already suffered a marked decline in status in American society over the past generation. It may be that they run to embrace methods like metacognition, because in an information society status comes with innovative-sounding technical expertise. It may also be that the coach-teacher is an irresistible ideal in a society which places autonomy on the top of its list of virtues and which is increasingly ambivalent about childhood. But whatever the cause, one can begin to see why the profession has been plagued by a 50 percent attrition rate in the first five years of work. Why would adults want to be teachers in a society that believes adults have nothing to teach? In

Japan teachers are called *sensei,* which means something like "wise counselor," and they are greeted by bowing children who say in unison, "Good morning, sensei." The best American teachers can hope for is a random "Yo, Miss Brooks, whasup?" At worst, they fear for their lives. For this they are paid poorly and widely viewed as chumps. In a study of the image of teachers on television and in movies, Barry Farber found "a slightly eccentric, well-meaning . . . camp counsellor" whose most notable qualities are forced jokes, earnest friendliness, and poor tailoring.[30]

Both cognitive science and the progressive tradition have encouraged the state of affairs wherein it is increasingly difficult to understand education in the usual sense of adults passing down valued knowledge to the young. Dewey spoke often enough about education as the "growth" of the child's individual powers to make it easy for his followers to forget this traditional view. In fact, progressive educators today often view the traditional disciplines (English, history, and the like) as the expendable products of arbitrary social convention. Stripping away this "artifice," they attend to what they view as the only true and natural fact—the solitary learner and his growth. Similarly, cognitive science directs educators' attention toward the activity of individual brains. As a result, the question of *how* children learn, which may be scientific, swamps the question of *what* children learn, which should be cultural. In the hands of contemporary educators, the knowledge contained in the disciplines is reduced to, in Jerome Bruner's critical words, "an indifferent flow of information to be processed . . . on [the child's] own terms."[31] Dewey himself once said that modernity had "liquefied" knowledge.[32] Contemporary educators have gone one step further and have turned knowledge into an invisible gas.

The perceived demands of a globalized information age have also undermined the notion of education as the passing down of knowledge, a word that is now used interchangeably with *information.* Rather than pass down knowledge that is changing so rapidly, the theory goes, teachers should simply teach kids how to find and use information as the need arises in their lives. Instead of teaching Shakespeare and other great writers to English students, for instance, teachers should simply instruct kids on where to find pertinent knowledge about them. In the information society the idea of an educated man or woman as someone who can quote the Gettysburg address or distinguish Renaissance from Romantic poetry is a quaint anachronism. Today's idea of an educated person is the creative problem solver and Internet explorer. Management guru Peter Drucker has a similar take: the educated person is someone with "the ability to present ideas orally and in writing; the ability to work with people; the ability to shape and direct one's own work, contribution and career."[33] To be educated, then, is to be a useful worker.

To be fair, some cognitivists do acknowledge the importance of learning the traditional disciplines, what they call "domains," and they distinguish between novice and expert thinkers within domains. But even when it comes to learning how to achieve expertise within specific disciplines, reformers attempt to mask, where it would seem impossible, the traditional distinction between ignorant child and experienced adult and undermine the notion of culturally valuable knowledge. In order to teach children to learn how to think like experts in a given domain, they recommend "situated" or "authentic" learning, that is, learning that takes place (supposedly) in circumstances approximating real life. Thus, when children study history, math, or English, they should as much as possible do what real, or expert, historians, mathematicians, and writers do. English teachers should not assign essays or book reports for their eyes only; instead, students should write poems or stories to read aloud in "writing celebrations" or publish in class newspapers. As they get older, they can write television scripts or ad copy for "authentic audiences." Likewise, whole math advocates tend to be disdainful of "paper and pencil work." They favor active engagement with real-life objects. Papert proposes that children design video and computer games, create music sound tracks, and engage in similar sorts of activities that would allow them to "construct knowledge" in a "personally meaningful" context. During the 1998 Winter Olympics, fourth and fifth graders in a Colorado school got to enjoy authentic learning when they designed snowboards using a new Web site. "My students are learning math in a real way," their teacher boasted.[34]

Here is the darkly ironic consequence of anticulturalism that we saw emerging in chapter 2: what seems like a generous concern for children's personal development turns out to be a narrow interest in their useful cognitive achievement. Anticultural theories challenge the entire idea of the school as an institution that separates children from the world at large; instead, these theories set out to turn the young almost immediately into productive workers. "The function of the school is no longer teaching as a mode of delivering information," John C. Hill of the Department of Educational Administration at the University of Cincinnati states, in the vocabulary common to his peers. "The function of the restructured school is to faciliate learning with the result that learners become the workers of their school."[35] Instead of a distinct stage of life that segregates children from the market and the workplace in order to enlarge their individuality in the broadest sense, childhood has become a kind of junior adulthood that takes place in a modified office or studio for the purpose of developing their work potential. The school is no longer School, as Papert capitalizes it to evoke its isolate and stodgy conventional character. It must be "real." Really innovative educators actually model the school on the workplace.[36] Child workers can design software or snowboards, write television scripts, and develop public policy on conservation or health care.

The sociologist Émile Durkheim once described education this way:[37]

> To the egoistic and asocial being that has just been born [society] must, as rapidly as possible, add another, capable of leading a moral and social life. Such is the work of education . . . It is not limited to developing the individual organism in the direction indicated by its nature, to elicit the hidden potentialities that need only be manifested. It creates in man a new being.

It appears that anticultural educators have no interest in creating a new being, one "capable of leading a moral and social life" or, for that matter, one with an enriched sense of personal possibility. Their underlying goal is to create self-sufficient workers with no special commitment to either the broader community or its cultural traditions.

They are creating citizens for an information age, where knowledge is valued only for its utility.

The paradox that what might seem to liberate individuals actually confines them is evident in another anticultural myth that is especially tenacious in education circles. This is the myth that children are naturally creative. The myth is based upon a misunderstanding about the source of creativity that we might call creativism. Creativism suggests that creativity stems from the ability to see things from an unexpected angle, to break through conventional perceptions. Thus it follows that children are naturally creative, because they have not learned the "right" or ordinary way of doing things and can thus see more unpredictable possibilities than adults can. Herbert Kohl, who made his reputation as the author of *Thirty-Six Children,* elsewhere recounts that he became a teacher because kids were "the saviors—they could dare to be creative where I was inhibited, they could write well because they didn't know what good writing was suppposed to be."[38] It also follows that education—and, in fact, culture in general—threatens to shackle the child's perceptions. Teresa Amabile, who writes frequently on the subject of children's creativity, includes on her list of "creativity killers" the following: rewards, competition, restricted choice, and teacher "surveillance," or "evaluation," meaning grades and tests.[39]

Educators' high regard for creativity arises from an insight that is neither new nor trivial. Beginning with Dewey, many education theorists have attempted to respond to the profound truth that modern life detaches us from primary experience. As the anthropologist Claude Levi-Strauss put it, the problem of the creative child "is first and foremost a problem of civilization rather than of education."[40] Educators became concerned that the schoolchild sitting at a desk and reciting multiplication tables is the very image of sterile, disembodied abstraction. Unfortunately, by the sixties these serious concerns began to overheat into a dubious romanticism. "It is as cruel to bore a child as to beat him," wrote one education writer in an essay entitled "How

School Stunts Your Child." Education should help kids to achieve "moments of ecstasy."[41] More recently, University of Chicago psychologist Mihaly Csikszentmihalyi has written of the need to inspire "flow" or "peak moments" in schoolchildren.[42] Others speak simply of classrooms "marked with exuberance, joy, laughter."[43]

Though it's unlikely that, say, math or history inspire such emotions even in those who feel strongly enough to pursue them as their life's work, this longing for intense experience is behind many creativist ideas. Yet the anticultural fallacy at the heart of creativism turns out to substitute superficial excitement for the deeper satisfactions that might come with genuine learning, the only route to creativity. To see how this occurs, consider the pleasures promised by one of the most well-known creativist approaches: the writing process. To be sure, the writing process, a popular method of teaching writing that originated at the influential Columbia Teachers College, is not without merit. It stresses the need for revision and daily writing; in this respect it is a valuable antidote to the years of neglect of writing instruction in American schools.[44] But undeterred by the legion of preliterate cultures that prove them wrong, writing process theorists insist that, like reading, writing comes naturally to children; it is a "natural desire," a "primal need" in the words of Lucy McCormick Culkins, one of the pioneers of the approach. Like some followers of whole language, writing process advocates believe children should use "invented spelling" rather than rely on dictionaries or adults for correct forms. In the hands of less perfervid educators, invented spelling might serve as a temporary measure to facilitate the writing of children in the early grades who have yet to learn the many irregularities of English and are too young to use a dictionary. But for fervent creativists, invented spellings are an end in themselves. These words "are not 'wrong,'" writes Culkins, "they are spectacular." Because written words bubble naturally from inside the child—writing is "an act of self-exposure and courage"—its products should not be held to a culturally defined form.[45]

By imagining expression as natural and joyous in this way, creativists are making a common anticultural mistake that goes beyond that made by their cousins, the whole language advocates. They are assuming, much like those who believe that the young child is an autonomous information processor, that expression is precultural. In reality, the opposite is true. Creative expression cannot occur without the architecture provided by cultural forms. Far from being blocked by excessive adult surveillance, it is stunted by poor grounding in the traditional disciplines. Read the memoir of any artist or, for that matter, any scientist or talk to any historian or software designer; you'll find they have immersed themselves in the history, traditions, and idioms of their craft. Artists and writers don't just "do" art and literature, they study them. Geniune creativity is possible only when one is so thoroughly versed in the laws of a discipline that they become a mode of thought. And it is only after becoming thoroughly versed that thinkers can bend the constraints of approved ways of seeing, constraints they have understood and mastered. "To break the rules you must know *about* the rules," Borges said.[46] Creativists like to think that creativity is a joyous experience one can leap into immediately, without dreary drill and practice. In truth, it is hard to know where practice and study stop and creativity begins. Creativists are confusing novelty, irregular ways of seeing or naming things, with creativity. It is rather like calling a student's amusing mangling of French verbs poetry.

When children are denied a real education in more traditional cultural forms, they simply turn to what they know, which today means television and the movies. The experience of a renowned turn-of-the-century Viennese art teacher named Franz Cizek, an apostle of innate creative vision for early progressive educators, demonstrates the problem: Cizek gave little instruction in technique or genre; he went so far as to forbid any art except his students' own work in his classroom. If a child asked, "How do I draw a horse?" he would answer, "You already know how, just do it and it will be good." The result? Observers found that the children's remarkably uniform drawings mimicked the style of street posters and contemporary book illustrations. These art students did what all of us, except a few (adult) geniuses, do: they stylized their perceptions according to the cultural forms available to them.[47] More thoughtful teachers are willing to admit something similar; upon telling children to write or draw what they wish, they find themselves knee-deep in Disneyfied Pocahontases and shoot-'em-up plots from TV series such as *The Power Rangers*. Instead of freeing children to express their creativity, teacher are simply chaining them to the Hollywood forms they already know.

Those who support trendy new approaches like interdisciplinary studies and assignments like journals, videos, and computer projects make a slightly different anticultural mistake in their efforts to inject creativity into the schools, but it is one that also ultimately leads children back to the mall. These creativists assume that the body of human knowledge is a large, free pantry of information available to everyone, expert or novice.

Consider interdisciplinary study (an increasingly popular approach of combining traditional subject matter like history and English into one class), which seems more substantial than other creativisit approaches. Its enthusiasts argue that the traditional school disciplines (math, English, history, etc.) are arbitrary categories imposed by factory-model educators of a bygone age. These categories result in what Theodore Sizer, founder of the Coalition of Essential Schools, calls "conveyor-belt" education, which holds students back from seeing the larger connections between ideas.[48] In an example of the interdisciplinary approach, a teacher at New York's School for the Physical City, an alternative school which uses "the city as its classroom," chose shadows as her theme for one lesson; she had her middle schoolers calculate the height of buildings by measuring shadows (math), read a poem about shadows (English), and observe the architecture of the Federal-style buildings (history and art) casting those shadows.[49]

The experience of Kathleen J. Roth, a science teacher writing in *American Educator,* illustrates how the appeal of this approach is more dazzle than substance. In the spirit of the holistic classroom, Roth and several colleagues developed a course of study for fifth graders centered around the theme of the 500th anniversary of Columbus' first voyage. She decided that the theme called for her students to study the diversity of plant species and the way plants adapt to their environments. As she proceeded, however, she found that her students, not yet familiar with the concepts of food chains and the interrelationship of ecosystems, could not understand the material the theme required of them. In effect, what Roth discovered was the reason students from all over the world study disciplines separately in the first place: science, history, literature, mathematics, and art each have a logic and language of their own that is independent of the individual mind that wants to make use of them.[50]

The novice needs to be led step-by-step through the dense structure of a specified body of knowledge. Yes, it is possible that on a limited scale—say, studying the westward expansion in history while reading *My Antonia* in English—interdisciplinary work can enrich understanding. However, simply snatching a theme for interdisciplinary study from the air—whether it be shadows or Christopher Columbus—demonstrates not genuine interrelationships but an educator's own desire to be seen as creative and, one suspects, the media age fear that there is nothing particularly interesting or relevant in the separate disciplines themselves. Lacking any real understanding of the meaning or source of creativity and, as we have seen, any commitment to passing down inherited knowledge, anticultural educators make the mistake of deeming an assignment creative simply because it imitates the glamorous nature of media entertainment.

This surrender to media glamour not only imprisons children in their own narrow, television-saturated world but also undermines the training of reasoned, logical thought, which republican theorists recognized was essential to life in a democracy. Following a line of argument and making reasoned judgments is an integral part of the "self-government" alluded to so often by the founders. The loss of these abilities is a logical outgrowth of the anticultural fallacy. Because anticulturalists tend to view children as innately and competently rational, they underestimate the difficulty—the unnaturalness, if you will—of the child's struggle to achieve mental discipline. They come to believe that educators can avoid the hard work of ordering the child's brain and that they can quickly move on to the supposed pleasures of creativity. Thus, they toss aside traditional exercises like comparison–contrast or persuasive essays and celebrate creative assignments like designing videos or board games. Yet the former demand sustained, analytic thinking while the latter require merely casual association. Take, for example, the projects by a high school class upon reading *Things Fall Apart* and *Cry the Beloved Country,* both novels set in Africa. One girl performed an interpretative dance based on Nigerian music; a team of students created maps of Africa with hypertext.[51] Computer-generated hypertext allows you to read a bit of text (explaining, say, the climate in Nigeria) and then click on another bit of semirelated text that appeals to you (e.g., nineteenth-century colonialism or Kenyan crafts). Its essence is whim and interruption, precisely what the child already has in abundance.

It's important to understand just how much this devotion to children's excitement undermines education in the United States and prevents the creation of what Durkheim called "a new being." The anticultural fallacy has prevented educators from realizing the simple fact that, rather than motivating children, the appeal to excitement and creativity distracts and overstimulates them. Anyone who has tried to balance a checkbook with a group of six-year-olds careening around nearby will recognize that excitement does not promote clear thinking. For children, tuning out the more primitive part of the brain that attends to light, movement, and noise in order to perform higher levels of abstract thinking is even more difficult. The brain is *supposed* to attend to novelty, after all, and for children everything is new. This is why Japanese teachers use the same set of tiles for teaching mathematical concepts all year (in contrast to American teachers, who use pieces of candy, buttons, and pennies); they have reasonably concluded, according to the authors of *The Learning Gap,* that "variety confuses conceptual learning."[52] It makes perfect sense: when you're looking at the familiar gray square objects you've used every day in school for the past year to learn addition, it's easier to think about five times six using them than if you are suddenly faced with a scoop of Tootsie Roll candies.

Of course, children need release from the mental work demanded of them throughout their early years. In fact, because it has always been clear that this work requires so much more energy from them than from their elders, children all over the world have recess. Yet in another symptom of the refusal to recognize children's disordered energies, American educators give fewer recess breaks to their students than do their foreign colleagues.[53]

The belief that children's brains are *naturally* ordered and compartmentalized is especially dangerous in an age when children's lives
are so harried and when so many are receiving two hours a day or
more of rapidly moving light and noise stimuli from the television set.
It is an error that has been particularly devastating to poor children
from chaotic homes, who have had even less opportunity to internalize orderly mental habits. "I love a noisy classroom," the principal of a
New York City elementary school once sighed to me as we entered a
hallway lined with classrooms that gratified his predilection. The
noisy classroom does more to appease his own wishful thinking than
to educate students. Holding fast to the fallacy that children are ordered and self-regulating rather than distractible and disorganized,
and confusing noise with mental energy and intense experience, he
was willing to trade the danger of boredom for that of incomprehension. What seems to be sensitivity to children's energy and creativity
turns out to be a surrender to their restless, excitable natures and to
the superficial pleasures they already know so well. The anticultural
educator avoids the work of creating "a new being" and leaves the
child's brain essentially as he found it—not creative but chaotic and
empty, not enriched but provincial and narrow.

There is considerable evidence that anticultural education has
failed to create the inspired and involved lifelong learners that are at
the heart of the theory. What we hear much more about is student apathy, restlessness, passivity, and, yes, ignorance. Let's begin with the latter. While it's often difficult to measure specific pedagogical innovations effectively because, regardless of their content, they tend to
invigorate teachers and bring about temporary improvements, whole
language, the only reform on which we have broad data, is a bust. California mandated whole language in 1987. By 1994 its reading scores
ranked last in the nation.[54] In a small experiment that compared discovery learning in mathematics with direct instruction of math facts
and concepts over two years in a Midwestern suburban elementary
school in 1992, researchers found significantly higher achievement for

those students who received direct instruction in both computation *and* concepts—as well as more positive attitudes toward math (ironically, one of the central goals of whole math reformers).[55]

Because we don't know precisely by what methods most American children are taught, it's difficult to cite cause and effect when it comes to more general findings about the academic performance of American children. Still, it's worth noting that over the last ten years verbal SAT scores have fallen even as the proportion of test takers with an A average has risen from 28 to 38 percent. This may reflect, said Donald M. Steward, the president of the College Board, "greater focus on personal qualities instead of academic achievement," a tendency which would be in keeping with the anticultural classroom.[56] International measures consistently show American kids doing mediocre work compared to their counterparts in other industrialized countries. Twelfth graders scored near the bottom of the Third International Math and Science Study (TIMSS); they placed 19th out of 21 nations in math and 16th out of 21 in science.[57] Americans are among the least literate populations of the industrialized world. The ignorance of students coming out of our public schools is a perpetual problem for employers and for teachers in colleges and universities. In one notorious example, in 1996 NYNEX had to test sixty thousand applicants before finding three thousand capable of filling entry-level positions.[58] The worst news of all is that the kids who are receiving anticultural education are the very people from whom the next generation of schoolteachers are to come, ensuring that even if educationists, in all their wisdom, wanted to return to a more traditional content-based education, it would be nearly impossible to do so. The nation's teachers simply won't know enough.

Anticultural educators have convinced themselves that by appealing to children's intrinsic interests and motivation they can inspire them to become lifelong learners. Yet here too results are at odds with theory. The authors of several studies of high schools, including the aptly titled *Shopping Mall High School,* found that when students are given the opportunity to decide what courses to take, they do not follow their interests so much as their whims: "My friends were taking it," "It was easy," or "I'm seeing a psychologist now, so I'll take psychology." As one perceptive teen at a Galleria-type school put it, "You can do whatever you want here . . . You can be a scholar or a total idiot." Guess which choice was more popular?[59] Counselors in schools with a lot of choice have reported a problem getting students to take harder courses.[60] In her children's novel *Are You There God? It's Me, Margaret,* Judy Blume captures the reality of what kids given open-ended choices come up with—and it's not what anticulturalists had in mind. Her sixth grade heroine is told to choose a personal project, and so she considers bras, boys, and God (in no particular order.)[61]

Appeals to their "innate interests" and "natural love of learning" have done little to inspire students. In fact, student apathy and restlessness are the most common complaints among teachers today. In a 1996 study, Temple University psychologist Laurence Steinberg found "an extraordinarily high percentage" of "alienated and disengaged" students. "Across the country," he wrote, "whether surrounded by suburban affluence or urban poverty, students' commitment to school is at an all-time low."[62] The UCLA Higher Education Research Institute confirms his description. It finds entering college students "increasingly disengaged from the academic experience," including the highest percentage ever reporting being bored in class.[63] Teachers all over the country complain about shorter attention spans among their charges and more resistance to challenging work. Between 1990 and 1995 alone, the United States has seen a doubling in the number of children diagnosed with attention deficit disorder, a disease that, strangely, no one had heard of in the days of rote learning and that is all but unknown in other countries.[64] It appears that the superficial excitement and creativity that educators have substituted for genuine mental work neither educates nor entertains students.

The final irony of anticultural ideas like intrinsic motivation and creativism is that they create precisely the kind of passive students that anticultural educators were so desperately trying to avoid. Not only do these theories neglect the young child's distractible, changeable nature; they also ignore the fact that the more attuned children are to novelty and sensation, the more they want them. Deprived of the conventional basis of their authority—superior knowledge and understanding—teachers are forced to resort to mere chumminess, personal charisma, or, worse, showmanship.[65] Teachers often complain that kids arrive in school sporting a challenging attitude that says "Here we are now/Entertain us," to quote the band Nirvana, and doubtless this is more the result of watching television for several hours a day than poor teaching. But, as we have seen, anticulturalism has made it difficult for the schools to construct a counterculture to the media's stranglehold on young minds. Between the tenets of creativism and intrinsic motivation, teachers naturally emulate the media's sensationalism and titillation.

Looking at the current crop of college students gives us some sense of how these popular approaches affect kids as they mature. Campuses all over the country report an increase in the number of students requiring remedial classes; nearly one-third of all undergraduates need a course in reading, writing, or math.[66] Fewer than a quarter of university and college faculty believe their students have been "well prepared academically."[67] More damaging to the convictions of educators is the intellectual apathy among students. The anthropologist Michael Moffat found that even college students do not choose courses on the basis of their interests: they merely think about whether a course meets early in the morning or on a Friday, whether the teacher is a hard grader or an easy one, or, at best, whether a course seems like a good career move.[68] One of the most common complaints among faculty today is the crude vocationalism reigning among students.[69] If they *are* intrinsically motivated, it seems to be largely because they are driven to get good jobs and fat paychecks. Arthur Levine, president of Columbia Teachers College and author of *When Fear and Hope Collide: A Portrait of Today's College Student,* finds that this is "a generation that overwhelmingly rejects the notion of learning for learning's sake."[70]

All of this is bad enough, but it neglects one other likely consequence of anticultural education: the diminution of a common civic culture. As we have seen, educators no longer take seriously their responsibility to create a democratic citizenry, one of the central missions of public education in the United States from its inception in the common school movement. In their presumption of children's inherent rationality, they neglect to train the next generation in habits of analysis, persuasion, and argument. It may well be that we're already seeing the fallout from this neglect in the disengagement from public affairs that characterizes twentysomethings.[71]

Worse, anticultural education advances a form of radical individualism that threatens a robust democracy. This is an individualism which goes far beyond the promise of self-government. It is one that says to the young, "You are entirely autonomous beings who have no deep connection to the world you have recently entered." The underlying message from adults who give students free choice about what to study is that the body of knowledge contained in the curriculum has no independent significance apart from what the student can make of it. It is merely, in the words of *Schools for the Twenty-First Century,* "the raw material for the knowledge-work process . . . to be worked on by students, processed by students, molded and formed by students."[72] The idea that knowledge is "raw material" for students to "mold" trivializes the past and children's relationship to it. For our young, according to anticultural educationists, the past—as represented in literature, philosophy, the arts and sciences—should have no weight. It is simply a theme park in which they can get "creative." At a middle school near my house several years ago, seventh graders were given "creative" assignments to do after reading *The Diary of Anne Frank.* Get ready for Anne Frank: The Board Game.

This glorification of individual skills and creativity at the expense of a serious encounter with the past and its continuing hold on us deprives the next generation of a foundation for social solidarity. Without a common curriculum, often without a single book in common, the next generation will never be part of what the authors of *Habits of the Heart* call a "community of memory."[73] Author E.D. Hirsch cites the case of identical twins in separate classes who already in elementary school were learning almost nothing in common.[74] David Marc polled a dozen graduate classes he had taught—small classes of around fifteen students—and could not come up with a single book that everyone had read.[75] This is not a trivial point. "A subject understood in common with other people is a social bond," Jacques Barzun has written.[76] Civil society depends on a sense of a shared past and a shared destiny.

In all fairness, educationists seem aware of the danger of the radical individualism inherent in their theories, and they have attempted to ballast it by several means. One is called "service learning," whereby students must perform a set number of hours of community service, like recycling projects or tutoring, in order to graduate. One school in Glendale, Arizona, focuses the entire curriculum each year on a different environmental issue, like water conservation or nuclear energy.[77] The other popular antidote to hyperindividualism is called cooperative learning. Cooperative learning descends from Dewey's sentiment that school ought to imitate the group activity of real life. Today this idea sometimes corrodes into a blunt vocationalism; kids must work in teams, the reasoning goes, because according to the latest management theories that's what they will have to do as workers in the new global economy. More typically, cooperative learning is viewed as having a moral purpose. Its advocates believe that in addition to learning through explaining problems to someone else, students develop tolerance and group feeling.[78]

Though judicious use of these approaches is not likely to do much harm, neither is it likely to counteract the message of radical individualism embedded in anticultural education. Concern for the downtrodden is surely part of our civic obligation, but the amnesiac, however compassionate, does not a citizen make. Volunteer work is another venue for personal choice, and it's not at all clear what someone measuring pollution levels in a local forest shares with a peer ladling stew at a soup kitchen. Nor does cooperative learning teach kids that they are living in a shared historical space. When Sol Stern asked the principal of his children's school why the students didn't have the slightest idea who William Tecumseh Sherman was when their school was named after the Civil War general, the principal answered in perfect edu-speak: "It's important to learn about the Civil War, but it's more important to learn how to learn about the Civil War. The state of knowledge is constantly changing, so we have to give children the tools to be able to research things, to think critically, to use a library."[79] But the question remains: Does it matter that kids know how to use a library, how to think critically, or how to work together in groups, if they don't know where they are and don't care?

The final message of anticulturalism is that there is no real reason to care. Although it may seem self-evident that a child who has freely chosen to do a project on turtles or to take a course in psychology instead of being assigned to write about the Gettysburg address or to take a course on the American novel would be more engaged or, as educators would have it, more "intrinsically motivated," choices like this finally tell kids that none of it matters very much. Children are wired to figure out what knowledge is considered meaningful in their culture and to internalize that meaning. Internal motivation is ultimately indistinguishable from cultural values. In the *Learning Gap,* Stevenson and Stigler conclude that it is the low expectations of teachers and parents that finally explains the poor performance of American students compared to their Asian peers.[80] Surveys find that teenagers themselves long for more structure and a clearer set of expectations from the adults around them.[81] Yet as we have seen, it is the very essence of anticulturalism—and this applies to educators above all—to refuse to give them that.

By turning knowledge into raw material, or information, on which students exercise their genius, anticultural education drains it of any real meaning. Even cognitive scientists, like Howard Gardner, who believe that kids need a rigorous introduction to the traditional disciplines or "domains" demonstrate a fundamental agnosticism about their value. They argue for studying traditional disciplines, but it is not because they are truly meaningful, that is, not because they represent the collected knowledge passed down over generations; not because they have anything to tell us about how to think about experience; not because, as T.S. Eliot once said simply of classical literature, "they are what we know"; not even because they are what we want to move beyond. No, children should study different disciplines because they provide them with useful ways to exercise different parts of their brains. In other words, we don't go to school to learn anything about the world that has been passed down to us and that we must eventually pass on to others; we go only to flex our cranial muscles. Like Matisse and Mozart for babies, American history, Shakespeare, and algebra for schoolchildren and adolescents have no intrinsic value; they are just brain food.

Thus it makes perfect sense that anticultural pedagogies produce apathy and alienation. Children learn from their elders, after all. And what they learn in America today is that adults are indifferent to their own society, to its accumulated knowledge, its history, its aspirations. The late philosopher Judith Sklar once said of her own experience teaching political theory: "I love the subject unconditionally and am wholly convinced of its importance and want others to recognize it as such. It has therefore been quite easy for me to avoid becoming a guru or substitute parent."[82] Or, it should be added, a facilitator or manager of instruction. What Sklar communicated in these words is a passionate belief in the inherent value not of her students' selfhood or of a vague process called "learning," though these surely matter, but, first, of a particular field of knowledge. For her, this field had a solid, toe-stubbing reality which involved her utterly. She was a guardian of cultural mysteries that she felt impelled to pass on to future generations.

Most American kids will never witness such a thing, much less experience it firsthand. They are told by their elders that the world outside has little to inspire their allegiance and that heaven lies inside their own narrow and unstructured minds. In the short term, it's a recipe for boredom and restlessness. Over the long run, it's a prescription for an anemic inner life. Despite the appearance that anticulturalist educators are committed to individual "needs," they do little to inspire in their students an interest in the inherited language and ideas that might sustain and enlarge private aspirations. Republican child theorists understood that adults needed to shape the individuality of the young; anticultural educators refuse this task. Assuming that culture might stifle the creative individual, they neglect the fact that culture gives shape to imagination and desire. Today's teachers do not merely leave kids ignorant and self-involved; they withhold from them a rich vocabulary for organizing their subjectivities and expose them to precisely those forces of the workplace and market-place progressive educators once hoped to escape.

Chapter 4

....

The Teening
of Childhood

"A kid's gotta do what a kid's gotta do!" raps a cocksure tyke on a 1998 television ad for the cable children's network Nickelodeon. She is surrounded by a large group of hip-hop-dancing young children in baggy pants who appear to be between the ages of three and eight. In another 1998 ad, this one appearing in magazines for the Gap, a boy of about eight in a T-shirt and hooded sweatshirt, his meticulously disheveled hair falling into his eyes and spilling onto his shoulders, winks ostentatiously at us. Is he neglected (he certainly hasn't had a haircut recently) or is he just street-smart? His mannered wink assures us it's the latter. Like the kids in the Nickelodeon ad, he is hip, aware, and edgy, more the way we used to think of teenagers. Forget about what Freud called latency, a period of sexual quiescence and naïveté; forget about what every parent encounters on a daily basis—artlessness, shyness, giggling jokes, cluelessness. These media kids have it all figured out, and they know how to project the look that says they do.

Throughout the previous chapters we saw many examples of the anticultural fallacy among educators, psychologists, and other child experts. The media doesn't explicitly add to the impressive list of innate talents advanced by these groups; it does not expressly argue that children develop best when they are free of cultural input. What it does do is provide a loud and raucous cheering section for these notions. The media's darling, like that of the other cultural arbiters we've looked at, is a child who barely needs childhood. In the movies, in magazines, and most of all on television, children see image upon irresistible image of themselves as competent sophisticates wise to the ways of the world. And maybe that's a good thing too, since their parents and teachers appear as weaklings, narcissists, and dolts. That winking eight-year-old in the Gap ad tells the story of his generation. A gesture once reserved for adults to signal to gullible children that a joke was on its way now belongs to the child. This child gets it; it's the adults who don't.

There are plenty of signs that the media's deconstruction of childhood has been a rousing success. The enthusiastic celebration of hipness and attitude has helped to socialize a tough, "sophisticated" consumer child who can assert himself in opposition to the tastes and conservatism of his parents. The market aimed at children has skyrocketed in recent years, and many new products, particularly those targeting the eight-to-twelve-year-olds whom marketers call tweens, appeal to their sense of teen fashion and image consciousness. Moreover, kids have gained influence at home. In part, this is undoubtedly because of demographic changes that have "liberated" children from parental supervision. But let's give the media their due. James McNeal, who has studied childhood consumerism for many decades, proclaims the United States a "filiarchy," a bountiful kingdom ruled by children.

But for all their power and influence, for all their apparent worldliness, for all their *stuff,* today's media children are Exhibit A of the costs of anticulturalism. Lacking a protected childhood, they come immediately into the noisy presence of the media carnival barkers. Doubtless, they learn a lot from them, but their sophistication is misleading. It has no relation to a genuine worldliness, an understanding of human hypocrisy or life's illusions. It is built on an untimely ability to read the glossy surfaces of our material world, its symbols of hipness, its image-driven brands and production values. Deprived of the concealed space in which to nurture a full and independent individuality, the media child unthinkingly embraces the dominant cultural gestures of ironic detachment and emotional coolness. This is a new kind of sophistication, one that speaks of a child's diminished expectations and conformity rather than worldliness and self-knowledge.

Nowadays when people mourn the media's harmful impact on children, they often compare the current state of affairs to the Brigadoon of the 1950s. Even those who condemn the patriarchal complacency of shows like *Father Knows Best* or *Ozzie and Harriet* would probably concede that in the fifties parents did not have to fret over rock lyrics like *Come on bitch . . . lick up the dick* or T-shirts saying KILL YOUR PARENTS. These were the days when everyone, including those in the media, seemed to revere the protected and long-lived childhood that had been the middle-class ideal since the early nineteenth century.

But the reality of fifties media was actually more ambiguous than the conventional wisdom suggests. The fifties saw the rise of television, a medium that quickly opened advertisers' and manufacturers' eyes to the possibility of promoting in children fantasies of pleasure-filled freedom from parental control, which in turn fertilized the fields for liberationist ideas that came along in the next decade. American parents had long struggled to find a balance between their children's personal drives and self-expression and the demands of common life, but television had something else in mind. It was fifties television that launched the media's two-pronged attack on the preconditions of traditional childhood, one aimed directly at empowering children, the other aimed at undermining the parents who were trying to civilize them. By the end of the decade, the blueprint for today's media approach to children was in place.

The first prong of attack was directed specifically at parents—or, more precisely, at Dad. Despite the assertions of those who see in *Father Knows Best* and *Ozzie and Harriet* evidence that the fifties were a patriarchal stronghold, these shows represent not the triumph of the old-fashioned family but its feeble swan song.[1] Dad, with his stodgy ways and stern commandments, had been having a hard time of it since he first stumbled onto television. An episode of *The Goldbergs,* the first television sitcom and a remake of a popular radio show featuring a Jewish immigrant family, illustrates his problem: Rosalie, the Goldbergs' fourteen-year-old daughter, threatens to cut her hair and wear lipstick. The accent-laden Mr. Goldberg tries to stop her, but he is reduced to impotent blustering: "I am the father in the home, or am I? If I am, I want to know!" It is the wise wife who knows best in this house; she acts as an intermediary between this old-world patriarch and the young country he seems unable to understand. "The world is different now," she soothes.[2] If this episode dramatizes the transgenerational tension inevitable in a rapidly changing immigrant country, it also demonstrates how television tended to resolve that tension at Dad's blushing expense. The man of the fifties television house was more likely to resemble the cartoon character Dagwood Bumstead ("a joke which his children thoroughly understand" according to one critic)[3] than Robert Young of *Father Knows Best.* During the early 1950s, articles began to appear decrying TV's "male boob" with titles like "What Is TV Doing to MEN?" and "Who Remembers Papa?" (an allusion to another early series called *I Remember Mama*).[4] Even *Ozzie and Harriet* was no *Ozzie and Harriet.* Ozzie, or Pop, as he was called by his children, was the Americanized and suburbanized papa who had been left behind in city tenements. Smiling blandly as he, apparently jobless, wandered around in his cardigan sweater, Ozzie was the dizzy male, a portrait of grinning ineffectuality. It is no coincidence that *Ozzie and Harriet* was the first sitcom to showcase the talents of a child character, when Ricky Nelson began his career as a teen idol. With parents like these, kids are bound to take over.

Still, the assumption that the first years of television were happy days for the traditional family has some truth to it. During the early fifties, television was widely touted as about the best thing that had ever happened to the family—surely one of the more interesting ironies of recent social history. Ads for the strange new appliance displayed a beaming mom and dad and their big-eyed kids gathered together around the glowing screen. It was dubbed the "electronic hearth." Even intellectuals were on board; early sociological studies supported the notion that television was family-friendly. Only teenagers resisted its lure. They continued to go to the movies with their friends, just as they had since the 1920s; TV-watching, they said, was family stuff, not an especially strong recommendation in their eyes.

In order to turn television into the children's oxygen machine that it has become, television manufacturers and broadcasters during the late forties and early fifties had to be careful to ingratiate themselves with the adults who actually had to purchase the strange new contraption. Families never had more than one television in the house, and it was nearly always in the living room, where everyone could watch it. Insofar as the networks sought to entice children to watch their shows, they had to do so by convincing Mom that television was good for them. It was probably for these reasons that for a few short years children's television was more varied and of higher quality than it would be for a long time afterward. There was little to offend, but that doesn't mean it was bland. In an effort to find the best formula to attract parents, broadcasters not only showed the familiar cowboy and superhero adventure series but also experimented with circus and science programs, variety shows, dramas, and other relatively highbrow fare, for example, Leonard Bernstein's *Young People's Concerts.* Ads were sparse. Since the networks had designed the earliest children's shows as a lure to sell televisions to parents, they were not thinking of TV as a means of selling candy and toys to kids; almost half of those shows had no advertising at all and were subsidized by the networks. At any rate, in those days neither parents nor manufacturers really thought of children as having a significant role in influencing the purchase of anything beyond, perhaps, cereal, an occasional cupcake, or maybe a holiday gift.

This is not to say that no one had ever thought of advertising to children before. Ads targeting youngsters had long appeared in magazines and comic strips. Thirties radio shows like *Little Orphan Annie* and *Buck Rogers in the Twenty-Fifth Century* gave cereal manufacturers and the producers of the ever-popular Ovaltine a direct line to millions of children. But as advertisers and network people were gradually figuring out, when it came to transporting messages directly to children, radio was a horse and buggy compared to the supersonic jet known as television, and this fact changed everything. By

1957, American children were watching TV an average of an hour and a half each day. And as television became a bigger part of children's lives, its role as family hearth faded. By the mid-fifties, as television was becoming a domestic necessity, manufacturers began to promise specialized entertainment. Want to avoid those family fights over whether to watch the football game or Disneyland? the ads queried. You need a *second* TV set. This meant that children became a segregated audience in front of the second screen and advertisers were now faced with the irresistible opportunity to sell things to them. Before television, advertisers had no choice but to tread lightly around children and to view parents as judgmental guardians over the child's buying and spending. Their limited appeals to kids had to be more than balanced by promises to parents, however spurious, of health and happiness for their children.

That balance changed once television had a firm foothold in American homes and advertisers could begin their second prong of attack on childhood. With glued-to-the-tube children now segregated from adults, broadcasters soon went about pleasing kids without thinking too much about parents. The first industry outside of the tried-and-true snacks and cereals to capitalize on this opportunity was, predictably, toys.[5] By the mid-fifties, forward-looking toy manufacturers couldn't help but notice that Walt Disney was making a small fortune selling Mickey Mouse ears and Davy Crockett coonskin hats to the viewers of his *Disneyland* and *The Mickey Mouse Club*. Ruth and Eliot Handler, the legendary owner-founders of Mattel Toys, were the first to follow up. They risked their company's entire net worth on television ads during *The Mickey Mouse Club* for a toy called "the burp gun"; with 90 percent of the nation's kids watching, the gamble paid off bigger than anyone could ever have dreamed.

It's important to realize, in these days of stadium-sized toy warehouses, that until the advent of television, toys were nobody's idea of big business. There simply was not that big a market out there. Parents themselves purchased toys only as holiday or birthday presents, and they chose them simply by going to a specialty or department store and asking advice from a salesperson. Depression-traumatized grandparents, if they were still alive, were unlikely to arrive for Sunday dinner bearing Baby Alive dolls or Nerf baseball bats and balls. And except for their friends, children had no access to information about new products. At any rate, they didn't expect to own all that many toys. It's no wonder toy manufacturers had never shown much interest in advertising; in 1955 the "toy king" Louis Marx had sold fifty million dollars' worth of toys and had spent the grand total of $312 on advertising.

The burp gun ad signaled the beginning of a new era, a turning point in American childhood and a decisive battle in the filiarchal revolution. Toy sales almost tripled between 1950 and 1970. Mattel was now a boom company with sales rising from $6 million in 1955 to $49 million in 1961.[6] Other toy manufacturers who followed Mattel onto television also watched their profits climb.

But the burp gun ad was also a watershed moment, because it laid the groundwork for today's giant business of what Nickelodeon calls "kid kulture," a phenomenon that has helped to alter the dynamic between adults and children. Television transformed toys from a modest holiday gift enterprise mediated by parents into an ever-present, big-stakes entertainment industry enjoyed by kids. Wholesalers became less interested in marketing particular toys to adults than in the manufacturer's plans for promotional campaigns to seduce children. In short, the toy salesman had pushed open the front door, had crept into the den while Mom and Dad weren't looking, and had whispered to Dick and Jane, without asking their parents'permission, of all the happiness and pleasure they could have in exchange for several dollars of the family's hard-earned money.

That the burp gun had advanced more power to children became more apparent by 1959, when Mattel began to advertise a doll named Barbie. Barbie gave a hint as to just how far business was ready to take the filiarchal revolution that had been set in motion by the wonders of television. Regardless of the promotional revolution it had unleashed, the burp gun was a familiar sort of toy, a quirky accessory to the battlefield games always enjoyed by boys. But Barbie was something new. Unlike the baby dolls that encouraged little girls to imitate Mommy, Barbie was a swinger, a kind of Playboy for little girls. She had her own Playboy Mansion, called Barbie's Dream House, and she had lots of sexy clothes, a car, and a boyfriend. The original doll had pouty lips—she was redesigned for a more open California look in the sixties—and she was sold in a leopard skin bathing suit and sunglasses, an accessory whose glamour continues to have iconic status in the children's market. In fact, though it isn't widely known, Barbie was copied from a German doll named Lili, who was in turn modeled on a cartoon prostitute. Sold in bars and tobacco shops, Lili was a favorite of German men, who were suckers for her tight (removable) sweater and short (removable) miniskirt.

Barbie has become so familiar that she is seen as just another citizen of the toy chest, but it's no exaggeration to say that she is one of the heroes in the media's second prong of attack on childhood. She proved not only that toy manufacturers were willing to sell directly to children, bypassing parents entirely, but that they were willing to do so by undermining the forced and difficult-to-sustain latency of American childhood. According to marketing research, mothers without exception *hated* Barbie. They believed she was too grown-up for their four-to-twelve-year-old daughters, the toy's target market. The complaint heard commonly today—that by introducing the cult of the perfect body Barbie promotes obsessive body consciousness in girls, often resulting in eating disorders—is actually only a small part of a much larger picture. Barbie symbolized the moment when the media and the businesses it promoted dropped all pretense of concern about maintaining childhood. They announced, first, that they were going to flaunt for children the very freedom, consumer pleasure, and sex that parents had long been trying to delay in their lives. And, second, they were going to do this by initiating youngsters into the cult of the teenager. If this formula sounds familiar, it's because it remains dominant today. Barbie began the media's teening of childhood; today's media images and stories are simply commentary.

Compared to today's sex-and-violence-obsessed media, all this may seem quite innocent. Things have gone so far beyond Barbie dolls and Dagwood dads that many parents, forced to rely on crude ratings and V-chips, have given up on asking for anything more from their children's entertainment than an absence of gunfire, four-letter words, and writhing, naked bodies. But this resignation is extremely shortsighted. The stories a culture passes on to its children not only tell a great deal about its aspirations and sense of human possibility; they also tell children what kind of people they are expected to become. Stories are not simply entertainment, pleasurable ways of passing the time; they mold children's imagination and desire. They provide cultural lessons as powerful as those learned in any school.

The cultural lessons offered by today's media are far more vulgar than, but actually quite consistent with, those we have seen coming from experts and educators. For one thing, parents—or, more generically, families—are seen as a drag on children's happiness. In the bitter words of Kevin McCallister, the child hero of the megahit movie *Home Alone,* "Families suck!" If the early days of television mildly evoked the tensions between future-minded children and their old-fashioned families, in these latter days families brim with barely suppressed rage. At various times during *Home Alone,* Kevin's family calls him an idiot, a jerk, an incompetent, a phlegm-wad, a disease. "Everyone in this house hates me!" he wails before being sent to the attic, where he will be forgotten the next morning when his family jets off to Paris. And there is little reason not to believe him. In *Home Alone 2,* Kevin befriends a homeless woman in Central Park, a suitable secret sharer for today's Hollywood child.

Occasional nasty evocations of family life may be nothing to worry about, but Kevin's sentiments find endless support from other screen characters. In fact, the media tirelessly repeats for children the lesson of family rot, reminding them that if they scratch the surface of the smiling family, they will find nothing but hatred, anger, disappointment, and cruelty—not to mention alcoholism, drug addiction, and abuse. Consider just a few examples from the year or so following the release of *Home Alone.* "Don't trust anyone," Junior's grandfather says to his father in the children's movie *Problem Child.* "Not even your own father?" Answer: "Especially your own father." In *Problem Child 2,* the grown son complains to his father, "Dad, you hate me." Response: "Okay, okay, you found me out." When the youngest child of the family in *Don't Tell Mom the Babysitter's Dead* whines to his mother as she takes off for two months, "Mom, you'll call every day?" she sneers back at him, "This *is* my vacation." On the small screen, things are even worse.

"I'm choking on my own bile," Al Bundy spits after kissing his wife on *Married with Children,* a top-rated syndicated program among children two to eleven years old.[7] In the opening episode of *My So-Called Life,* a critically successful series that was resurrected on MTV, the fifteen-year-old heroine muses, "Lately I can't seem to even look at my mother without wanting to stab her repeatedly."

Lest children be put off by this, Hollywood insists that they compare their own superior knowingness to that of sentimentalists of the past, who never had the honesty to look family rot directly in the face. In *Problem Child,* Junior's adoptive father, a decent but foolish fellow, finds himself ready to smother the boy with a pillow embroidered with the words HOME, SWEET HOME. *Married with Children* uses (wink, wink) Frank Sinatra's *Love and Marriage* as its theme song. In *Home Alone,* advertised by Fox as "a family comedy—without the family," the classic film *It's a Wonderful Life* flickers on the TV in the background as Kevin's parents are on the phone arranging their flight back from Paris to the son they left behind. The television series *The Simpsons* embellishes the theme of what critic Josh Ozersky calls the "anti-family."[8] The show, which its creator, Matt Groening, has dubbed a "mutant *Ozzie and Harriet,*" takes place in a town called Springfield, a smirking allusion to the setting of *Father Knows Best.* This is Dagwood Bumstead with a vengeance. "A role model in my very own home," Lisa sneers after her father Homer wins the employee-of-the-month prize at the nuclear plant when he averts a meltdown—which would have been caused by his own stupidity in the first place.

Of course, all of this ignores the obvious point that these are comedies—and in the case of *The Simpsons,* at any rate, very funny ones. In fact, according to conventional wisdom, these shows represent an improvement over the past. Yesterday's picket fence banality has given way to second-shift realism. "Thankfully we are past the days of the perfect Mom and all-wise Dad and their twin-beds," sighs a reviewer in the *New York Times* in a statement characteristic of our times.[9] Others argue that shows like *Married with Children* and *The Simpsons* are in the vital tradition of American popular culture, using the earthy "take-my-wife" tone of vaudeville. They point out that comedy thrives on subversion, undercutting the pretensions of daily life and the puffed-up self-importance of the boss, senator, or prince. Surely, according to this line of thinking, the polished veneer of domestic life can afford to be dented by a hefty laugh or two. It was precisely this human urge toward ridiculing the powerful and the sacred that was prissily repressed in the *Father Knows Best* fifties, when much of television was scrubbed clean of any lingering vaudevillian raunchiness.

But shows like *The Simpsons* are part of an anticultural project that goes well beyond reviving the earthy origins of comedy, a fact that should be abundantly clear from a perusal of contemporary children's literature. Many children's authors seem to view their job as topping TV's "mutant *Ozzie and Harriets*," though without the laughs. They are the professional pathologists of parental weakness. In a survey of recent children's literature, Anne Scott MacLeod found a Hobbesian domestic scene.[10] *The Late Great Me* (1976) by Sandra Scoppettone begins, "We were the all-American family because at the core, like every other typical family, there was rot." The opening of another children's novel, titled *The Foxman*, reads, "And that night my mother got me under the kitchen table and tried to kill me with a butcher knife." More recent works not covered by MacLeod prove her perspicacity. Two books for toddlers about mothers are entitled *Why Are You So Mean to Me?* and *Mommy Go Away!* Michael Dorris' 1997 posthumous novel for eight-to-twelve-year-olds, *The Window*, portrays a world where adults are forever disappearing. The main character's mother is in a detox program, and her thoughtless and incompetent father shuffles her from place to place. Brock Coles' *The Facts Speak for Themselves* concerns a thirteen-year-old girl whose lover—the middle-aged father of one of her friends—is shot by her mother's ex-boyfriend. The list could go on.[11]

The only younger citizens suitable for a nation beset by this epidemic of family rot are self-reliant, competent children, and the media, like the expert and pedagogical literature, is full of them. "We must stop treating children as helpless, gullible sheep who need to be carefully watched and protected," writes Cy Schneider, the onetime head of the Mattel ad account and one of the founding intelligences behind Nickelodeon, in a familiar sort of statement among advertisers, screen writers, publishers, and the like. "In reality, children are intelligent, discriminating, and skeptical."[12] But the truth is that the frequent appearance of the savvy child over the past fifteen years speaks less about the media's clear-eyed realism than of our anticultural obsessions. Consider prodigies like the hero of the aptly titled *Little Man Tate,* the sixteen-year-old doctor in the TV series *Doogie Howser,* the fourteen-year-old "modern pre-woman" in Nickelodeon's series *Clarissa Explains It All* and the nine-year-old lawyer on *Ally McBeal.* In the movies *Vice Versa, Freaky Friday, Like Father, Like Son,* the three *Back to the Future* movies, and, in a slightly different vein, *Big,* children become their parents and parents become children. On television adults are forever reminding us how smart kids are these days: "I remember when I realized I could beat my dad at most things," muses Homer Simpson in a cartoonish spin on the theme. "Bart could beat me at most things when he was four."

Particularly striking is the same uncanny maturity in Hollywood's new crop of orphans. Orphans have long served as a catalyst for sentimental, protective feelings in audiences; think of Oliver Twist, Little Orphan Annie, or the pleading waifs of wartime photojournalism. The anticultural orphans, however, are cool and resourceful survivors; they don't need your sympathy, thank you. Certainly, there's no need to worry about a roof over their heads. These orphans live in a consumer heaven, which their parents' absence only improves. Richie Rich, in a film by that name, is the twelve-year-old orphan CEO of his father's candy corporation; manicured and barbered, dressed in power tie and suspenders, the whiz kid reaches the cover of *Fortune* and *Business Week.* The five children in both the movie *Don't Tell Mom the Babysitter's Dead* and the TV series *Party of Five* live a life of yuppie ease without Mom and Dad. In *Don't Tell Mom,* Sue Ellen eagerly takes charge of the house and her younger siblings after her single mother leaves for a vacation in Australia and the babysitter drops dead. Classily made up and dressed for success, she finds a job as an executive assistant at $37,000 a year, balancing career and home far more successfully than her hopeless mother ever did. When Mom was still on the scene, the house was a landfill of junk food remains; by the end of the movie, it is immaculate. Lights gleam on the water of the repaired swimming pool, and the children serve gourmet hors d'oeuvres to Sue Ellen's business guests. Even TV's more insecure Blossom, in a show by that name, has the spunk and style to cruise through her early teen years apparently undamaged by her mother's desertion and her father's hippie spaciness.

The producers of *Rugrats,* the top-rated cable series, apparently see their job as introducing mutant Ozzies and Harriets and their competent offspring to our youngest children. Of course, this is not the way the show is hyped. "It's about a contemporary American family that lives in the real world," says Herb Scannell, Nickelodeon's president, using what has become the conventional Hollywood justification for a lot of family rot entertainment. "It just happens to be animated."[13] But *Rugrats*—the title is a sour term for young children old enough to spend a lot of time playing on the floor but too young to merit the label *brat*—is less a reflection of real life than a Head Start for the bitter new conventions of Hollywood family fare. The three-year-old main character, ironically named Angelica, is simply a Bart Simpson in training—a bully, an egotist, a smart aleck *extraordinaire* who spends her days ordering around the diapered toddlers in the neighborhood. Her family portrait is completed by a father, a doting simp who responds lovingly to each of his obnoxious daughter's screaming commands, and a mother, a monomaniacal, power-suited Wall Streeter who barks sell orders into the phone glued to her ear. So negligent is this mother that in one episode her daughter actually tries to sue her. It's funny satire all right, but real it is not.

This irony and satire, so pervasive in the American media that they saturate the tales for toddlers on up, brings into focus a more subtle problem with the family rot genre: they demonstrate a sneering disdain for both the imagination and the emotions that good stories should engage.[14] Beginning in the nineteenth century, as republican childhood took hold in the United States, children for the first time in history were able to enjoy stories designed specifically to appeal to their sense of adventure and imagination, to open up new vistas of experience, to widen the self. Books that were intended as more than amusement and that acknowledged children's serious concern with serious questions began to appear. Is the world a good or bad place?

How will I make my way in it? Whom should I trust? But imagination and serious probing are not for today's child. Instead of feeling fear, longing, wonder, sadness, or triumph, today's child is supposed to stay safely in the detached ironic mode. This is the devil's bargain shadowing anticulturalism that we've encountered before. In order to live up to the self-sufficiency his elders so value, the child must sacrifice any emotions that might threaten it. The competent child cannot risk feelings of neediness, vulnerability, or even imagination. These are old-fashioned kid stuff. Children of anticulturalism, particularly as the media would have them, are not only competent, but tough, cool, and sophisticated. They're not even suppposed to *like* stories.

A comparison between traditional fairy tales and our own newfangled versions captures the shift. Fairy tales, according to Bruno Bettelheim in his *Uses of Enchantment: The Meaning and Importance of Fairy Tales,* engage children because they address their psychic dilemmas. They are more than therapy, however. Tales can enrich children's imagination by offering resonant new imagery for their private struggles. Many fairy tales, with their frightening images of cruel adults and abandoned children, dramatize one of those central dilemmas: "the child's desire for and anxiety about independence." Bettelheim's discussion explains perfectly the young child's fascination with superheroes:

> These stories [about abandonment] direct the child toward transcending his immature dependence on his parents and reaching the next stage of development . . . The child of school age cannot yet believe that he ever will be able to meet the world without his parents . . . He needs to learn to trust that someday he will be master of the world.[15]

If you remove the message of family rot, *Home Alone* might succeed on this account. Its story line is not so different from classic plots like "Jack and the Beanstalk," which may account for its success: a resourceful, clever child outwits the giant adults out to devour him. Ultimately, however, having successfully accomplished his challenge, Kevin in *Home Alone* is reunited with his family.

The media's new breed of fairy tales not only shrugs off these psychic dilemmas and their resolution but scorns the imagination and children's pleasure in narrative enchantment altogether. Using humor as a defensive device, these tales refuse to let their listeners immerse themselves in their drama. In Jon Scieszka's *The Frog Prince, Continued,* for instance, toddlers begin their education in family rot and the irony they must adopt toward it. The heroine has become such an unrelenting nag that her amphibious husband sets out on a journey to find a witch to turn him back into a frog. "Okay, so they weren't so happy," the tale begins. "They were miserable." In the original "Frog Prince," a princess comes to transcend her self-centered immaturity and childish fears and learns to love despite unpleasant appearances. In Scieszka's version we find out it was all a sham, since love stinks and the best thing to do is just snicker at it.[16] Actress Shelley Duvall's video series *Fairy Tale Theater* is an elite preschool in "feeling neither highs nor lows." In Duvall's trendy hands, the emotional tension and meaning of the story are repeatedly interrupted by snide one-liners, irrelevant but archly amusing flashbacks, and off-color jokes. Child-deaf wisecracks abound in *Sleeping Beauty:* for instance, one of the sprites who comes to bless the princess is a lisping, obviously male . . . well, fairy, and when the prince must pull the pearls off the belly shirt of the princess (played by Bernadette Peters) with his teeth, her perky breasts and bare midriff dominate the screen. "Let's just hope there's a prince out there with more courage than brains," quips one of the fairies; cut to the stupid prince. And so forth.

The universally beloved *Sesame Street* is Fairy Tale Theater's cultural Siamese twin, another upscale tutor in the virtues of irony and detachment. Its infatuation with the idioms of television, in the form of numerous celebrity appearances and quick cuts, renders it, like Duvall's series, astonishingly impatient with engrossing and meaningful storytelling. Early on in its development, the creators of this extensively researched show were informed that children love slapstick humor; they ignored the advice.[17] They chose instead to soak their two-to-five-year-old audience in a cool bath of irony. Kermit the Frog dresses in the belted mackintosh and brimmed hat of the 1940s newspaperman—details meaningless to the show's intended viewers except as training in the media symbols required for future TV watching—when he interviews a smarmy wolf from "Little Red Riding Hood" or a vain, lisping prince from "Cinderella," to mention just two of many portrayals of characters that children once were allowed to think of as villians, heroes, and heroines but that are now portrayed as simpering fools. Don't get caught up in any of this, the writers seem to be saying; you're too sophisticated to fall for these ridiculous fairy tales.

Anti–fairy tales of this sort are often praised because they are supposed to be fun and because they critique traditional antifeminist stories, with their powerful princes and passive princesses.[18] Both of these positions fall prey to the anticultural fallacy and ignore the fact that the anti–fairy tale is also a sermon—on the value of ironic distance. Writers of the anti–fairy tale and their enthusiasts presume that young children not only need no acculturating but are ready to render an autonomous critique of the culture they already magically possess. A parody like *Sesame Street*'s "Cinderella" is only funny when the viewer has ironic distance from the original source of parody. But two- and three-year-olds are incapable of such distance from anything, much less stories they are just coming to know. Moreover, adults are always acculturating children even when they think they are not. Rather than teaching children to critique convention, the ironic tone of the anti–fairy tale serves only to create a new one. It instructs them in the dominant aesthetic pose of the ironic sophisticate. The eye-rolling pose kids learn from these stories is as much a goal of a specific attempt at socialization—or, to use academic language, coercion—as is a curtsy or handshake. In fact, by telling preschoolers to mock something whose power they cannot yet discern and whose meaning they have not yet understood, the anti–fairy tale undermines real criticism. Rebellion is only meaningful, after all, when it arises out of conviction, something our cultural arbiters on the West Coast seem set on extinquishing.

Recently Hollywood has given us engrossing children's stories that take the child's dilemmas seriously and eschew irony, all of them, notably, orphan or quasi-orphan stories: *E. T., Fly Away Home, The Little*

Princess, and *Little Women.* But these are the exceptions. By the time they are ready for school, American children have been shown repeatedly what is expected of them: they must repress their feelings of vulnerability under a thick layer of stylized hip pseudo-irony. Moviegoing children find that the rare moments in which childhood loneliness threatens to burst through the slick celluloid surface are coolly put down. Strong emotions are to be vigorously swept out the French doors. When the youngest child in *Don't Tell Mom* cries, "I miss Mommy!" his older siblings adopt that familiar put-down sneer, that pose of utter exasperation which has become as familiar a comedy trope as the double take. "Nobody—not my parents, not the police, not the U.S. Air Force—will look after me," chirps Alex in *Home Alone 3* as he prepares to battle the international spies who are after his toy car. Playing on kids' love of stories about their babyhood, the creators of *Rugrats* have Angelica recall her own birth as her mother is pushed in a wheelchair down the hospital corridor holding her as a baby: "It's a girl," the not-so-proud, new mother announces all business into her cell phone. "And her name is . . . ah, ah . . . What's her name again?" she asks her husband. Today's child, suckled on the glowing screen, should be able to shrug off her isolation with a knowing laugh. "Oh, we can take anything," second grade Lisa Simpson reassures her father when he announces to his family that he has terrible news. "We're the MTV generation. We feel neither highs nor lows."[19]

None of this is to argue that there is no place for subversive humor in children's lives. Friendly observers of children's media correctly point out that children have always shared in a rebellious subculture. The demands of the ordered, adult world are a burden to young children who still find it a struggle to control their impulses. The subversive rhymes and jokes of children's culture provide them with the opportunity to let off steam during the inevitable frustrations that build with the eat-your-peas commands that bombard them during the years of their socialization. At seven my daughter and her friends were singing "I hate you, you hate me" in parody of the "I love you, you love me" theme song on *Barney.* Sympathetic media critics might also rightly point out, as Alison Lurie did in her book *Don't Tell the Grownups: Why Kids Love the Books They Do,* that popular children's stories also often have a subversive side.[20] Peter Rabbit, to take one classic example, defies his mother and escapes into Mister MacGregor's garden to scavenge for treats.

But it's important to distinguish between what amounts to an indigenous kid folk culture and the images and stories presented to them by adults. To confuse the two is to enter into the anticultural fallacy and to obscure the icy purpose of today's media stories. Adults are instructors in culture. As we have seen in previous chapters, they are always interpreting the world for children—and never so much as when they think they are refusing to do so. Far more than does the self-generated tribal culture of dead-baby jokes or Barney put-downs, adult stories give shape to children's desires, providing them with names and scenarios. When children listen to a story or observe images of other children, they grasp not so much what life is like as *how adults want them to see it.* In *Alice's Adventures in Wonderland,* a story discussed by Lurie, Lewis Carroll has great fun parodying children's school lessons in the Caterpillar's unanswerable, ponderous questions and in the Mock Turtle's course of instruction in "Ambition, Distraction, Uglification, and Derision." Lurie seems to assume that children will respond to this because, in fact, they share Carroll's sentiments. Of course, they probably do. But Lurie misses the larger point, namely, that stories are conduits of cultural wisdom. By poking fun at school lessons the way he does, Carroll, an adult, communicates his own vision of the life-affirming value of imagination, pleasure, and wit to his audience of children. He himself is a teacher.

Prime-time cartoons, such as *The Simpsons, Daria,* and *South Park,* offer the newest way to reduce the child's predicament to a stock comic formula. Cartoon figures fly in under the radar of whatever sensitivities on these matters are left in the American consciousness. An audience would have trouble sitting comfortably through a scene in which a little girl cries as she sings "Happy birthday to me" because everyone has forgotten about her birthday, but it's just more Simpsonian hipness when Lisa Simpson does it. "You can get away with stuff in animation you can't get away with in live action," says David Pritchard, president of the animation house Film Roman, which produces *The Simpsons* and *King of the Hill.* "The audience is more forgiving . . . When Bart Simpson insults his father, it's a joke, not something that offends the real parents watching." Nor is anyone put off by MTV's Daria, a teenaged Dorothy Parker whose knowing put-downs completely elude her dim-witted parents and teachers. One family rot episode of *South Park* is entitled "Cartman's Mom Is a Dirty Slut" and concerns a major character's search for the identity of his father. Because *South Park*'s third graders swear like sailors, the creators and enthusiasts of *South Park* congratulate themselves for their cartoon's realism, a weird feat of logic that, we have seen, has become a Hollywood commonplace. The fact is, part of the cartoon's appeal is that it relieves us of contemplating the complex actuality of childhood. If he were real, the obese, TV-addled, junk-food-obsessed, and fatherless Cartman would stop us in our laugh tracks. No, far from real, *South Park*'s kids and their compatriots, who curse but don't cry and who jeer but don't ache, are cultural personae as stylized and unreal as the pigtailed Kitten on *Father Knows Best*.

Ads targeting children make perfect companion pieces to stories of family rot and children savvy enough to roll their eyes amusingly through all the misery. In ads today, the child's image frequently appears in extreme close-up—the child as giant. Appealing to children's fantasies of omnipotent, materialistic freedom, advertisers portray an anarchic world of misrule in which the pleasure-seeking child reigns supreme.[21] Spot, the red dot on the logo of containers of 7 Up, comes to life, escapes from the refrigerator, and tears through the house causing riotous havoc.[22] A Pepsi ad shows screaming teens and preteens gorging themselves with cake, pouring Pepsi over their heads, and jumping on the bed with an electric guitar. "Be young, have fun, drink Pepsi," says the voice-over.[23] Adult characters—even adult voice-overs and on-camera spokespeople—have been banished in favor of adolescent voices in the surfer-dude mode.[24] Any old folks left standing should prepare to be mocked. Perceived as carping, droning old-timers who would deny the insiders their pleasure or fun, adults are the butts of the child-world joke. They are, as the *New York*

Times' Charles McGrath noted after surveying Saturday morning cartoons, "either idiots, like the crazed geek who does comic spots on 'Disney's 1 Saturday Morning,' or meanies, like the crochety, incompetent teachers and principals on the cartoons 'Recess' and 'Pepper Ann.'"[25] Teachers are, of course, citizens of the adult geekville as well: in one typical snack food ad, kids break out of the halls of their school or behind the back of dim-witted teachers droning on at the chalkboard.[26]

The misleading notion that children are autonomous figures free from adult influence is on striking display in ads like these. Children liberated from parents and teachers are only released into new forms of control. "Children will not be liberated," wrote one sage professor. "They will be dominated."[27] Nineteenth-century moralists saw in the home a haven from the increasingly harsh and inhuman marketplace. The advantage of hindsight allows us to see how this arrangement benefited children. The private home and its parental guardians could exercise their influence on children relatively unchallenged by commercial forces. Our own children, on the other hand, are creatures— one is tempted to say slaves—of the marketplace almost immediately.

The same advertisers who celebrate children's independence from the stodgy adult world and all its rules set out to educate children in its own strict regulations. They instruct children in the difference between what's in and what's out, what's hip and what's nerdy—or, to quote the inimitable Beavis and Butthead, "what's cool and what sucks." Giving new meaning to the phrase *hard sell*, today's ads demonstrate for children the tough posture of the sophisticated child who is savvy to the current styles and fashions. In a contest held by Polaroid for its Cool Cam promotion, the winning entry, from a Manassas, Virginia, girl, depicted a fish looking out a fishbowl at the kids in the house and sneering, "The only thing cool about these nerds is that they have a Cool Cam." Polaroid marketed the camera with a pair of sunglasses, the perennial childhood signifier of sophistication. A candy called Nerds, put out by Nestle, has been tremendously successful, though the only thing that distinguishes it from a dozen others that have a similar taste is its winking name.[28]

It should be clear by now that the pose the media has in mind for children—cool, tough, and sophisticated independence—is that of the teenager. The media's efforts to encourage children to identify with the independent and impulsive consumer teen—efforts that began tentatively, as we saw, with Barbie—have now gone into overdrive. Teenagers are everywhere in children's media today. Superheroes like Mighty Morphin Power Rangers and Teenage Mutant Ninja Turtles are teenagers. Dolls based on the TV character Blossom; her suggestively named friend, Six; and her brother, Joey, portray teenagers, as do the dolls based on the TV series *Beverly Hills 90210,* not to mention the ever-popular Barbie herself. Even the young children dressed in baggy pants who sing *A kid's gotta do what a kid's gotta do* for Nickelodeon are, for all intents and purposes, teenagers.

By populating kids' imaginative world with teenagers, the media simultaneously flatters children's fantasies of sophistication and teaches them what form those fantasies should take. Thus, the media's "liberation" of children from adults also has the mischievous effect of binding them more closely to the peer group. In turn, the peer group polices its members' dress and behavior according to the rules set by this unrecognized authority. In no time at all, children intuit that teens epitomize the freedom, sexiness, and discretionary income—not to mention independence—valued in our society. Teens do not need their mommies to tell them what to wear or eat or how to spend their money, nor do they have sober responsibilities to restrain them from impulse buying.

These days, the invitation to become one of the teen in-crowd arrives so early that its recipients are still sucking their thumbs and stroking their blankies. During the preschool lineup on Nickelodeon one morning, there was a special Nickelodeon video for a song entitled "I Need Mo' Allowance." In this video the camera focuses on a mock heavy metal rock band consisting of three teenaged boys in baggie pants and buzz cuts who rasp a chorus that includes lines like *Mo' allowance to buy CDs!* A dollar sign flashes repeatedly on the screen. This video was followed by an ad for a videotape of *George of the Jungle.* "This George rides around in a limo, baby, and looks great in Armani," jeers the dude announcer. "It's not your parents' *George of the Jungle!*" Change the channel to *Sesame Street,* and although the only ads you'll get are for the letter *H* or the number *3,* you may still see an imitation MTV video with a group of longhaired, bopping, stomping muppets singing *I'm so cool, cool, cool!* That few three-year-olds know the first thing about Armani, limos, or even cool is irrelevant; it's time they learned.

Many companies today have "coolhunters" or "street teams," that is, itinerant researchers who hang out in clubs, malls, and parks and look for trends in adolescent styles in clothes, music, and slang to be used in educating younger consumer trainees. Advertisers can then broadcast for children an aesthetic to emblazon their peer group identity. Even ads for the most naive, childlike products are packed with the symbols of contemporary cool. The Ken doll, introduced in 1993, has hair tinted with blond streaks and wears an earring and a thick gold chain around his neck. The rock and roll which accompanies many of these ads is the pulsing call to generational independence now played for even the youngest tot. The Honey Comb Bear (in sunglasses) raps the virtues of his eponymous cereal. The 1998 Rugrats movie is accompanied by musicians like Elvis Costello and Patti Smith. With a name like Kool-Aid, how could the drink manufacturer continue its traditional appeal to parents and capture today's child sophisticate as well? The new Mr. Kool Aid raps his name onto children's brains.

Unlike the education offered in our public schools, this curriculum of family rot, answered by teenage independence and cool spending, appears to have been highly successful. As math or geography students, American children may be mediocre, but as consumers they are world-class. They learn at prodigiously young ages to obey the detailed sumptuary laws of the teen material world, a world in which status emanates out of the cut of a pain of jeans or the stitching of a sneaker. M/E Marketing Research found that kids make brand decisions by the age of four.[29] *Marketing to and Through Kids* recounts numerous stories of kids under ten unwilling to wear jeans or sneakers without a status label. One executive at Converse claims that dealers inform him that children as young as two are "telling their parents what they want on their feet." Another marketing executive at Nike notes, "The big shift we've been seeing is away from unbranded to more sophisticated branded athletic shoes at younger and younger ages." At Nike the percentage of profit attributable to young children grew from nothing to 14 percent by the early nineties.[30]

Nowhere has the success of media education been more dramatically apparent than among eight-to-twelve-year-old "tweens." The rise of the tween has been sudden and intense. In 1987 James McNeal, perhaps the best-known scholar of the children's market, reported that children in this age group had an income of $4.7 billion. In 1992 in an article in *American Demographics* he revised that figure up to $9 billion, *an increase of almost 100 percent in five years.*[31] While children spent almost all their money on candy in the 1960s, they now spend two-thirds of their cash on toys, clothes, movies, and games they buy themselves.[32]

The teening of those we used to call preadolescents shows up in almost everything kids wear and do. In 1989 the Girl Scouts of America introduced a new MTV-style ad with rap music in order to, in the words of the organization's media specialist, "get away from the uniformed, goody-goody image and show that the Girl Scouts are a fun, mature, cool place to be."[33] Danny Goldberg, the chief executive officer of Mercury Records, concedes that teenagers have been vital to the music industry since the early days of Sinatra. "But now the teenage years seem to start at 8 or 9 in terms of entertainment tastes," he says. "The emotions are kicking in earlier."[34] A prime example is Hanson, a rock-and-roll group whose three members achieved stardom when they were between the ages of eleven and seventeen. Movie producers and directors are finding it increasingly difficult to interest children this age in the usual children's fare. Tweens go to *Scream,* a horror film about a serial killer, or *Object of My Affection,* a film about a young woman who falls in love with a homosexual man.[35] After the girl-driven success of *Titanic,* Buffy Shutt, president of marketing at Universal Pictures, marveled, "They're amazing consumers."[36] Mattel surely agrees, as evidenced by their Barbie ad. "You, girls, can do anything." Clothing retailers are scrambling for part of the tween action. All over the country companies like Limited Too, Gap Kids, Abercrombie and Fitch, and Gymboree have opened stores for six-to-twelve-year-olds and are selling the tween look—

which at this moment means bell bottoms, ankle-length skirts or miniskirts, platform shoes, and tank tops.[37] Advertisers know that kids can spot their generational signature in a nanosecond—the hard rock and roll, the surfer-dude voices, the baggy pants and bare midriffs shot by tilted cameras in vibrant hues and extreme close-ups—and they oblige by offering these images on TV, the Internet, in store displays, and in the growing number of kid magazines.[38]

The seduction of children with dreams of teen sophistication and tough independence, which began with Barbie and intensified markedly in the last decade, appears to have had the desired effect: it has undermined childhood by turning children into teen consumers. This new breed of children won't go to children's movies and they won't play with toys. One of the stranger ironies of the rise of the tween is that toy manufacturers, who with the introduction of Barbie began the direct hard sell to children and were the first to push the teening of American childhood, have been hoist with their own petard. The 1998–99 Toy Industry Factbook of the Toy Manufacturer's Association says that the industry used to think of kids between birth and fourteen as their demographic audience, but with the emergence of tweens they have had to shrink that audience to birth to ten.[39] Even seven- and eight-year-olds are scorning Barbie.[40]

Who needs a doll when you can live the life of the teen vamp yourself? Cosmetic companies are finding a bonanza among this age group. Lines aimed at tweens include nail polish, hair mascara, lotions, and lip products like lipstick, lip gloss, "lip lix." Sweet Georgia Brown is a cosmetics line for tweens that includes body paints and scented body oils with come-hither names like Vanilla Vibe or Follow Me Boy. The Cincinnati design firm Libby Peszyk Kattiman has introduced a line of bikini underwear for girls. There are even fitness clubs and personal trainers for tweens in Los Angeles and New York.[41]

Marketers point at broad demographic trends to explain these changes in the child market, and they are at least partially correct. Changes in the family have given children more power over shopping decisions. For the simple reason that fewer adults are around most of the time, children in single-parent homes tend to take more responsibility for obtaining food and clothes. Market researchers have found that these kids become independent consumers earlier than those in two-parent homes.[42] Children of working mothers also tend to do more of the family shopping when at around age eight or nine they can begin to get to the store by themselves. Though candy, toy, and cereal manufacturers had long been well aware of the money potential of tween cravings, by the mid-eighties, even though their absolute numbers were falling, tweens began to catch the eye of a new range of businesses, and ads and marketing magazines started to tout the potential of this new niche. The reason was simple: market research revealed that more and more children in this age group were shopping for their own clothes, shoes, accessories, and drugstore items—indeed, they were even shopping for the family groceries. Just as marketers had once targeted housewives, now they were aiming at kids.[43] Jeans manufacturer Jordache was one of the first companies to spot the trend. "My customers are kids who can walk into a store with either their own money or their mothers'," the company's director of advertising explained at the time. "The dependent days of tugging on Mom or Dad's sleeve are over." Now as the number of children is rising again, their appeal is even more irresistible. Packaged Facts, a division of the worldwide research firm Find/SVP, has said that the potential purchasing power of today's kids "is the greatest of any age or demographic group in our nation's history."[44]

And there is another reason for the increasing power of children as consumers: by the time they are tweens, American children have simply learned to expect a lot of stuff.[45] Many of them have been born to older mothers; the number of first babies born to women over thirty has quadrupled since 1970, and the number born to women over forty doubled in the six years between 1984 and 1990. Older mothers are more likely to have established careers and to be in the kind of financial position that allows them to shower their kids with toys and expensive clothes.[46] Also, grandparents are living longer and more comfortably, and they often arrive with an armload of toys, sports equipment, and fancy dresses. (The products of the children's clothes company Osh Kosh B'Gosh are known in the trade as "granny bait.") Divorce has also helped to inflate the child market: many American children divide their time between parents, multiplying by two the number of soccer balls and Big Bird toothbrushes they must own.

But as we have seen before, impersonal social forces have found support in human decisions. Important as they are, demographics by themselves can't explain ten-year-olds who have given up dolls for mascara and body oil. Throughout this chapter we have seen that the teening of childhood has been a consummation the media devoutly wished—and planned. The media has given tweens a group identity with its own language, music, and fashion. It has done this by flattering their sense of being hip and aware almost-teens rather than out-of-it little kids dependent on their parents. On discovering the rising number of child customers, Jordache Jeans did not simply run ads for kids; they ran ads showing kids saying things like "Have you ever seen your parents naked?" and "I hate my mother. She's prettier than me." When Bonne Bell cosmetics discovered the rising sales potential of younger shoppers, they did not merely introduce a tween line, which some parents might think bad enough; they introduced it with the kind of in-your-face language that used to send children to bed without dinner: "We know how to be cool. We have our own ideas. And make our own decisions. Watch out for us." Sassaby's "Watch your mouth, young lady" is a smirking allusion to old-fashioned childhood that is meant to sell a line of lip "huggers" and "gloss overs."

There is little reason to think that children have found the freedom and individuality that liberationists assumed they would find now that they have been liberated from old-fashioned childhood and its adult guards. The rise of the child consumer and the child market itself is compelling evidence that children will always seek out some authority for rules about how to dress, talk, and act. Today's school-age children, freed from adult guidance, turn to their friends, who in turn rely on a glamorous and flattering media for the relevant cultural messages. Recent studies have found that children are forming cliques at younger ages than in previous years and that those cliques have strict rules about dress, behavior, and leisure. By the fifth or sixth grade, according to *Peer Power: Preadolescent Culture and Identity,* girls are gaining status "from their success at grooming, clothes, and other appearance-related variables."[47] Teachers and principals also see an increasing number of ten- and eleven-year-olds who have given up toys for hair mousse and name-brand jeans and who heckle those who do not. What matters to this new breed of child is, according to Bruce Friend, vice president of worldwide research and planning at Nickelodeon, "being part of the in-crowd" and "being the first to know what's cool."[48] These "free" children "are extremely fad conscious"; moreover, according to *American Demographics,* tweens' attraction to fads has "no saturation points."[49] Look for the tween consumer to become even more powerful.

A diminished home life and an ever more powerful media constitute a double blow against the conditions under which individuality flourishes. Whereas in the past eccentric or bookish children might have had the privacy of their home to escape the pressures of their media-crazed peers, today such refuge has gone the way of after-school milk and cookies. And if you think that at least such children have been freed of the pressure of yesterday's domineering fathers and frustrated mothers, you might want to reconsider. As Hannah Arendt once noted, "The authority of a group, even a child group, is always considerably stronger and more tyrannical than the severest authority of an individual person can ever be." The opportunity for an individual to rebel when bound to a group is "practically nil"; few adults can do it.[50] The truth is, as we have seen, yesterday's parent-controlled childhood protected children not only from sex, from work, and from adult decisions but also from the dominance of peers and from the market, with all its pressures to achieve, its push for status, its false lures, its passing fads.

But in the anticultural filiarchy which is replacing traditional childhood, adults no longer see their job as protecting children from the market. In fact, it is not that the child's hurried entrance into the market means that parents are increasingly failing to socialize children. It's the other way around. Children are viewed by manufacturers as the "opinion leaders in the household," according to a vice president at Keebler.[51] Manufacturers believe that children are exercising influence over family purchases never before remotely associated with the young. Holiday Inn and Delta Airlines have established marketing programs aimed at children, and *Sports Illustrated for Kids* publishes ads from American Airlines, IBM, and car manufacturers.[52]

While simply turning off the TV would help, at this point television is only one part of the picture. Kids learn of their sophisticated independence from retail displays and promotions, from magazines and direct mailings. With their captive audience, schools have become an advertiser's promised land. We saw in chapter 3 how much educators have surrendered to the media in their preference for "creative" assignments like videos and board games. But the schools' capitulation to the media goes beyond that: kids see ads in classrooms, on book order forms, on Channel One, on the Internet, on school buses, and now even in textbooks. Book order forms distributed in schools throughout the country from the putatively educational firm Scholastic look like cartoons and provide children with the opportunity to order stickers, autograph books, fan biographies, and books based on popular movies and television shows. Practically every Fortune 500 company has a school project, according to the *New York Times,* and many administrators expect that in the near future we will be seeing signs like CHEERLEADERS BROUGHT TO YOU BY REEBOK in school gyms.[53] "It isn't enough just to advertise on television," Carol Herman, a senior vice president of Grey Advertising, explains. "You've got to reach the kids throughout their day—in school, as they're shopping at the mall . . . or at the movies. You've got to become part of the fabric of their lives."[54]

The scorched earth policy in the name of the filiarchy requires that ever younger children be treated as potential customers, once again in the guise of education. When *Sesame Street* arrived on the airwaves in 1969, no one imagined that preschoolers could be a significant market segment. In fact, the improbability of preschool purchasing power was the reason *Sesame Street* had to appear on public television in the first place; no one wanted to put a lot of money into creating and broadcasting a program for kids who had no purchasing power. How shortsighted that was! By 1994 Children's Television Workshop was bringing in $120 million a year largely on the strength of its over five thousand licensed products. The list includes not just educational items like books and audiotapes but bubble bath, pajamas, underwear, and Chef Boyardee Sesame Street pasta. Toy manufacturers gradually caught on to the power of the littlest people, especially where their education was concerned. The number of preschool toys exploded in the decades after *Sesame Street* was introduced, and many of them were stamped with a seal of approval from some expert or other—or with the image of Ernie or Big Bird, which in the minds of many amounted to the same thing.

And now *Teletubbies* has arrived to help carve out the *pre*-preschool market and to give power to the littlest people. *Teletubbies* was designed for one- and two-year-olds, and though no one has ever explained how it could possibly be educational for babies to watch television, it is clear that when toddlers see pictures of the four vividly hued plush and easily identified characters (with television screens on their stomachs) on bottles or bibs, they will cry for them and PBS will rake it in. In anticipation of opening up this new market segment, the media went into overdrive. Pictures of the characters appeared in ads in trade and consumer magazines and were plastered on buses in New York City and on a giant billboard in Times Square. The show was a topic on *Letterman, Today,* and *Nightline.* "If this isn't the most important toy at Christmas this year, then something desperately wrong will have happened," gloated Kenn Viselman, whose Itsy Bitsy Entertainment Company has the rights to *Teletubbies* products. "This show had more advance press than *Titanic.*" Wondered one critic, "Where does it end: A TV in the amniotic sac?" But marketers were thrilled; according to the president of another licensing company, before now "the 1-to-2-year-old niche hasn't been filled very well."[55] The 1-to-2-year-old niche? McNeal has said that children become aware of the market as early as two months of age.[56] There is no more unmistakable sign of the end of childhood as Americans have known it.

Chapter 5

Fourteen-Year-Old Women and Juvenile Men

Parents having trouble with their teenagers or teens who are sick of their parents might be interested in hearing about the Emancipation of Minors Act, passed by the California legislature in 1982. Initiated by youth rights organizations, the act allows minors who petition for "emanicpation" to become legal adults. True, emancipation is limited—an emancipated minor still cannot buy liquor, for instance—but the act enables teenagers to sign contracts, own property, and keep their earnings. Hopes were high that the act would allow smart, competent teens to assume more independence. As the president of Youth Advocates Inc. wrote to Governor Jerry Brown, "Within our experience requests for emancipation come from the 'good kids' . . . These minors are usually the brighter, more industrious, self-reliant youngsters who have matured earlier than the arbitrary eighteen year designation . . ." All kids have to do is get their parents' signature, have a short hearing with the judge and voila!—they are quasi adults. It is easier than getting a driver's license.

So how have the liberated teens fared? A few have used their emancipation to get ahead—to work longer hours or enter into business contracts—but only a few. Most simply wanted to escape the usual hassles with parents over curfews, drugs, smoking, and driving. Many of them dropped out of school. Forced to rely on the kindness of friends and acquaintances for beds to sleep in and food to eat, these "industrious, self-reliant youngsters" complain of loneliness and financial worries. No wonder. It turns out that in most cases the parents were pleased to be rid of the kid; in fact, they were the ones who had come up with the idea of the kid's emancipation in the first place. What the Emancipation of Minors Act has accomplished, in other words, is the legalization of child neglect.[1]

The Emancipation of Minors Act exquisitely captures the unintended consequences of the law's changing attitude toward teenagers over the last thirty years. As the courts intended, the "legal march away from the conception of the child as a dependent person," in the words of legal scholar Martha Minow,[2] has gone some way toward protecting kids from the arbitrary decisions of authorities like judges, police, and, to a lesser extent, principals, teachers, and parents. But, at the same time, this journey has also "protected" adolescents from adult guidance and support. Swayed by anticultural ideas, lawmakers have posited adolescents not only as "industrious" and "self-reliant" young people but also as rational and self-aware actors who are independent of, and often in opposition to, the mature representatives of the society into which they must move. And so judges, legislators, and lawyer-advocates, like the media, educators, and child experts we've already discussed, have helped to undermine the meaning and goals of traditional American childhood and have made it ever more difficult for adults to socialize children.

Put in these terms, it may seem that lawmakers are making a glaring mistake, but they have their own reasons for being sympathetic to anticultural ideas. Western legal tradition is predicated on the idea that the individual is a solitary and autonomous decision maker.[3] As Americans began to hear more and more often from the academy and the media that they had underestimated children's innate cognitive and moral capacities, it seemed to them only natural for the law to reflect the way in which children could benefit more directly from our individualist tradition. The troubling irony is that by submitting to the anticultural notion that children are innately equipped for freedom, lawmakers in fact have subverted the liberal democratic principles the law is supposed to be upholding. The rights movement of the last several generations has made it increasingly difficult for young people to be trained properly for citizenship. The bureaucratic and technical proceduralism that has resulted from all this, which now passes as society's way of respecting the young, is a recipe for cynicism and alienation rather than for the sense of conscious moral agency and civic obligation that a free society demands.

A ny discussion about the law's current attitudes toward children and childhood must begin with the case that announced the coming of anticulturalism into the justice system: *In re Gault*.[4] Decided by the Supreme Court in 1967, *Gault* introduced to America a child-citizen who stood in a more adultlike relationship to society. If this child-citizen needed any shaping or socializing, the law certainly wasn't going to get involved. And it was going to make it more difficult for parents and teachers to do so too.

This is not to say that the *Gault* decision wasn't inspired by a serious injustice. It was. On a June morning in 1964, fifteen-year-old Gerald Gault made an obscene phone call from his Arizona home to a Mrs. Cook. Such a prank might not seem serious enough to merit more than a parental lecture and punishment, but Gerald's parents never had the chance to discipline him. Notified by a distressed Mrs. Cook, the police arrived at Gerald's home, hauled him into headquarters, performed a cursory investigation, and sent him on to a juvenile court hearing. As if this wasn't an extreme enough response to such common adolescent mischief, the juvenile court judge committed Gerald to the state industrial school until majority. In other words, a fifteen-year-old boy was condemned to *six years* in a state institution for one dirty phone call. One could hardly blame Gerald's parents—who were at work when their son was taken into custody and who, at any rate, had no recourse to stop it, since under Arizona law no appeal was permitted—when they sued the state; they must have felt as if their son had been kidnapped by government officials.

The Gaults did not find much sympathy for their plight in the lower courts, but when after several years the case finally reached the United States Supreme Court, the time was right for their son's mistreatment to take on historical significance. The justices not only agreed with the Gaults, noting the injustice of confining a fifteen-year-old for six years for a crime which might have provoked nothing more than a $50 fine if committed by an eighteen-year-old, but did so in the most dramatic and pathbreaking terms: "[N]either the Fourteenth Amendment nor the Bill of Rights is for adults alone," they proclaimed, in words that would ring repeatedly in future lower judicial decisions. Like adults, minors had the right to due process, to "principle and procedure," including the right to counsel, the right to remain silent, and the right to confront witnesses.[5]

In order to grasp the enormity of this decision, it's important to understand how much it represents a break from the way Americans had previously dealt with children and teenagers who had gotten into trouble with the law. Until the turn of the twentieth century, despite the republican tradition of sheltered childhood, children were sentenced and imprisoned no differently from adults. Kids who pilfered coal from the train tracks might find themselves sharing quarters with horse thieves and murderers or, even worse, rapists. Recognizing the dangers latent in this treatment and believing that those under seventeen should be handled differently than adults, Progressive reformers in 1899 inaugurated the first juvenile court for troubled youth, who at that time were most commonly petty thieves and street corner bullies. The judge in the new court was to be recast; no longer an impersonal agent of the law meting out retributive justice, now he was to be something closer to "a wise parent . . . deal[ing] with a wayward child," in the words of Julian Mack, one of the first Chicago juvenile court judges.[6] In street clothes rather than a robe, at a desk rather than the bench, the judge was to put aside the stern demands of justice and set about pondering the "best interests of the child" by delving into his "soul-life." "I talk with the boy, give him a good talk, just as I would my own boy," explained Judge Richard S. Tuthill,

Mack's predecessor, "and find myself as much interested in some of these boys as I would if they were my own."[7] In this spirit, one well-known judge, Benjamin Lindsey, sometimes sent "lads" in need of it—most delinquents were male—to the courthouse shower.

The problem with this arrangement, as countless boys doubtless discovered, was that it opened the door to a dangerous expansion of capricious state power. Judges had extraordinary discretion over their cases. Short of a lengthy appeals process, there was no way to argue their decisions, no matter how whimsical or intemperate. There were no defense lawyers, juries, or rules of evidence. It was no wonder that the justices in *In re Gault* slammed the institution as "a kangaroo court."[8] If the judge thought your son was guilty, he was guilty. If the judge thought your daughter needed a three-year respite in a reform school, well, you could say good-bye for three years no matter how petty her crime. Reformers often demonstrated breathtaking arrogance: "We are saying to the father and the mother that they have not the wisdom, or the ability, or the willingness, properly to train that child," Judge Mack announced.[9] As Christopher Lasch, one of a number of critics of Progressive benevolence who began to voice their concern in the late 1960s argued, the juvenile court "created new varieties of arbitrary power. Neither children nor their parents, it turned out, had much recourse against authorities who were 'only trying to help.'"[10]

But for all the substantial dangers built into its design, the juvenile court was nonetheless founded on a humane and important truth in modern American life: the adolescent is no adult. The founders of the juvenile court were dedicated to the emerging view of American adolescence as a separate life stage, one as much like dependent childhood as autonomous adulthood. In their view, adolescent judgment and moral sense were still incomplete; they believed, for instance, that "the peculiar weakness [of adolescents'] moral nature" made them ill-equipped to resist "the manifold temptation of the streets."[11] Such immature beings needed adult guidance. The absence of procedure, though it came to seem to its later critics merely an invitation to judiciary mischief, was actually intended to allow adolescents to avoid the full brunt of the law. It gave the judge flexibility to take into account such considerations as: Had the youth gotten into trouble before and why? What were things like at home? Did he need to be removed from a brutal home, or did he just need additional supervision from a parole officer? In short, the juvenile court was designed to be a socializing institution, one that was, in some respects, more like a school than a court.

Unfortunately, when the Supreme Court announced in *Gault* that the constitution applied to children as well as adults, it started a process that ensured the unraveling of both the strengths and weaknesses of the juvenile system. For while in *Gault* and related subsequent decisions the justices assured that due process safeguards could coexist with "every aspect of fairness, of concern, of sympathy, and of paternal attention," this has not been the case.[12] The post-*Gault* court endorsed a highly problematic trade-off: while it has protected children from certain kinds of injustices, particularly an unwarranted loss of liberty like that suffered by Gerald Gault, it has introduced bureaucratic impersonality and has eroded the court's traditional child-rearing values of protection and socialization. Simply put, by introducing the image of the child as a young citizen who needed protection *from* the state, *Gault* erased the image of the child who needed the protection *of* the state. The decision transformed the image of the child before the court from a youngster entrusted to the care of a father substitute to a young adult benefiting from the services of a professional lawyer. Like the expert's "competent infant," the educator's "learning machine," and the media's sophisticated consumer, the law's child has innate capabilities; he stands proud, an independent—and sometimes unsupported—citizen.

When we consider how actual teenagers have reacted to their new-found rights, we begin to get a good picture of the anticultural misunderstanding under which the justices labored. Surely, for a democracy to thrive, its citizens must first of all have the capacity to understand the meaning and obligations of their freedom. But this is often not the case with adolescents, who tend to view the post-*Gault* court with either incomprehension or suspicion. Studies of the juvenile court find that teenagers, particularly those under fifteen, commonly waive their rights because they don't know what they mean. They fail to grasp that lawyers are there to protect them whether they are guilty or not;

instead, they tend to view lawyers as working for the judge. They do not grasp that the law is a suprapersonal set of rules; they perceive it as personified in the police or the judge, who in their view can make it up as he or she wishes. "In general," one researcher has written, "it would appear juveniles tend to perceive their legal rights not as entitlements but as privileges which may be revoked at the whim of adult authorities."[13] To put it simply, they think like kids.

Though it did nothing to shift the law's new definition of the child-citizen, a good example of the adolescent's immaturity came before the Supreme Court twelve years after *Gault* in *Fare v. Michael C.*[14] Michael C. was a sixteen-year-old California boy with a long record of delinquency who was arrested for murder; he was, as required by *Gault,* advised by the police of his Miranda rights, that is, the right to remain silent, the right to an attorney, and so forth. The transcript of his meeting with the police illustrates how the *Gault* justices may have overestimated kids' ability to grasp the nature of their new relationship to the state:

Q: Do you understand all of these rights as I have explained them to you?

A: Yeah.

Q: Okay, do you wish to give up your right to remain silent and talk to us about murder?

A: What murder? I don't know about no murder.

Q: I'll explain to you which one it is if you want to talk to us about it.

A: Yeah, I might talk to you.

Q: Do you want to give up your right to have an attorney present here while we talk about it?

A: Can I have my probation officer here?

Q. Well, I can't get a hold of your probation officer right now. You have the right to an attorney.

A: How I know you guys won't pull no police officer in and tell me he's an attorney?

Q: Huh? . . . If you want to talk to us with an attorney present, you can. If you don't want to, you don't have to . . . That's your right. Do you understand that right?

A: Yeah.

Q: Okay, will you talk to us without an attorney present?

A: Yeah, I want to talk to you.[15]

Though he was an older juvenile with a long record and though he had been told repeatedly that he had a right to an attorney, Michael apparently didn't understand the technical legal difference between his parole officer, who worked for the state, and an independent lawyer, who would work for him. This "immature, emotional, and uneducated" boy, as Justice Powell called him in his dissent, cried through much of his questioning and pleaded for the person he knew and trusted, even though that person could not help him in a court of law and could even do him some harm.[16] Forced to follow the logic of their own portrait of the child-citizen, however, the justices decided that Michael was a fully responsible actor and that he was mature enough to understand his predicament. If he was citizen enough to be granted his rights, then he was citizen enough to understand them. His confession and conviction could stand.

The fact that Michael C. was in all likelihood guilty should not blind us to the inherent unfairness of asking kids to play a role which is so at odds with their abilities. In recent years, as the number of younger adolescents and even preadolescents accused of crime has increased, the problem has edged into absurdity. In Pontiac, Michigan, an eleven-year-old boy (who was dressed in his Halloween costume at the time of his arrest) waived his right to remain silent, which he later said he thought meant "can't go nowhere," and confessed to shooting an eighteen-year-old boy coming out of a convenience store.[17] In July of 1998 two Chicago boys, ages seven and eight, confessed to the murder of eleven-year-old Ryan Harris. Though people who knew the boys, the larger of whom was four feet two, questioned how they could have dragged a five-foot-one-inch, eighty-eight-pound body across a well-traveled street stealthily enough to avoid witnesses, it was only when semen was discovered on the girl's body and DNA tests were completed that the boys were released. Later it was revealed that though officers referred to the boys as "young men," they knew enough to elicit the boys' confession through the promise of a

MacDonald's Happy Meal.[18] If there's any picture that captures the confusion in current American beliefs about children—ironic in that it arose in part out of the benevolent wish to extend the Constitution to them—it is surely that of the police intoning to a bewildered eight-year-old, as they sometimes do today, "You have the right to remain silent . . ." while promising him a treat.

The post-*Gault* court gives us numerous examples of how anticulturalism seems an excuse for adult negligence. For all its considerable faults, the old juvenile court was designed so that all adults—parents, teachers, judges—were in a conspiracy to teach adolescents their moral and civic responsibilites. *Gault* forced that conspiracy to disband. It not only stripped adults of their role as teachers and guides but made them adversaries both of the child and of each other. Kids in trouble who already have a precarious sense of right and wrong receive enough ambiguous lessons on the subject to leave them permanently confused. Fearing they might be subpoenaed by the prosecution, lawyers often tell their clients not to talk to their parents–even about decisions that could drastically alter their future.[19] And consider what happens to the parent-child relationship by the mere fact that kids have the right to remain silent. When their child is in trouble with the law, most parents, one researcher has found, want them to take responsibility if they have in fact done something wrong. "He should tell the truth," they say, or "If he's guilty, he should own up."[20] This is what a society needs its parents to believe. Studies have shown what most parents have seen firsthand in less serious circumstances: guilty kids are prone to blame their victim or a peer.[21] The resistance to admitting guilt for a misdeed runs deep in human nature; owning up comes only with careful teaching, and even then it's precarious. Yet premature due process rights subvert the required repeated lesson of moral responsibility. It gives sullen adolescents the opportunity—no, the *right*—to act out their worst instincts. It forces them into an adversarial stance with those who should be supervising them. And as we have seen, it does so for the sake of principles that the adolescent often doesn't even understand.

What all of this suggests is that far from advancing liberal principles, treating kids as adults actually undermines them. The justice system can no longer presume a responsible and competent citizenry, a necessary precondition for a democracy. It's not enough to argue, as many advocates do, that the young are no different than many adults who do not fully understand their rights to due process. For one thing, we run the risk of trivializing or even transforming the meaning of citizenship when we grant rights to those we *assume* are not fully capable of exercising their responsibilities. It suggests that we value entitlement more than obligation and muddies the relationship between government and citizen. For another, adolescents are not the same as ill-informed adults. Adolescents are unfinished beings, and adults are obliged to continue the work of shaping them, a process that can and sometimes must include serious punishment. Indeed, though most Americans believe punishments are too lenient, 85 percent of them, according to a report from Public Agenda, still feel that given the right guidance, teens in trouble with the law can be straightened out.[22] As "works in progress" and as dependents, they live in an entirely different relation to authority than adults do. They are still learning from authority—even as they test its boundaries—the rules of the world they must live in.

Instead of grappling with this problem and facing the faulty premises of the *Gault* decision, judges, lawyers, and child experts have simply scrambled for ways to prop up the straw man of the autonomous child or teen rights bearer. One influential forensic psychologist has urged that schools begin teaching children about their legal rights beginning in the third grade.[23] The dissenters in the *Fare* case, namely, Justices Thurgood Marshall, William J. Brennan, and John Paul Stevens, argued that juveniles should be determined to have invoked their right to silence simply upon asking for *any* friendly adult. Justifiably wondering how kids can waive something they do not understand, psychologist Thomas Grisso of the University of Massachussets Medical School has gone further: he recommends that instead of being *allowed to remain silent,* kids should be *required to remain silent* unless an interested adult is in the room.[24] Several states have agreed and have passed laws that parents must be present before a minor waives his or her rights or confesses. Some advocates go further yet, pointing out that in many cases parents themselves are not adequately concerned or informed about their kids' rights; they think minors should be *required to have a lawyer* before they can talk.[25] No one seems to notice that going this far subverts the very intention of due process rights. Here is the state from which individuals supposedly need protection—hence, their right to a lawyer— *ordering* them to protect themselves from the very power it uses to make the order in the first place.

Advocates assumed that increasing children's rights would teach them the principles of fairness.[26] But by asking kids to take part in a rule-bound drama they don't understand, the post-*Gault* court has often had the effect of teaching the principles of advanced hustling and cynicism instead. To an adolescent in trouble, lying, manipulating, and stretching the rules are bound to look much more appealing than playing fair and square. Kids often figure out that by failing to show up, they can add to the likelihood that exasperated witnesses won't come back again and that their case will be dropped. Edward Humes' account of the juvenile court *No Matter How Loud I Shout* confirms this by noting that kids are sometimes helped by their lawyers to find ways to delay, an especially disturbing effort given their need for clear and swift responses from adults.[27]

In the end, then, the law simply assists the troubled adolescents of anticulturalism to remain in their amoral, unfinished state. Liberated from the shaping influence of their elders, they are also freed from the experiences that might force them to reckon with their own conscience and bring them to self-awareness. A New York case illustrates the point. In 1992 Juan C., a fifteen-year-old student at New York City's Taft High School, one of the tougher schools in the Bronx, was stopped by a security guard who noticed a bulge in his jacket. Though Juan tried to run away, the guard was able to reach into his pocket and find a loaded semiautomatic pistol, leading to the boy's suspension and arrest. However, the judge in Juan's case ruled the search illegal because it violated the Fourth Amendment requirements for reasonable search and seizure. There is a peculiarly absurd American quality to the fact that a potentially dangerous fifteen-year-old went free because he was able to demonstrate to a judge just how well he had hidden his gun.[28] The message for this teen and the legions of others going free on this kind of technicality is that the adults around them are indifferent toward their adolescent deceptions, bravado, and, in all too many cases, cruelty.

In its heyday, the juvenile court had the potential to uphold the best tradition of American childhood. It took seriously society's obligation to form self-governing citizens. And it set out to do so by attending to the adolescent's individual nature and circumstances. But in its embrace of technical legalisms, the anticultural court has turned its back on this tradition. Its heart belongs to correct procedure rather than to the troubled child. Symbolic of this shift is how little meaningful attention the post-*Gault* court pays to more malleable kids, the ones teetering on the edge of the criminal abyss, even when their parents are crying for help. Humes recounts how one mother called the police repeatedly about her son, who was joining street gangs, skipping school, and staying out all night. She was told, "There's nothing anyone can do unless he commits a crime."[29] Although we know that young lawbreakers usually commit a number of minor offenses of the kind the courts have no time to monitor and then work their way up to commit serious crime, there is little effort to keep track of this evolution. Humes also tells the following woeful but common tale: George came into the system at age six, a victim of abuse, and was passed around a series of neglectful foster homes. In his early teens, he was arrested after being found joyriding in a stolen car and was found guilty of burglary. At this pivotal moment, he was neither punished nor guided onto a different path, both of them necessary for shaping any child. Instead he was placed under "supervision," a laughable word for the cursory attention he received from an overworked probation officer with two hundred other kids to monitor. By age sixteen, George had been charged with robbery, and after his conviction in adult court he received a twelve-year prison sentence.[30]

Examples of innovative approaches that speak to the adolescent's continuing need for coherent, informal socializing can be found scattered throughout the country. In Philadelphia, for instance, a Youth Aid Panel made up of local citizens has the authority to punish "minnows" like shoplifters and marijuana smokers by making them clean up local parks, write letters of apology, and the like.[31] But such innovations face considerable obstacles in today's legal atmosphere. Judge Roosevelt Dorn, a juvenile court judge in Los Angeles who plays a major role in Humes' book, let the word out that he would be available to help parents whose kids seemed beyond their control, whether or not the kid had committed a crime. Though the experiment was publicized only by word of mouth, four hundred desperate parents dragged their kids into Judge Dorn's chambers in less than ten months. According to Humes, several defense attorneys overheard the judge as he threatened to detain a young truant brought in by his mother. Judge Dorn was performing—he had no authority to detain a child who had not actually committed a crime—but the attorneys, incensed at the judge's attempt to scare this boy into good behavior, asserted that it violated the youngster's rights.[32]

The post-*Gault* court tells kids—worse, it tells kids who are in trouble—that they are free, isolate, adult actors and that their elders' only responsibility toward them is to ensure that the complex rules they can't understand are being meticulously followed. "I'm a technician," says a legal aid lawyer in another study. "I help these people by getting them their freedom."[33] Yet most of the adolescents who find their way into juvenile court these days have been neglected by families, by teachers, by just about every adult they've ever encountered. They often live in a half-conscious, irresponsible condition, which one writer aptly calls "drift," their only ballast a dangerous peer group.[34] Now they come to juvenile court, and what do they get? Lawyers who are technicians aiding them in their natural desire to avoid confronting their misdeeds.

Here once again is the familiar irony of anticulturalism: to liberate children is to undermine their liberty. Thirty years ago, advocates were convinced that turning the child into an adultlike citizen would be a clear-cut victory for fairness and justice. But the logic that gives children adult rights also subjects them to adult punishments. Justice Potter Stewart warned of this danger in his dissent in *In re Gault*. "So it was that a twelve-year-old boy named James Guild was tried in New Jersey for killing Catherine Blakes," he wrote about juvenile justice before the days of the juvenile court. "A jury found him guilty of murder, and he was sentenced to death by hanging. The sentence was executed. It was all very constitutional."[35] Today, although a 1988 Supreme Court decision—*Thompson v. Oklahoma*—makes it unconstitutional to put to death anyone who committed a crime while under the age of sixteen, the decision seems a shaky one.[36] As one scholar has cautioned, *Thompson* was decided by a vote of five to three and one of the five, Sandra Day O'Connor, seemed willing to revisit the question.[37] Indeed, under the terms of anticulturalism, where is the argument for protecting children from hangings and lethal injections?

In the Supreme Court's decisions concerning a minor's right to an abortion, similar and even more tenacious anticultural misconceptions are at work, with the same neglectful consequences.

In its landmark 1973 decision *Roe v. Wade,* the Supreme Court explicitly avoided consideration of whether the constitutional right to abortion was shared by minors. It was an understandable evasion. Historically, the court had been loath to allow the state to interfere with the parent–child relationship, and if any subject seemed designed to roil up family life, it was teen sex. Even though *Gault* and several other subsequent decisions had pronounced minors citizens with constitutional rights, in each of these cases the interests of the child and the parents had been identical. In fact, parents had inititated these suits on behalf of their children. When the issue of abortion rights for minors finally came before the court later in the 1970s, it was a very different matter. This time it was doctors and interest group advocates who came forward first in *Planned Parenthood of Missouri v. Danforth* and then in *Bellotti, Attorney General of Massachussetts, et. al. v. Baird et al.* to plead on behalf of children the constitutional right to obtain an abortion without involving their parents.[38]

It is true that in their decisions the justices attempted to avoid the extremes of anticulturalism. Although, on the one hand, they reiterated the terms of *Gault,* proclaiming that "[m]inors, as well as adults, are protected by the Constitution and possess constitutional rights,"[39] they nevertheless allowed states to require girls to involve their parents when seeking an abortion. However—and here's where the justices tipped the balance—they allowed states to do this *only* if those girls who could not or would not involve their parents were allowed instead to receive permission from a judge, a practice known as judicial bypass.

An escape hatch like judicial bypass may well be necessary in the event that a girl finds herself a victim of incest or abuse or if she is being coerced by her parents into bearing a child or having an abortion. But it's important to understand that by insisting on judicial bypass even when a state law requires a girl merely to *inform* her parents of her intention to get an abortion, the court went much further than that. For the first time ever, the law made an explicit provision for minors to subvert the wishes of their parents—and even to withhold knowledge from them—and thereby proclaimed the unmarried pregnant girl to be the most sovereign and independent of the new generation of minor rights bearers.

In order to land in this peculiar situation, the justices once again came under the sway of anticulturalism and failed to note the grey shades of real kids. It's not surprising that some of their decisions cite anticultural child experts whose ideas we've already encountered in chapter 2. Like the expert's child, the teenaged girl who appears in their decisions is a rational, independent-minded, clearheaded—and wholly mythological—creature. Both experts and advocates pronounced adolescents to be equal to adults when it comes to decision making. "There is no factual justification for treating fourteen-year-old women [*sic*] differently, in this regard, from eighteen-year-old women," the American Psychological Association announced in an *amicus* brief submitted in one Supreme Court parental notification case. Urging the court to attend to their own "empirical" rather than culturally "normative" ideas about adolescence, the experts went on to insist that the relevant literature "consistently indicates that for most purposes, there is no basis for the differentiation of adolescents from adults on the ground of competence alone."[40]

Instead of puzzling over expert conclusions that were so wildly out of sync with ordinary experience, the justices assented. They concluded that America's competent and logical girls would use judicial bypass only when necessary, that is, when they had good reason to fear for their safety if their parents found out they were pregnant. They assumed that girls from well-functioning families would seek their parents' support and consent. But the justices were wrong. The most common reason for girls to avoid going to their parents is simply that they are afraid of disappointing them, as doubtless they would be.[41] Thus, around 40 percent of all girls who are seeking an abortion would rather tell a stranger than their parents—though clearly few of them have real cause to fear for their safety. One study found that girls informed their parents at the same rates in Minnesota, where there is a statute for notification, as in Wisconsin, where there is none.[42] Similarly, a 1992 study by the Alan Guttmacher Institute reported that about 40 percent of girls do not notify their parents at all, regardless of law.[43] In other words, give kids in trouble a way to avoid telling their parents and many will seize it.

The justices fell for another anticultural myth proposed by rights advocates. According to this myth, it is not teenaged girls but adults who are prone to irrationality and confusion. Parents hearing of their daughter's pregnancy, they believed, were likely to assault her, kick her out of the house, or force her to bear an unwanted child, one who, it was sometimes hinted, could well be the product of an incestuous union. The reality is that girls who get pregnant often want to have babies and find support for their dreamy plans from friends and boyfriends—and not from their parents. Frantic parents are more likely to talk reluctant daughters into getting an abortion than to prevent them from seeking one.[44] Some have reasonably speculated that whatever enthusiasm ambivalent Americans do muster for abortion rights is largely because they want the option for their underage daughters.

The justices' failure to heed what adolescents are really like has led to unhappy consequences that echo those in the post-*Gault* court. Kids in trouble are abandoned to an anonymous procedural void that seems to follow from anticultural practice. In Massachussetts, from the moment the state's judicial bypass was passed, judges were inundated with requests from pregnant and frightened minors. They granted interviews rarely lasting more than fifteen minutes, during which they would attempt to determine, as the law stipulated, whether the girl was mature enough to decide to have an abortion without help from her parents. Inevitably, their tools were crude. "How old are you?" they would ask. "How long have you been pregnant?" "Do you understand the nature of an abortion procedure?" Some judges would ask more personal questions about why a girl did not want to go to her parents, but many would not. Of the thousands of girls who requested judicial approval between 1981 and 1991 in Massachussetts, only thirteen were denied it; of those, eleven quickly got an okay from another judge. Though Massachusetts lawmakers had imagined the judge's chambers as a somber retreat for careful consideration of an individual girl's predicament, they had instead created an office for bureaucratic rubber-stamping.[45]

Not that things are much better in more conservative jurisdictions. These offer a somewhat different encounter with adult negligence, this time in the form of impersonal arbitrariness. Some girls are told by authorities that they are not competent to decide whether to have an abortion—and yet that they *are* old enough to bear a child. In some states, like Indiana, judges wouldn't confirm the request of anyone. In Ohio, a judge denied permission to a seventeen-and-a-half-year-old straight-A student who stated she was neither financially nor emotionally prepared for motherhood. In some of these places, pregnant girls merely crossed state lines to more generous courtrooms, a practice that probably only increased their disaffection from adults. In Massachussetts, judges who had avidly opposed abortion rights realized that there was no way a girl could be too immature to make an abortion decision yet mature enough to have a baby, and they began okaying petitions.[46]

In substituting bureaucratic impersonality for potential parental anger, the justices advanced the cause of the isolate child-citizen in ways that adolescents do not need and may not even want. Conventional wisdom has it that teenagers are natural rebels seeking freedom from their parents' rules and strictures. But recent studies suggest this is not the whole story. In his study of adolescents from varied economic and social backgrounds, entitled *The Search for Structure*, Francis Ianni found "considerable evidence . . . of the turning to adults for information, validation, and guidance about the future."[47]

The 1997 National Longitudinal Study of Adolescent Health found that in order to thrive, teenagers need to be closely involved with their parents and their schools.[48] Another study, entitled *Talented Teenagers,* put it more baldly in concluding that the best environment for teenagers is really not so different from that for infants. Teenagers need "continuing security and support for the emergence of exploration and independence," the study argued. Such support leaves teenagers free to pour their mental energies into their interests, talents, and the difficult cognitive tasks that they are, or at least should be, encountering in school.[49]

The court has sided with the chaotic and confused adolescent rather than with the needy one evoked in these studies. In effect, it has written an adversarial relationship between parent and child into solemn law. It is true that kids who are in trouble—whether they have failed a test or have been caught smoking marijuana or have become pregnant—are afraid to go to their parents. The large proportion of girls who take advantage of judicial bypass is proof of that rule. But promoting a young pregnant girl's fearful escapism and discouraging her from seeking attention from her parents only leaves her stranded in an anticultural void. No matter how we try to refashion her and remove the stigma from her predicament, the unmarried pregnant girl is still a girl in trouble. Either she is going to become a mother at an age when she is incapable of taking full responsibility for a child—in which case the parents or the state will have to take up the slack—or she is going to go through a painful and troubling procedure that she may find herself confronting again. Few discussions of abortion rights for minors acknowledge that there is reason to believe that 20 percent of teenagers who get pregnant will become pregnant again during their teen years, but it is a useful reminder.[50] Despite the anticultural decisions of the Supreme Court, fourteen-year-olds are not women and they need adults who are more than lawyers and judges.

Of course, Americans have not given up on the idea of a dependent adolescence, nor have they granted kids anything like full legal autonomy. A certain ambivalence about the full-grown but still dependent teenager is mirrored in the many inconsistencies in the law. To cite just a few: In many states a girl can get an abortion without telling her parents, but she must obtain a note from them in order to miss school on the day she goes to the clinic. For that matter, she may need permission to get a tattoo, have root canal surgery, or procure an aspirin from the school nurse. A seventeen-year-old could be put to death for killing a policeman, but he would have to ask his parents' permission to marry before the sentence is carried out and he could not order a beer for his last meal.[51] In some jurisdictions sixteen-year-olds might be able to run for parks commissioner, but they could not be held responsible for a contract they signed granting management of a concession stand.

At first glance, the schools would seem to have escaped these inconsistencies by holding fast to old-fashioned notions of the adolescent as an ungainly child. After all, kids still *have* to go to school. When they are there, teachers and principals can search their lockers and give them random drug tests, both of which would be violations of the Fourth Amendment for their elders. Authorities can also censor their student council speeches and, in many states, their newspapers. In a good number of states—as long as there is a witness and parents have been notified in writing—they can even paddle their backsides.[52]

But by most accounts, the rights revolution that began with *Gault* has had an enormous impact on the schools. True to their anticultural vision, the Supreme Court neglected the simple fact that individuals must be citizens-in-training before they can be actual citizens and that much of that training must take place in schools. Instead, it rendered decisions that have armed students with both legal ammunition and "attitude" and have made it increasingly difficult for educators not only to shape their character or to prepare them for responsible citizenship—always a central purpose of public education in the United States—but even to protect them from each other. Nowhere are the demoralizing consequences of the anticultural fallacy more prominently on display than in the disciplinary climate of today's schools.

The reign of anticulturalism in the schools was inaugurated in 1969, two years after *In re Gault,* with the Supreme Court's decision in the case of *Tinker v. Des Moines Independent Community School District.* In 1965, a group of adults and students from Des Moines donned black armbands in protest against the Vietnam War. The issue for the adults involved was moot, of course, but not for the children. The principal of the local school demanded that the students remove their armbands or else face suspension. One of them, a fifteen-year-old named John F. Tinker, sued and the Supreme Court took his side. "It can hardly be argued," wrote Justice Abe Fortas for the majority, "that either students or teachers shed their constitutional rights to freedom of speech or expression at the schoolhouse gate . . . Students in school as well as out of school are 'persons' under our Constitution."[53] Six years later, the Supreme Court followed up with another decision in this vein after riots in several Columbus, Ohio, schools resulted in the suspension of several students, at least one of whom claimed to be innocent of any involvement in the mayhem. *Goss v. Lopez* granted kids the right to due process in hearings that threatened a suspension over ten days.[54]

Construed narrowly, these Supreme Court decisions seem fair and correct. *Tinker* supported students who expressed opinions at odds with the government, a seemingly necessary protection, especially at a time of profound political turmoil. It also reduced the possibility that educators could simply indoctrinate children with their own beliefs. As for *Goss,* the court was careful to insist that schools need only provide informal hearings, not elaborate procedures. Such hearings, it seemed, could guard against feared abuses of power without seriously disrupting principals' authority.

However, a closer look at these cases might have foretold the troubles to come. The students in *Tinker* ranged from eight to fifteen years old, the younger age being one that might make even the most vociferous free speech supporter think twice. And hearings required by *Goss* were really not so informal. They had to include "effective notice," a chance for accused students to give their version of what happened, to summon the accuser, to cross-examine and to present their own witnesses, and possibly even to have legal representation.[55] Moreover, the fact that *Tinker* and *Goss* were handed down at a time of increasing centralization—the number of school districts shrank from 127,000 in 1932 to 16,000 in 1980—increased their power. Fears of litigation fueled the growing anxiety of teachers and principals about supervisory disapproval as they warily watched their newly empowered students.[56] If what has followed is not an absolute breakdown of adult influence over children and general chaos, it is not for want of repeated and exhausting trying. The philosophy behind anticultural education that we encountered in chapter 3 has spread beyond the classroom into principals' and superintendents' offices.

Gerald Grant's *The World We Created at Hamilton High,* a study of a city high school in the decade and a half following *Tinker* and *Goss,* provides a complex account of the rise of the rights-armed student and the fall of the socializing teacher. Like many such schools, Hamilton High suffered through riots and shutdowns in the late sixties as it became more integrated and was forced to confront its own racist past. As the smoke cleared over the next decade, however, it became clear that the new order, though more egalitarian, had created a seriously demoralized "just get through the day" institution. Simply put, teachers had come to fear their students. "Assemblies often degenerated into catcalls and semiobscene behavior while teachers watched silently," Grant writes. "Trash littered the hallway outside the cafeteria, but it was a rare teacher who suggested a student pick up a milk carton he or she had thrown on the floor." Cheating was widespread, but "few adults seemed to care."[57]

Small wonder. Given the decisions now coming from the courts, teachers who accused kids of cheating found themselves feeling as if they were the ones who had done something wrong; they were required to produce documentation and witnesses to counter the "other side of the story." One teacher who had failed a boy for plagiarizing a paper had to defend herself repeatedly before a supervisor after being harassed by daily phone calls from the student's parents and the lawyer they had hired on their son's behalf. Another teacher, asked why she didn't report several students who were making sexually degrading remarks about her in the hallway, shrugged and replied, "Well, it wouldn't have done any good . . . I didn't have any witnesses." The phrase "You can't suspend me" became the taunt of many a disruptive student.[58]

The "you can't do anything to me" attitude of students toward their schools, promoted under the new dispensation, comes through loud and clear in the numerous rights manuals now available to adolescents. With titles like "Up Against the Law," "A High School Student's Bill of Rights," and "Ask Sybil Liberty," these manuals provide nourishment for the many adolescents looking to add to their disaffection from adults. They enumerate for kids all the impermissible things adults, particularly teachers, are going to try to make them do. Kids learn that you don't have to answer a school official if he or she questions you; that a teacher can't make you do anything that violates your conscience; that if you don't like the way the school makes you dress, you can go to court; that you can demand to see your school records. Some advocates have also sought due process in academic placement and grading.[59] Although thus far they've been unsuccessful, their attempts have fueled the adversarial feelings between teachers and students.[60]

This new state of affairs is not merely a management and morale problem; it also serves to dumb down the curriculum already weakened by the forces of progressive theory. Another study, this one of three high schools (two urban and biracial and one suburban and white), describes how in each institution a fear of new adolescent power drove administrators and teachers to keep classes amiable and nonthreatening—or, in other words, unchallenging. Teachers accepted talking, laughing, spitballs, and even card playing as long as they didn't get out of hand, for "the principal obligation of the teachers . . . was to 'get along with the kids.'"[61] Fearful of inspiring conflicts, all but a handful of charismatic teachers studiously avoided giving low grades, demanding homework, and challenging tests. Further, the school curriculum degenerated, as we saw in Chapter 3, into an assortment of faddish, gimmicky selections providing students free choice about what to study. After all, courses like "Music as Expression," dedicated to the study of rock and roll, are much less likely to make a kid testy than "Nineteenth-Century American Literature."

Like their peers in juvenile court, disruptive and manipulative students benefit most from the new order, for they are most impressed by the fact that the adults around them are relatively powerless. They quickly figure out that no authority is legitimate or final, that there's always a way to get around the rules. To suspend a student in Los Angeles, for instance, a principal has to go to the school system's Student Discipline Proceedings Unit, which then has to go the Board of Education—if, that is, the case reaches the board before the statute of limitations expires.[62] In 1995, school principals in Montgomery County, Maryland, recommended 1,090 expulsions. The superintendent and school board approved only three.[63] As a result of increased due process in the schools, Jackson Toby has written, "unruly students get better protection against school officials and most students get less protection from their classmates."[64]

This is bad enough, but a more subtle and corrosive problem attending the arrival of the rights-bearing student affects more than just the kids; it bodes ill for all citizens in a democratic society. Just as *Gault* has spawned an unintended and unfortunate consequence, namely, empowering teenagers to use the law's requirements to delay and manipulate, so too has *Tinker* done less to advance political maturity than to empower the obsessions of the teen imagination. *Tinker* has indeed encouraged free expression—on the issues that really concern the Darwinian teen: sex and violence. Meanwhile, educators, forced to allow speech to flow freely and to remain neutral about its content, are rendered impotent in any attempt to instruct students in the responsibilities of democratic debate and rational deliberation or to enlarge their capacity to distinguish between momentary pleasure and long-term benefits.

A 1986 Supreme Court case, *Bethel School District v. Fraser,* illustrates the problem perfectly.[65] Matthew Fraser, a high school senior, was suspended for a speech he gave during an assembly, a speech filled with sexual innuendo and greeted by his grateful classmates with hoots and obscene gestures. When Matthew's father sued over his punishment, the lower courts not only supported his son's free speech rights as defined by *Tinker,* but went so far as to question the Bethel district's efforts at "cementing white, middle-class standards for determining what is acceptable and proper speech and behavior in the public schools."[66] Mr. Fraser was awarded damages from the school, and Matthew, whose violation of "white, middle class standards" had (predictably) turned him into a local hero in the eyes of his peers, was voted valedictorian in a write-in campaign. Appalled at the results of their own handiwork, the Supreme Court justices reversed the decisions of the lower courts. *Tinker* had not meant to hold, wrote Chief Justice Warren Burger, quoting Justice Black's dissent in that case, "that the Federal Constitution compels the teachers, parents, and elected school officials to surrender control of the American public school system to public school students."[67]

Many have viewed *Bethel v. Fraser* and several ensuing decisions that seem to dampen the spirit of student rights as a sign that the Supreme Court is ready to shift the balance of authority back from students to school officials.[68] But regardless of their outcome, lawsuits that leave teachers unsure of the distinction between instructing kids in the norms of civil language and moral behavior and violating their rights to free speech or due process are a victory for the forces of anticulturalism. And *Bethel v. Fraser* has hardly solved the problem. In 1997 a New York State school district was permitted to suspend a senior for distributing articles urging students to urinate in hallways, scrawl graffiti on the walls, and riot when the police arrived—but only after two years of effort and enormous amounts of money finally brought the case to the attention of the state's highest court.[69] In his dissent in *Tinker,* Justice Hugo Black had written that the majority's decision condemns "all the public schools in the country to the whims and caprices of their loudest mouthed, but maybe not their brightest, students."[70] He was exaggerating, but not by much.

Once teenagers think of being a loudmouth as a personal right, the entitlement itself becomes the chief good while the higher goal of free speech in educational settings fades into insignificance. "Rights talk," in Harvard law professor Mary Ann Glendon's phrase, ultimately has the effect of bestowing high moral purpose on adolescent obsessions and making the already difficult tasks of training teenagers' judgment and refining their sensibilities seem quaintly irrelevant. One recent case involved the existence of *YM* and *Teen* magazines in a middle school library. Their appearance in the library was condemned, because these magazines print fairly explicit advice about condoms, masturbation, and the like. The critics failed to raise the more pertinent question: How could these magazines, the bulk of whose articles concern fashion and dating, possibly be construed as educational, and how could librarians argue that "the issue is intellectual freedom"? Turning *Teen* magazine into a symbol of "intellectual freedom" tends to promote juvenile complacency rather than intellectual exploration.[71] In San Francisco, a student gave a speech alluding to the length of his penis. When the principal admonished him, he was duly informed by the rest of the student body that the boy had a right to free speech.[72] Patricia Hersch in *A Tribe Apart*, a study of teenagers in suburban Virginia, reports that many times when educators tried to cut short the inevitable adolescent tangents on sexual topics, kids would raise the flag of free speech. They "demand their rights . . . They refer to the First Amendment, hint at discrimination."[73]

To make matters worse for educators, some parents have also come to believe that the right to self-expression should preempt all concern for intellectual or moral seriousness. As long as kids are speaking up, it must be a good thing—no matter how difficult it makes the task of education. In 1994 eighth graders in a Hershey, Pennsylvania, school engaged in a disruptive protest when they learned they had to go to school for several extra days in June to make up for snow days. Parents supported their children rather than the school because they were "good kids [who] . . . just wanted to make a statement." As Laurence Steinberg, who relates this incident in his *Beyond the Classroom*, remarks, this kind of support for the kids over the school was unheard of in other times and still is in other countries.[74] Yet this situation is minor compared to a case in Half Moon Bay, California. There, a fifteen-year-old who wrote several English compositions, one about torching the school library and beating up the school principal and another, called "Goin' Postal," about taking a gun to school and putting seven bullets into the principal's body, was suspended. His parents sued the principal and the school district for damages and to have the boy's suspension expunged from his record. They found support among many of their fellow parents, who believed the school had overreacted.[75]

Examples like these begin to suggest how much is at stake when kids are never taught the responsibilities that accompany the right to free speech. Speech can be dangerous. It can wound and it can provoke. A democratic society relies on its citizens' comprehension of the dangers as well as the more constructive uses of free speech. But when will the next generation have the opportunity to learn this lesson? Only when words have turned to sticks and stones. In a Colorado high school, a principal, forced to respect the law as determined in *Tinker,* could not stop a student from wearing Ku Klux Klan insignia to school. That is, until a black student punched the student. Only then, when the Klansman's "speech" could clearly be construed as threatening school order, could the principal call the insignia a danger and therefore forbid it.[76] In Springfield, Oregon, fifteen-year-old Kip Kinkel gave a report in science class on how to build a bomb, and in his literature class he read from his journal about his dreams of killing. No one made particular note of what in another era would have been clear red-flag behavior. "He was a typical fifteen-year-old," the Springfield superintendent of schools said—until the boy shot and killed his parents and two classmates in a rampage. School officials noted that classroom talk of murder is common, a truth borne out by reports that Dylan Klebold and Eric Harris made videos about shooting up their school before they did precisely that in Littleton, Colorado.[77] In other words, given free rein to say whatever they want, kids talk casually of murder, bombs, and suicide and adults do nothing about it until someone gets hurt.

Given all this anticultural paralysis, it shouldn't be surprising that public school students find discipline more ineffective than do their disenfranchised private school counterparts. The increase in public school violence has been widely documented. *American Educator* found 36 percent of inner-city junior high teachers report that they have been threatened by a student. The same goes for 11 percent of suburban and 7 percent of rural teachers. Until Congress passed the Gun Free Schools Act in 1994 mandating expulsions of a year, in a number of jurisdictions kids caught with guns might be suspended for a week, only to return to school or, at most, be transferred to another school.[78] What is more surprising is that public school kids also find their schools *more unfair.*[79] Some child advocates of the sixties and seventies referred to schools as prisons, but it is only after several decades of the supposedly liberating forces of anticulturalism that resentful students must march through metal detectors, get sniffed for guns by trained dogs, give up the privacy of lockers and book bags (because they are effective places to hide weapons), look out at the street from barred windows, and watch police and security guards patrolling the hallways.

This all goes to prove the sociological truth that as informal cultural controls disappear, raw, policelike power steps into the breach. The irony of the legal revolution that turned students into "citizens" is that authority in the school has not been made more intelligible. With consequences similar to those following the *Gault* decision and the institution of judicial bypass for girls seeking an abortion, authority has only been shaped into what for kids are alien, legalistic forms. As the school, like the courts, becomes less of a flexible training environment where adults intuitively induct students into the norms of their culture, it becomes more of a technical and legalistic institution, like any other government agency. When the presumption is, in author Gerald Grant's words, that "children are adults capable of choosing their own morality as long as they do not commit crimes,"[80] they are turned into fake adults, subject to the same rules as their elders. Anything goes except the outright illegal.

And since society can't merely ignore most of the cruelty and high jinks kids inevitably engage in, that means more of it has to become illegal. If you're not allowed to teach 'em, book 'em. Consider the age-old kind of bullying that is today called sexual harassment. Probably everyone has acute memories of how cruel kids can be, teasing each other about their breath, their clothes, their breast size, their weight. Given the respect for children's free speech rights, it may well be that cruel taunts are on the rise. Certainly there is plenty of evidence that sexual taunts and grabbing are commonplace; according to one study, 62 percent of girls and 42 percent of boys in grades 8 through 11 report experiencing harassment.[81] But whereas in the past it was clearly the job of adults to restrain such bullying, today's teachers are unsure. Do they risk a confrontation with the child's parents or the principal? Do they know beyond a reasonable doubt what happened? Even without these fears, they have no widely accepted cultural ideals of kindness or good manners.

What they have instead is Title IX of the Federal Education Act. In Title IX the Office of Civil Rights of the Department of Education adapted (adult) workplace guidelines on sexual harassment to make schools liable for creating "a hostile environment." You could argue that Title IX has the virtue of reinvesting school officials with the power to do some of what they're supposed to do: discipline rowdy students, or at least those whose sins can be construed as sexual. But it does so in the very narrow, legalistic terms which began the school's descent into bureaucratic paralysis in the first place. And it does so not just for adolescents but for children whose idea of a hostile environment is along the lines of the witch's castle in *Wizard of Oz*. In a 1992 case marking the first time sexual harassment charges trickled down into the elementary schools, a six-year-old named Cheltzie Hentz of Eden Prairie, Minnesota, was found by the Office for Civil Rights and the Minnesota Department of Human Rights to have been taunted in her elementary school about her body and a supposed sexual relationship with her father. Both agencies chastised the school for failing to treat elementary school nastiness as a legal matter instead of a disciplinary one.[82] Other schools have been more energetic. In Minneapolis, where even kindergartners are subject to sexual harassment laws, a thousand children were expelled or suspended during the 1991–92 school year on charges relating to sexual harassment.[83] Jonathan Prevette, a six-year-old North Carolinian, was called into the principal's office and informed that, in accordance with the guidelines, he was in danger of being suspended if he tried again to kiss a classmate on the cheek.[84] In California "unwelcome sexual advances," including "flipping" (i.e., lifting a girl's skirt), can be used to suspend fourth graders.

The case of an eleven-year-old California girl, Tianna Ugarte, illustrates how the law's extended reach, though no triumph for children, can only grow longer. When Tianna's family repeatedly complained about a boy who called her a bitch and a whore, the school superintendent, fearing a lack of verifying evidence, did nothing. Saying that her rights had been violated, Tianna's family sued and won.[85] The success of the suit is filled with demoralizing irony. First, the schools can now be held liable for violating the rights of girls bothered by boys whose own celebrated rights (remember the superintendent's fear of disciplining the offender) may have allowed the harassment to get out of hand in the first place. Second, making kids legally responsible for behaving according to norms they have yet to internalize does not help them in that project. In fact, it is a dangerous return to outmoded methods of childrearing. It substitutes the threat of alien force for personal persuasion and introduces peremptory power instead of the tedious and subtle work of socializing the young. Such threats, as nineteenth-century republican child theorists recognized, do not go far toward shaping a democratic personality.

Thus it is that the anticultural assumptions behind decisions like *Gault* and *Tinker,* far from advancing freedom, threaten its foundations. A free society rests on a contract between intentional, responsible selves and a state which they support and which, in turn, respects their competent autonomy. When we lose a shared understanding of when or how that self is achieved—or, to put it another way, of when or how the child becomes an adult—we undermine the terms of the contract. Today's children and adolescents may be guaranteed rights to due process, to privacy, and to free speech but not for a responsible, democratic future.

Chapter 6

Sex and the Anticultural Teenager

Everyone knows that teenagers today are more likely to have sex than kids of previous generations. What most people probably don't know is how little joy attends these encounters. Eric Konigsberg, a journalist who followed the sexual exploits of students at Vassar College for *Spin* in 1998, found "an environment that seemed melancholy, nihilistic, groping, purposeless, apathetic, lifeless." Students sometimes get in the mood by composing computer billboards with categories like "Freshmen I Want to Fuck" or "Top Ten Whores."[1] At Georgetown University undergrads have sponsored "money parties," for which they pay a cover charge of twenty dollars in exchange for a fistful of Monopoly money. The goal is to earn as much money as you can by performing sexual favors.[2]

The younger brothers and sisters of these college kids also aspire toward the "nihilistic" and "groping." The infamous Spur Posse of California, a group of high school boys who "hooked up" with up to sixty girls each in a sexual competition, are perhaps not a completely new breed. But today girls have joined in the once male-only sexual competition. Take, for instance, the sixteen-year-old interviewed by the sociologist Lillian Rubin who had sex with "forty, maybe fifty different guys."[3] Even middle schoolers can be blasé these days: "It was sort of the thing to do," shrugs one girl, remembering her seventh grade sexual initiation. "It wasn't supposed to be a big deal."[4] To be fair, for most kids it *is* still a big deal. On school buses and in hallways they mimic sexual intercourse and masturbation and grab at each other's buttocks and breasts. They lie about being virgins. According to Michael Cohen, a research psychologist and principal of Arc Consulting, nine- and ten-year-old girls, whose counterparts in the past always looked forward to becoming teenagers, now say they are afraid.[5] Even as, in recent years, the number of teenagers engaging in early and promiscuous sexual intercourse is declining, their foreplay, which increasingly and at younger ages includes oral sex—and, if the teen grapevine is to be believed, anal sex as well—remains casual.[6] Though it has been obscured by the threat of disease and pregnancy, the real news on the teen sex front is that there has been, regardless of what form sex takes, a radical downsizing of the emotional side of sexual desire. "None of us will ever have a normal relationship," the heroine moans in an episode of the teen hit TV series *Buffy the Vampire Slayer,* expressing what is perhaps the latent fear of a generation. "We're doomed."

It wasn't supposed to be like this. When they were young adults, the parents of today's teenagers, a generation that came of age in the sixties and seventies, believed they were going to hand down to their children a freer and more honest world than the one they were just escaping. That generation understood, in a way their own parents had not, that teenagers are fully sexual beings. They hoped that by escaping the Puritan hang-ups that plagued their parents and grandparents their kids would have "healthy" sexual attitudes. They hoped that their daughters would no longer experience the fear and shame that had once shadowed the girl who had done "it" and that they would be confident enough to admit, to act on, to "own" their desire. This generation hoped that they would demystify sex, free it from the control of church ladies and what sexual reform advocates had long called the "conspiracy of silence." In this new world, sex would be better and so would kids.

So why hasn't this dream come true? The answer becomes clear enough when you take a careful look at the statements of sex educators, curriculum planners, public health officials, psychologists, and those popular writers who have sought to lead kids out of a sexual Egypt and into the promised land. There's not a recognizable teenager in the lot. And the sex these experts evoke is no more familiar. Drained of all feeling but physical pleasure, rationalized into Filofax personal organizer entries, the sex given to us by this ministry is little more than techno-fantasy. They do not see the alternately insecure and grandiose, idealistic and crude, perpetually glandular teenager most of us know. Their teenager, like that of so many other experts, is rational, self-aware, and autonomous. Information is all these kids need, they say. Information and some deprogramming to counteract society's continuing efforts to pervert their healthy sexual natures. So now we have a nation of teenagers who are information rich but knowledge poor. They—and their ten-year-old brothers and sisters, for that matter— may be adults when it comes to technical information; certainly their putative sophistication about sexual matters is the subject of endless head shaking by parents and the media. But as they approach graduation in the anticultural school of self-sufficiency, they remain predictably illiterate when it comes to real human connection.

Sherril Jaffe, who wrote about her experience as the mother of a troubled fifteen-year-old in a book entitled *Ground Rules,* describes what happened when she asked the family therapist what she should tell her lost and miserable daughter about sex. The minidrama that ensued is absurd and poignant in a particularly contemporary way:

> "All you should say," he said, "is 'I hope you practice safe sex.'"
>
> "I hope you practice safe sex," I said to her one day. She gave me a look of disdain.
>
> "I hope you practice safe sex," she had said back to me in a mocking tone.
>
> Why had she mocked me? Because she didn't need to be told

to practice safe sex, because of course she would practice safe sex?
... Or was she taunting me because she bitterly resented me making assumptions about her sex life? The last possibility I thought
of was that she was mocking me because she could tell my words
were from the therapist's script. These weren't my words at all. I
was a foolish woman without any words of her own.[7]

It may seem odd that this grown woman and mother of two has no
words of her own, but she is hardly alone these days. Many uncertain
parents find themselves mouthing bromides that have the sound of
common sense but that feel false or strangely inadequate when they
are earnestly delivered to their children. "Be careful." "Respect yourself." "Don't let anyone force you to do what you don't want." Told
that their own views on these matters are likely to be out of date or irrelevant, parents are reduced to giving grim admonitions about safety
and health, admonitions that are, ironically, often no more welcome
to their listeners than Victorian-style moral treatises would be. Some
shrug and give up, simply allowing their sons and daughters to have
their girlfriend or boyfriend spend the night.[8]

In the past twenty-five years or so, sex specialists—officials from
influential organizations like Planned Parenthood and the Sexuality
Information and Education Council of the United States (SIECUS),
educators, counselors and curriculum planners—have set out to redefine sex and teenagers in ways that have led parents like Jaffe to this
impasse. This redefinition has become so familiar as to seem like
transparent truth, but a careful examination of its assumptions reveals
it to be yet another example of the anticultural fallacy. In the minds of
experts, at any rate, the competent infant has grown up to become a
competent teenager.

It is worth noting that experts today no longer talk about sex and
sex education. They talk about sexuality and sexuality education, and
the distinction is more than semantic. Sex referred to a specific act—
heterosexual intercourse—and sex educators of the past attempted to
explain its biology while making it clear that it was off limits for
teenagers. Sexuality, on the other hand, refers to something far more
than specific acts. It is about identity. "Sexuality is much more than

'sex' or 'sexual intercourse,'" announces *Bodies, Birth, and Babies,* a manual endorsed by both Planned Parenthood and SIECUS. "It is the entire self as girl or boy or man or woman . . . Sexuality is a basic part of who we are as a person and affects how we feel about ourselves and all our relationships with others."[9]

Despite the fact that sexuality has become a commonplace term today—it is the language used by Oprah and *Seventeen* as well as by professionals—it is, in truth, a strangely vague concept. It appears that sexuality is something inside every person, including every child. It is a pure part of our biological inheritance. "You are a sexual being from the day you are born," a book called *You're in Charge: A Teenage Girl's Guide to Sex and Her Body* tells its young readers. "Your sexuality reveals itself to you through feelings, desires, sensations, and fantasies. You reveal your sexuality to others simply by being yourself."[10] Furthermore, sexuality appears in the child's everyday behavior and is as much a part of the child's experience as it is of the adult's. Supporters of "comprehensive sexuality education" believe classes should begin as soon as children enter school. As Susan Wilson of the New Jersey Network for Family Life Education explains, "You are not just being sexual by having intercourse. You are being sexual when you throw your arms around your grandpa and give him a hug."[11]

Sexuality appears to be benign as well as natural. Experts tend to believe that it is only society, with its suffocating rules and lingering puritanism, that complicates the child's sexuality. "It's the 'should' aspect of morals that is the most sexually damaging," writes Lynn Leight in *Raising Sexually Healthy Children.* "'Should' is a word that sets up standards that usually are in conflict with our actions. In defying this perfect set of values, a person often feels guilty."[12] Unsurprisingly, feminists have been highly influential in advancing these notions. Women have suffered most from societal "shoulds" about sex, they argue; society's obsession with female virginity and its fear of female desire have made many women lose touch with their natural and true sexuality.

This model applies to kids as well. Following in the footsteps of Carol Gilligan, Naomi Wolf argues that prepubescent girls are fully at ease with their bodies and themselves. But because society cannot embrace their sexuality, at adolescence they lose "the 'voice' of their own desire" and become "denatured." In the minds of many feminists like Wolf, this explains the problem of teen pregnancy; because "the culture that surrounds girls signals to them that they must sexually forget themselves," they fail to plan ahead by carrying condoms in their backpacks or taking birth control pills regularly.[13] Mary Pipher, the psychologist-author of the bestselling *Reviving Ophelia,* also argues that girls are suffering from their "rigorous training for the female role." Though many of the patients she describes would make their grandmothers weep with despair, she concludes that "the rules remain the same: be attractive, be a lady."[14]

At this point, it should be clear that the red-faced, sex-segregated, just-the-biological-facts sex education courses familiar to anyone over forty had to go. Sexuality educators have an entirely new mission—to inoculate children's natural sexuality from society's poisonous attitudes. Their first job is to help kids remain "comfortable" or "relaxed" about sex. This explains how so much of current sexuality education has moved toward a highly rationalistic—and highly controversial— attempt at social engineering. Educators set out to defuse any messy or unruly emotions kids might have picked up outside school walls. "Be prepared for some silliness and embarrassment about body parts," a curriculum guide published by Rutgers University Press warns teachers. "Children have picked up societal attitudes and know that certain parts of the body are usually not talked about."[15] Learning to use proper language, to speak openly and rationally, is the key to overturning these damaging emotions. In a private school near my house, fifth graders are required to pronounce the words for the genitals at increasingly louder volume; their classmates down the hall solve algebra equations to a chorus of "Penis!" "Vagina!"

So where do parents fit into this picture? It's easy to see how mothers like Sherril Jaffe, though terrified that their children will contract a sexually transmitted disease, have become paralyzed with confusion and resignation. Experts blame parents, viewing them as the serpent in the garden of children's sexuality: parents use imprecise and euphemistic language, they are embarrassed, they impose "moral agendas" on their kids.[16] "In a variety of subtle ways, most parents instruct their children that sexuality is not a topic to be discussed," asserts a well-known advocate. "Most parents do not tell their children anything about sexuality—not even the basics of sexuality . . . If teenagers were to ask important questions their parents would be most uncomfortable."[17] Teachers "are the best role model for creating comfort";[18] parents, on the otherhand, to quote the poet Philip Larkin, "fuck you up."

The official redefinition of sexuality is a perfect example of the anticultural fallacy. To anticulturalists, sexuality is something good and tame that exists inside the child. Left to flourish on its own, it would be "healthy." Exposed to society, it becomes sick or distorted. It's useful to contrast this view with that of Sigmund Freud, the inventor of the idea that children possess sexual drives. For Freud, children's sexual desires were neither temperate nor rational. Their urges were directed primarily at their parents, and they were as intense as they were twisted. Freud believed children's early desires were tinged with rage and sadism as they came to realize that they were being thwarted by a rival, namely, the same-sex parent. Unlike the comfortably rational creature of today's psychologists, Freud's child was devoted to his or her primitive misunderstandings. Education, no matter how comfortable and straightforward, would fail to straighten out such a child.

Freud had another theory that stands in stark contrast to today's thinking. He believed that somewhere around six or seven years of age children entered a relatively calm, asexual period called latency, which lasted until the storms of puberty. According to Freud, latency was essential for children in modern societies, for it was during this time that they were able to focus their restless energies on cognitive achievement. He acknowledged that some cultures give free rein to sexual curiosity throughout childhood. But he believed these societies paid the great price of technological and economic backwardness for their easy sensual pleasures. Freud believed that there is no easy answer to the conflicts of the human predicament, that the struggle between individual urges and cultural achievement, between our longings and the requirements of social life, is inevitable and tragic.[19]

By contrast, anticultural approaches to this subject are vague and superficial. For anticulturalists, children's sexuality is a simple matter.

They are desirous of sex in much the same way they are hungry for food. There are no stages, no conflicts, no irrational fears—in short, no psychology. Whereas Freud saw the child's sexual longings as grandiose and colored by jealousy, sexuality theory (like all anticultural ideas) simply waves away the problem of the child's egotism. Moreover, today's experts entirely dismiss latency and sublimation; these notions would severely challenge their belief in a laid-back, natural sexuality. It is significant that educators never consider the possibility that when kids giggle and turn red during frank class discussions, it is because they are aroused. It is also significant that they assume that it is parents, not kids, who are uneasy discussing sex.[20] According to the anticultural philosophy of sexuality, kids may be sexual but they are sexual in an easygoing, benign, "natural" way. Their desires never boil over at inopportune times or in unkempt form. Bathroom jokes, dirty rhymes, and giggling are never signs of primitive sexual urges nor of discomfort when vulnerable private impulses are aired in public; they are proof only of societal hang-ups.

This background information should make it easier to understand how experts have once again altered the way we think about adult obligations toward the young. If you take seriously the ideas of sexuality, it becomes hard to believe that teenagers might need guidance, as opposed to information, about how to behave as they reach sexual maturity. Certainly no hard-and-fast "no intercourse" rule for unmarried adolescents seems in order.[21] At any rate, anticultural teenagers create themselves outside cultural rules of this sort. The wording of the 1991 "Teenager's Bill of Rights" published by the New York City Department of Health (and funded in part by the federal Centers for Disease Control) suggests that ideas about sexuality are entwined with the adolescent rights revolution we saw in the previous chapter: "I Have the Right to Express Myself." "I Have the Right to Decide Whether to Have Sex and Who to Have It With." "I Have the Right to Think for Myself."[22] By the early 1970s, as sexuality theory took hold, educators began to view their job as including such tasks as "reduc[ing] anxieties and fears [in students] about personal sexual development," anxieties that society might have imposed, and even "facilitat[ing] rewarding sexual expression."[23] To this end, some might try to teach sexual technique. "If you are having intercourse with a girl," the 1987 *Changing Bodies, Changing Lives* instructs, "and want it to last longer, you can stop thrusting for a few moments when you feel yourself getting aroused. If the girl is on top and controlling the movement you can ask her to stop for a minute or to move more slowly."[24]

For the most part, however, educators, fearful of creating controversy, stuck to the more neutral and more strictly anticultural policy of encouraging teens to "make their own decisions." By 1981, according to the Guttmacher Institute, 94 percent of school districts agreed that the major goal of sex education ought to be "informed decision-making."[25] The decision-making model assumes that kids already possess the values, beliefs, and self-awareness that go into such decisions. They are their own parents and teachers. The psychologist Mary Pipher tells her young patients to find a quiet place and ask themselves, "How do I feel right now? What do I think? What are my values?" "Once they have discovered their own true selves," she continues, "I encourage them to trust that self as the source of meaning and direction in their lives."[26] Even younger teens seem to have access to "their own true selves." Human Sexuality: Values and Choices, a program for seventh and eighth graders, uses the same model.[27] In fact, the ideal of informed decision making is instituted as early as elementary school. During a dispute over an AIDS education program in the New York City schools, one member of a district school board said, "The more information you give people, the better choices they make." She was referring to lessons for nine- and ten-year-olds.[28]

Experts never seem to consider where the beliefs, values, and self-awareness behind these choices come from. Though these are all clearly a product of gradual cultural learning, experts act instead as if they are magically part of teen identity. And because anticultural teenagers already possess all this cultural content necessary for making their choice, educators see their job as teaching only the procedures—or skills—of determining whom to sleep with and when.

These include decision-making skills, refusal skills, and communication skills—and, if these don't work, stress management skills and goal-setting skills. A lot of the press surrounding sexuality education curricula has made them sound like pornography. But, in practice, skills instruction makes sexuality education more like a how-to manual than like a XXX-rated movie. Take this astonishing example, a video produced by the Massachusetts Department of Public Health in 1989 to teach AIDS prevention: The narrator, a hip, young nurse, distributes flash cards to her class depicting the fourteen stages of condom use. The students get together, look at one another's cards, and decide the proper order, which looks like this: TALK WITH PARTNER. DECISION BY BOTH PARTNERS TO HAVE SEX. BUY THE CONDOM. SEXUAL AROUSAL. ERECTION. ROLL CONDOM ON. LEAVE SPACE AT TIP (SQUEEZE OUT AIR). INTERCOURSE. ORGASM/EJACULATION. HOLD ON TO THE RIM. WITHDRAW THE PENIS. LOSS OF ERECTION. RELAXATION. And, finally, an environmental skill: THROW CONDOM OUT.[29] "We teach them what to do in the front seat of the car," former surgeon general Jocelyn Elders announced in the same techno-spirit, "we can teach them what to do in the back seat."[30]

Doubtless, the threat of AIDS and other sexually transmitted diseases has cast a shadow on much of this optimism. The potentially destructive power of sexual desire, common wisdom in most societies up until recently, seems to have returned with a vengeance. In the past several years, educators have taken to enumerating the risks of early intercourse; some advise kids to wait either until they are older or until they are married. But, surprisingly enough, even conservative, abstinence-based curricula also subscribe to the basic notion of sexuality; one well-known curriculum entitled Sex Respect defines sexuality as "the total of all the traits and values—physical, mental, emotional, and spiritual—that make a person male or female . . . Our sexuality is part of our personality. We couldn't escape it, even if we wanted to (and think of all we'd miss!)." The only way to justify abstinence, given this definition, is personal danger.[31] Critics of such programs reasonably object to their excessive "fear-mongering" on this score—the risks of premarital sex are ennumerated in Sex Respect as "disease, pregnancy, infection, sterility, guilt, doubt, fear, self-hatred."

But despite the long shadow cast by AIDS, many educators continue to bask in the sunshine of their sexuality theory. After making a pitch for abstinence as one of the possible decisions kids might make—"You have to decide for yourself how important these messages [about abstinence] are for you," state the authors of *Changing Bodies, Changing Lives*—they go about teaching kids more contemporary forms of "rewarding sexual expression." In the interests of safety, they extol the joys of "outercourse," that is, oral sex, body massage, and masturbation.[32] Masturbation has become a particularly hot topic recently; as one enthusiastic Los Angeles schoolteacher says, it "is *a way to express yourself sexually* without actually having sex [my italics.]"[33] "Before becoming involved with someone else's sexuality," recommend the authors of *You're in Charge,* "why not explore your own?" Masturbating increases "self-understanding and self-worth."[34] According to William Kilpatrick, author of *Why Johnny Can't Tell Right from Wrong* and professor of education at Boston College, one lucky sophomore class at a Massachussetts high school was told to masturbate for one of its homework assignments.[35]

"I hope you practice safe sex," Sherril Jaffe said helplessly to her fifteen-year-old. Her words now make a good deal of sense. Having learned that adults have nothing to teach kids, that kids make their own decisions, discover their own values, and, like their elders, have a need to express that part of their identity called sexuality, there seems to be no other choice for a parent than to utter clinical platitudes.

Unless, that is, teenagers are not the calmly sexual, rational, freely choosing, information-organizing, independent individuals described by experts. And, of course, it turns out they are not.

In one respect the expert vision was correct. When given the okay, teens *will* have sex. Before the days of sexuality theory, in the mid-1950s, only a little over one-quarter of girls under eighteen were sexually experienced.[36] As of 1995, half of all fifteen-to-nineteen-year-old girls and 55 percent of boys in that age range reported that they had had sexual intercourse. In the 1970s, 39 percent of sexually active adolescent girls reported multiple partners; as of 1988 that number had grown to 55 percent. Thirteen percent of those girls reported having had sex with at least six men.[37] And childbearing too—perhaps inevitably, given this shift in sexual mores—has become child's play. While only a few decades ago a pregnant schoolgirl was forced to disappear in a fog of lies and shame, today's pregnant teenagers are role models serving as cheerleaders, homecoming queens, and class presidents.

But sexuality specialists couldn't have been more wrong in assuming that teenagers are autonomous and competent decision makers who need only a crash course in refusal and communication skills. Another example of the anticultural fallacy, this presumption ignores two facts: First, since kids naturally seek rules of behavior and meaning from the culture around them, they do not ultimately make their own decisions, even about sex. Second, turning the child into a competent, independent decision maker is a far more complicated task than simply providing skills instruction.

Let's begin with the first point. All signs point to the fact that kids act according to collective expectations of their specific cultural environment. Those who are having sex early are doing so primarily because their peer group has determined that they should. A 1986 Planned Parenthood poll revealed that 58 percent of sexually experienced kids cite forces like pressure from a partner or a desire to boast to friends or to be popular as the reason they and their friends began sexual relations. Almost none of these kids, incidentally, were looking to "explore their sexuality" and only 12 percent of them—most of them boys—said they were driven by a desire for sexual gratification. Girls in particular seem prey to peer pressure. A 1996 poll released by the Ms. Foundation for Women found that 73 percent of girls think most girls have sex not because that's what they want, but because it's what their boyfriends want. In that same poll, 81 percent of the girls fifteen and over who had had sex wished they had waited and 60 percent of the boys said the same. As the writer Wendy Shalit has noted, in the current atmosphere the choice of abstinence doesn't help, because kids view it as the choice for losers, those who are not "ready yet."[38]

The way teenagers actually talk is entirely different from the way the fictitious, autonomous decision maker whom the experts imagine would speak. Sexually active kids know full well how enslaved they are to the cultural control of their peers. A sixteen-year-old mother I interviewed several years ago told me she had been "sick of being the only fourteen-year-old virgin around." She explained, "I didn't really like the guy that much; I was just trying to get my friends off my back. When he started telling people 'Oh, I had her,' I got really mad. I told everyone, 'No, I was using *him*.'"[39] When kids resist, they feel shame similar to what kids of several generations ago felt when they *did* have sex. Listen to a fifteen-year-old Chicago girl interviewed by Lillian Rubin:

> I haven't found someone I feel comfortable with, so I haven't felt the need to have sex yet. I don't see the point in rushing anything. I'm young; I have time. [Here she demonstrates unusual maturity—and, it needs to be said, rhetoric she doubtless heard from some adults along the way.] But only my very best friend knows the truth. The other kids don't know because I lie and say I'm doing things I'm not. As long as you say what they want to hear, nobody bothers you. It's when you're different that they don't like it.[40]

"This is what you are supposed to do," one fourteen-year-old told Patricia Hersch about her own decision to have sex. "It is our teenaged phase."[41]

Feminist-inspired sexuality experts insist that a repressive society continues to make it difficult for girls to be consciously and fully sexual. But, as we have seen, the words of teenagers suggest that the opposite is true: these days girls are often worried about *not* having sex. In the past, college counselors were sought out by the most sexually active kids; now it's the virgins who come in wondering if something is wrong with them. Teens as young as thirteen or fourteen are sometimes embarrassed by their virginity, the exact reverse of a generation ago. Polls confirm this picture: girls are more concerned about being the only virgin on the block than about having what used to be called "a past." The 1986 Harris Poll reported that fewer than 30 percent of teens (including twelve- and thirteen-year-olds) believe that having

sex would "ruin their reputation" with their friends, a finding repli-
cated in a more recent Ms. Foundation for Women poll.[42] Somehow,
it's no surprise to hear from the 1992 National Health and Social Life
Survey that nearly a quarter of teenaged girls describe their first sexual experience as "voluntary but not wanted."[43]

Despite a massive disinformation campaign on the subject from
sexuality experts, it has become increasingly clear that parents are the
only ones who can help kids resist these inevitable pressures of the peer
group to act grown-up. Parents remain *the* main predictor of sexual attitudes. Researchers analyzing recent data from the National Longitudinal Study of Adolescent Health (Add Health) have concluded that
kids with parents who disapprove of early sexual activity *and* of the
availability of teen contraception are less likely to engage in early sex.[44]
Other studies support the view that while there will always be exceptions, kids from close, intact families tend to delay sex until their late
teens. In fact, half of all kids, interestingly enough the approximate
number of those living in such homes, are virgins until seventeen.[45]
Kids from religious homes tend to be late-bloomers regardless of de-
nomination, as do those from families who highly value education.[46]
Asian American adolescents, well known as high achievers, have a significantly lower rate of sexual activity than their white, black, and His-
panic counterparts. They cite as reasons for their reticence clear messages against early sex from their parents and, consequently, less
pressure from their peers.[47] On the other hand, kids who start having
sex early—and this means those who are most likely to become pregnant and who are most susceptible to disease—have mothers who engaged in early sexual activity, come from single-parent homes, and live
with families relatively uninterested in education.[48]

As a rule, anticulturalists understate the amount of learning and
experience required to become an autonomous individual, and such is
the case in the optimism of sexuality educators who recommend
teaching skills. The word *skill* implies technical know-how, or competence in a rationalizable series of actions, like those needed to drive
a car or build a bookcase or, yes, place a condom on a penis. But to
make a decision independent of the group or to refuse the importun-
ing of a boyfriend is of another order entirely. Experts forget that to

say no assumes that you know what you think and what you want. "I think by talking about these things and by role playing," says Susan Wilson, "you give kids control and you give them the language to say 'That's enough—I don't want any more. I don't want to have intercourse.'"[49] Anyone who recalls being fifteen will know that teens often have only a hazy sense of what they want. They live in a floaty, "I dunno" condition that can be maddening to adults. The phrase "voluntary but not wanted" is a fitting motto for much of their experience. They do things without a clear sense of their own motivation or purposiveness. "[I] never really thought about it," answers one fourteen-year-old when asked why she decided to have sex at twelve. "It's usually a spur-of-the-moment type of thing. I guess it, like, makes us closer friends."[50]

Teens like this are not self-reflective, self-determining individuals who can carry the full weight of autonomous decision making. It's not because they lack skills but because they don't yet have "their own true self," to use Mary Pipher's terms. They do not possess the judgment, self-control, foresight, and self-awareness that are needed to be full, independent beings. When kids are asked why they do not use birth control, it is not for the reasons one might expect—because they don't know how to use it or how to get hold of it. Nor is it because, as feminists charge, they are paralyzed by "social ambivalence" about their sexuality. It is because they are not yet thinking, planning masters of their destiny. Consider the sixteen-year-old mother I mentioned above: "I was on birth control pills," she explained. "But then I slept at my cousin's house and missed a day. I took two pills the next day. I guess that happened a few times. The nurse told me I had to take them every day, but I couldn't."[51] Adolescents also tend to subscribe to what David Elkind calls the "personal fable," the belief that they are exempt from the natural laws that apply to others.[52] The response give by a fourteen-year-old when she was asked during an interview with Lillian Rubin whether she had considered the consequences of having sex without a condom dramatizes this illogic: "I did but . . . I mean, it's really hard to believe it can happen to you. I know that's stupid, but . . . well, it's true."[53]

Given these weaknesses, it's not surprising to hear that even though the percentage of adolescents using contraception at first intercourse has increased markedly—from 45 percent in 1976 to 65 percent in 1988 to 73 percent among boys and 78 percent among girls in 1995—teens remain flighty when it comes to birth control.[54] According to one study, only 35 percent of fifteen-to-seventeen-year-old girls relying on condoms reported consistent use. Only 40 percent of those girls relying on oral contraception took the required pill every day.[55] As anyone with firsthand experience with teenagers could have predicted, adolescents experience higher rates of failure than their elders with all methods of contraception. Another reason to doubt that the recent drop in pregnancies is cause for optimism about teen self-control is that much of the recent improvement in birth control use appears to be the result of new drugs like Norplant, which is implanted in a woman's arm every five years, and Depo-Provera, which is injected every three months—that is, drugs that don't require care and planning. Neither of these drugs, by the way, offers protection from sexually transmitted diseases. Three million teenagers contract some kind of STD every year, even though most of them have learned in their sexuality classes that some of these diseases are incurable and that some cause sterility.

That teenagers are not yet compartmentalized, self-controlled masters of their destiny is clear from another fact: they have trouble being simultaneously sexual and academic strivers. Higher-achieving students are far less likely to be sexually active than their lower-performing peers. The 1986 Harris poll revealed that 57 percent of kids with averages of C or lower said they had engaged in sexual activity, as compared to 26 percent of those with averages of B+ or above. In the 1993 Survey of High Achievers only 19 percent of boys and 27 percent of girls said they had had sexual intercourse. A study of talented teenagers found them markedly more conservative in sexual attitudes than their peers.[56] According to Frank Furstenberg of the University of Pennsylvania, teenagers from the inner cities—who, though they are described by their obstetric nurses as thoroughly versed on the subject, are notoriously bad at consistent use of birth control—"dislike contraception precisely because it transforms sex into the realm of rationality."[57] It appears that Americans have been a little too quick at throwing out Freudian notions about latency and sublimation. Peaceful coexistence between reason and desire does not come naturally and quickly to kids. The better academic performance of the sexually reticent, a statistic widely ignored by the popular media as well as by advocacy groups, demands clear-eyed attention in a society that rests its egalitarian hopes on successful schooling.

Many sexuality experts scold that the greater competence European kids appear to have in using birth control—they have both lower rates of adolescent pregnancy and abortion and more access to reproductive health clinics than their Yankee counterparts—suggests that American sexual hang-ups are getting in our kids' way.[58] But they ignore the fact that European kids also have earlier and more aggressive help from adults in building the psychic infrastructure needed to turn them into autonomous actors. Where many of our children grow up under a reign of anticulturalism that asks them to determine their own rules and make their own decisions, European kids learn from an early age to live within the preexisting cultural boundaries passed on to them by their elders. One study comparing French and American children found that the French "are taught very early the importance of man-made limits" and the need to compartmentalize behavior.[59] Another study discovered that while Danish teenagers live with less parental supervision—the Danish adolescent is subject to fewer rules at fourteen than an American is at eighteen—younger Danish children are confronted with higher expectations for self-control, a requirement which, the authors reasonably speculate, makes them more competent adolescents.[60] You can give your kids more freedom, but you can't expect that to mean they'll grow up faster. In fact, it may be the opposite.

Wedded to the anticultural myth that American teens are capable of being autonomous individuals with a clear sense of who they are and what they want with miraculously little guidance, sex experts continue to place the blame for current woes on a repressive, rather than a negligent, society. This flawed thinking is worth repeating not only because it exemplifies how the creed of sexuality is so powerful that it has become resistant to the evidence of experience but because it reflects the inevitable tensions between our most cherished liberal tenets and the predicament of the child. For all the believers in the creed of sexuality, and indeed for many parents who have internalized it, teenagers are individuals worthy of full autonomy, selves whose individuality we risk violating when we restrict their range of choices, sexual or otherwise.

Yet this generous show of respect has turned out to be the very destructive failure of anticultural thinking. To talk to kids with a weak capacity for foresight and judgment about "skills" they are incapable of using and about "making decisions" or "sexually expressing" an autonomous self that is only struggling to be born is to engage in a particularly American form of well-intentioned, anticultural neglect. The results, as we have seen so often, are never the utopian ones imagined by anticulturalists. Where adults intended to give their children freedom to be themselves, they have ended up condemning them to mindless conformity and bewildered isolation. "It's not like you just decide to have sex," a middle school girl explained to one interviewer. "It's like you don't have a choice. You're so emotionally torn, you just say, 'Do it, get it over with, nothing will happen.'"[61] "Everyone is so mixed up," another girl tells Mary Pipher, "that they just get drunk and do it. They try not to think about it the next day."[62] Autonomous and free decision making? Not by anyone's definition.

"The end and aim of sex education," wrote child expert Dorothy Baruch in a 1959 manual for teens, "is developing one's fullest capacity for love."[63] How quaint these words sound today! And yet it's worth pausing to consider their implications, not just for the young person who read them but for the wider society. In the days before the rise of anticulturalism, love provided a myth that both organized and lent symbolic meaning to sexual urges. Human beings naturally try to make meaning of experience with whatever tools their culture gives them, and this is especially true for sex. Society has always had to find a way to accommodate those human drives which have so much potential for disruption—venereal disease, fatherless babies, jealous rages, even murder and war. Love enriched society's inevitable strictures against certain kinds of sexual activity by endowing them with imaginative meaning. It told young people *why,* that is, why they couldn't—or, as prohibitions against sexual activity began to ease, why in some cases they could.

Equally important, love was a central component of Western, and particularly American, individualism. A young country which allowed its youth unprecedented freedom, America gave love a central role in the individual biography. It was a pivotal part of the task of adolescent and young adult self-discovery. By falling in love, the young were intended to develop their "full emotional capacity," as Dorothy Baruch put it in 1959, and by choosing their own future spouse they were able to shape their lives according to their own design. The mythology of romantic love was clearly individualistic; it both heightened and enlarged the realm of one's inner life and provided moral legitimacy for private choice. At the same time, love's culmination in marriage promised social order and continuity. Through its association with marriage, then, love merged individual desire and social need; as sociologist Ann Swidler put it, it "fus[ed] the problem of the search for one's true self with the quest for one's right mate."[64] In short, the mythology of love satisfied both egoistic and social needs.

Sexuality theory, on the other hand, while it set out to more fully gratify the former, has ended up satisfying neither. A radically individualistic and body-centered creed, it has conceived of individual fulfillment in the most narcissistic and shallow terms and has all but emptied sex of meaning. If the aim of sex education was to develop "one's fullest capacity for love," the aim of sexuality education appears to be developing one's fullest capacity for self-sufficiency. This anticultural ideal has threatened to smother the imagination and the capacity for strong bonds in contemporary teenagers.

So much attention has been given to the young ages at which teenagers today begin their sexual activity that the real issue has been obscured. They are having sex in a radically changed emotional climate.[65] Sexuality has offered kids a rich banquet of bodily pleasures— oral sex, body massage, homosexuality, masturbation—but it has maintained a grim, thin-lipped silence about Eros—what Christopher Lasch calls "the union of esteem and sexual desire."[66] Love has disappeared in this peculiar new kind of puritanism; so has longing, jealousy, and self-transcendence.[67] "Sex is too important to glop up with sentiment," shrugged a Planned Parenthood pamphlet for teens from the mid-seventies. "If you feel sexy, for heaven's sake admit it to yourself. If the feeling and tension bother you, you can masturbate."[68] More recent statements, though less bald, reveal the same attitudes. Experts write as if they no longer imagine that love enlarges and enriches private life; on the contrary, they believe it blocks people from an authentic exploration of their sexuality. "When girls speak of being swept away by passion and desire," write two Massachussetts educators, "they may be reflecting traditional cultural values saying that females should not learn and know about sexuality."[69] Girls "need help separating affection from sex," Mary Pipher asserts.[70] Desire for another inhibits self-fulfillment. "A woman without a man," Gloria Steinem once famously said, "is like a fish without a bicycle."

Of course, under the spell of sexuality, there is the danger that the lover—or "partner," to use the telling current term—will become little more than an instrument to advance an individual's pleasure and self-discovery. Experts are not completely unaware of this potential contradiction between the egoistic goals of sexuality and the intimate reality of sex. They make a special effort to address the dangers of coercion in seminars on date rape and to emphasize that "no means no." A few brave souls have even made an effort to break the conspiracy of silence about emotions, though only coyly. The author of *Bringing Up a Moral Child* goes about as far as experts can go these days when he recommends that parents teach children "not to think of sexual intimacy as *taking* but as *sharing*. Sharing means that you regard the other person as a whole person—not just something for your enjoyment."[71]

Similarly, experts seeking to transcend the egotism latent in the theory of sexuality believe in what they call "communication skills." But having deprived kids of a meaningful shared mythology—indeed of a language—communication can only sputter ineffectually. Take this boy speaking in a focus group for Massachussets high school students: "I don't like lasting relationships . . ." he says. There is "too much work involved . . . too much talking on the telephone . . . you have to spend all your time with her and that fucking sucks; you can't spend it with your friends." A teen mother in the same group sees things a little differently: "That's why I think I ended up having sex with him [her baby's father]. 'Cause, like, he talked to me and stuff, and I know that he trusted me to talk to me."[72] What exactly is there for these kids to communicate?

In truth, these efforts to get around the miserly egotism at the heart of sexuality theory are too little, too late. Like all anticultural theorists, sexuality experts have tried to ignore children's egotism, and now we can see the results in school hallways, at adolescent parties, and on college campuses. Emotionless sex abounds, mostly among boys who "don't like lasting relationships," but a striking number of girls have adapted to the new sexual order as well. "I never really understood the whole emotional part of it," one such teenager tells Hersch. "I thought it was really awkward and everything. But what's there to handle? I guess there are feelings, but I really don't quite understand the big deal."[73] SEX IS MIND OVER MATTER was the nonchalant emblem on a T-shirt popular some years ago; IF SHE DOESN'T MIND, IT DOESN'T MATTER.

Of course, love has not been entirely erased from the adolescent imagination. Teen magazines put the term in bold, colorful letters on their covers, and Hollywood and the record industry, though increasingly inept at evoking any real emotion outside of rage, occasionally give kids stories and lyrics that might stir their dulled romantic sensibilites. Despite the best efforts of feminists to get them to embrace emotionless sex, girls continue to be more interested in these messages than are boys, who are colder and more calculating in their pursuits, an approach which has now been approved by their elders.[74]

Denied the kind of education that might have given imaginative depth to their desires, many kids experience only a vague emotional hunger. In her book *Promiscuities,* Naomi Wolf reports that most of her friends complained of feelings of emptiness and longing for tenderness during their first sexual encounters in the seventies, as the reign of sexuality began, and things do not appear to have changed.[75] Significantly, girls with many partners (who, sexuality theorists might argue, are freely expressing themselves) are rarely orgasmic.[76] It is girls who are in close, loving relationships, about which adults have been mum, who enjoy sex most.[77] "Utopia for teenage girls would be a place in which they are safe and free," states Mary Pipher, who, having achieved bestsellerdom for her poignant descriptions of numerous lonely and neglected girls, ought to know there is a great deal more to it than that.[78] But sexuality, that is, sex purely as pleasure and self-expression, is a stubborn creed.

Teen pregnancy is another perverse consequence of the new disdain toward love. For many kids, especially those from broken homes, sex is a way to counter loneliness. As we saw, kids with little parental involvement are much more susceptible to early sexual initiation and much more likely to become pregnant. The vast majority of teen mothers have grown up without fathers at home and with little sense of what it is to be loved by a man. They often fall for older men who flatter and woo them with promises of the male attention they've never had. Many of these girls, inevitably disappointed by these men, come to see a baby as a love object who will compensate them for their losses. In reality, nothing shatters the ideal of a rational teen performing a rationalized though pleasurable act entirely divorced from its traditional associations with marriage, reproduction, and emotional bonds more than the rise of out-of-wedlock teen motherhood during precisely those years that birth control became more widely known and available to youngsters.[79]

Deprived of a resonant set of beliefs and values that were once provided by culture and meant to curb aggressive drives, kids today are engaging in more sexual boasting, teasing, and fondling. Beginning in elementary school and intensifying in middle school, boys who have been successfully scrubbed clean of all shame and all aspirations toward tender feelings go out into the world and do what such boys might be predicted to do: mock girls' breasts, simulate sex and masturbation, brag about having sex with friends' mothers, pinch girls' buttocks and breasts, and call them hookers, ho's, and sluts. Nor are these just the so-called bad boys, says Peggy Orenstein in *Schoolgirls: Young Women, Self-Esteem, and the Confidence Gap.* Boys with good grades also jeer and mock.[80] A Harris survey under the auspices of the American Association of University Women found that 33 percent of girls among a sample of students in grades eight to eleven were harassed so often and so aggressively that they tried to avoid going to school.[81] However, many observers find that girls have also begun to enter into the battle.

But perhaps all these kids are only the unlucky minority? To see how the creed of sexuality has been transmitted to America's most privileged and successful kids, it's instructive to take a look at social life on the nation's elite campuses. Arthur Levine, whose book *When Fear and Hope Collide: A Portrait of Today's College Student* gives perhaps the most complete account of the current crop of undergraduates born in the late seventies and the early eighties, entitles his chapter on social life "Retreat from Intimacy."[82] And, in fact, kids have been remarkably successful at accepting the general terms of loveless sexuality that serve as today's cultural wisdom.

Most college students are treated to a refresher course in the new sexual mores when they first come to campus. Orientation week always includes required meetings where students learn where to get their free condoms and hear warnings about clear communication. Humanities teachers also sometimes help remind students of the demands of emotionless sexuality. At one time an aid to young men and women in their quest for identity, one of whose central adventures was the search for love, these courses now stubbornly recite only the vocabulary of "gender roles" and "power." When a middle-aged David Denby returned to his alma mater, Columbia University, for a refresher course, he found that "in two classes about feminism and the relations between the sexes, I doubt I heard the word 'love' spoken once . . . One now got the impression that for many students power was sexy, but sex was not."[83]

Some college students couple up in serious relationships and are half bitterly, half longingly known as "married." But for the most part, not surprisingly under these circumstances, college kids avoid intense involvement with the opposite sex. *The Princeton Review's Guide to the 310 Best Colleges* includes a survey of student opinion about campus life. In the 1997 edition the list of colleges where complaints about "no dating" ring in the air is a who's who of elite institutions: Williams students "don't date much"; Amherst's social scene is "nonexistent"; there is "no dating" at Colgate, Dartmouth, University of Chicago, Bryn Mawr, Brandeis, and many others. "The dating scene here is as much fun as a root canal," writes a Yale student. A highly experienced Vassar student told Eric Konigsberg about having sex the previous night with another student: "And then afterward, we went out to dinner. That was amazing. My first date in my life."[84]

The intimacy of coed dorms combined with the creed of emotionless sex lends a paradoxical quality to campus relationships. On the one hand, men and women develop close friendships with each other. In dorms they come to live like brother and sister, clad in their boxers and T-shirts, chatting till all hours of the night, stopping by each other's rooms during study breaks. Yet a deep mistrust lurks behind this undergraduate friendliness. Undergrads are warned by residence advisors not to get involved with dormmates; to do so is sometimes called "dormcest." In a casual group, they are at ease with each other; in couples, they watch each other as warily as strangers on a dark and empty street. Visiting college campuses in the years after the publication of her first book in the late 1980s, Katie Roiphe was "astonished at how many students conceptualized the average date between two undergraduates as if it were the opening of a horror movie. Dinner and a movie, according to this point of view, was likely to lead to date rape or worse."[85] "People I know who graduate are terrified of losing those intimate groups," says one Yale student, "and having to date."[86]

So how do college kids today get together? To replace one-on-one dating, students today have introduced new rituals in keeping with the mores of low-intensity sex. They turn to what Levine calls "a succession of one-night stands fueled by alcohol."[87] Students go in large groups to parties or bars, where they often bump and grind to rave music (generally in groups rather than as couples) and drink themselves unconscious. Emboldened by alcohol, they might finally couple up for some "scamming," "scrumping," "mashing," or "hooking up," which can mean anything from a sweaty twenty-minute make-out session to intercourse. Rarely do these meetings mark the beginning of a long-term relationship. Usually they are one-nighters repressed into the fog of a drunken haze. "In a normal Brown relationship," one student told the campus newspaper, "you meet, get drunk, hook up

and then either avoid eye contact the next day or find yourself in a relationship." Students unable to avoid the previous night's partner in a
class or in the cafeteria studiously avoid any mention of their encounter.[88] Of course, Brown is not unique. It's been estimated that 44
percent of college kids binge on alcohol at least once every two weeks.
Twenty percent of those have unplanned sex. More worrisome, 10
percent have unprotected sex.[89] Sixty percent of college women diagnosed with a sexually transmitted disease were drunk at the time of
infection.[90]

Older observers of the scene have a number of theories about the
origins of these puzzling new tribal practices. Some speculate that
anxiety about AIDS has made kids so scared of sex that they must be
smashed beforehand, though it makes no sense that a fear of disease
would promote precisely the sort of casual and unprotected sex that
increases its risk. Others believe this generation is fearful of repeating
the pattern that led to the type of miserable relationship their parents
had. But while commonsensical, this interpretation is also flawed.
There is some evidence that children of divorce get involved in close
relationships earlier, albeit in the long run less successfully, than their
peers.[91] Some speculate that college kids, having to hold down jobs to
help with high tuition costs (over 60 percent of students work while
attending college) have no energy or time for real relationships.

These theories avoid the obvious: these are smart kids doing more
or less what is expected of them. The generation that has breathed the
haunted air of nonchalant bodily pleasures carries on as they have
been taught. They talk about sex in great detail and without emotion.
They try not to confuse sex with emotion. And they "explore their
sexuality" even when that means denying the inherent dignity of another. "On any given night," a Vassar junior told a reporter, "you can
go down to the Mug [a local bar] and get whatever you want." At one
point, he continued, he would order his partners like brands of beer:
"Tonight I want a long-haired girl, then a short-haired girl, then a tall
girl, and so on."[92]

The prevalence of binge drinking before sex and the anxiety surrounding dating suggests that kids may sense the limitations of the
new dispensation. It's understandable. A philosophy of sexuality

which denies both rules of conduct and any aspirations higher than "communicating" or "sharing," might, after all, leave a few souls hungry. This longing for something more emerged loud and clear when one enterprising Brown senior started a computer dating service called Helping Undergraduates Socialize, or HUGS. On Valentine's Day 1996, *one-third* of the campus signed up—"athletes and artists, fraternity brothers and rebels, heterosexuals and members of the gay and lesbian alliance."[93]

And many kids clearly hope for more clarity from their elders. "But what *are* the new rules?" students would ask Katie Roiphe during her campus speeches. "How *should* we act when we're out on a date?"[94] Like the public school principals who were forced to replace informal cultural rules with the law, college administrators are forced to turn to legal sanctions. Most campuses have introduced speech codes, antiharassment regulations, and councils to replace the loss of cultural rules and sustaining myths. But the effect of such procedures and codes, as we saw in the previous chapter, is likely to be perverse. In this case it pushes college kids even further into loveless sex. There can be no more glaring example of the disenchantment of sex than the sexual offense policy introduced at Antioch College in 1993, a policy that reduces the most intimate of human relations to the terms of an apartment lease. "Obtaining consent is an ongoing process in any sexual interaction," the code reads. "Verbal consent should be obtained with each new level of physical or sexual conduct in any given interaction . . . The request for consent must be specific to each act." According to Marian Jensen, dean of students at Antioch, wine and candlelight have been replaced by this seductive come-on: "Would you like to activate the policy?"[95] What a perfect example of the triumph of the rationalized sex sought by experts!

Though only dimly understood, this waning of the centrality of love represents a profoundly important cultural shift. It has helped to transform the nature of adolescence over the last thirty years and has also signaled the triumph of the anticultural ideal of chilly autonomy. For today's kids, sexual activity is no longer situated within a framework of larger social goals, namely, courtship, marriage, and adulthood. It no longer has anything to teach them about the possibilities of

mature and enduring connections. For this generation, sexual fulfillment is a goal in its own right. It has no larger meaning. "The decision to sleep with someone," Roiphe writes, "which feels so pressing,
so momentous, so absolutely crucial means nothing. It will vanish into
the spin cycle of the washing machine with the sheets."[96] This is a kind
of freedom, to be sure, but it's not one to celebrate.

....

Chapter 7

Postmodern
Postadolescence

Imagine being frozen in 1965. Then imagine coming back to life today and turning on the television. You would immediately notice two changes: first, the abundant and graphic sex and, second, the frequent and detailed violence. These changes in the fare offered by televison are generally recognized and often lamented, but another change seems so banal as to be just about invisible. I'm referring to the number of shows concerning young, affluent singles, such as *Seinfeld, Friends, E.R.,* and *Ally McBeal.* The genre is so popular that it has revived dying networks and given birth to a few new ones.

Marketers and television executives are apt to argue that young, affluent, and single characters merely reflect real life. Free from many responsibilities, young singles often have tempting quantities of discretionary income for expensive clothes, electronic equipment, and other luxuries in their bank accounts. But this fairly new economic group adds up to something far more significant than an attractive marketing niche. The explosion of these shows and the viewers to whom they are targeted foretells the emergence of a new social animal, one we might call the "postmodern postadolescent": a single, childless, and relatively affluent twenty- or thirtysomething. What's striking about postmodern postadolescents is their hazy status. Are they children? No. Adults? Not exactly. So what are they?

Postmodern postadolescents represent the consummation of anticultural childrearing. They are the first generation to reap the benefits of a philosophy that has thoroughly endorsed the notion of self-creation. Despite their reputation as slackers, these postadolescents demonstrate a strong work ethic and a great deal of entrepreneurial spunk. In time, doubtless, the vast majority will marry and have children. The republic will survive. But there are disturbing signs that their tendency to loiter on the outskirts of adulthood is something more than a desire to extend the playful irresponsibility of childhood or to continue the adolescent project of finding themselves. They stall because of confusion about their adult role in a culture suspicious of aging. And they stall out of fear, mistrust, and what Elizabeth Wurtzel in her memoir *Prozac Nation* has called "a low grade, terminal anomie."[1] They can permit themselves friendships but not love affairs, cohabitation but not marriage, sociability but not interdependence. In fact, this seems the logical response to years of training in radical autonomy and the emotional minimalism that goes along with it.

W hat I call postadolescence has evolved in the space of a little more than a generation. The young people of today take considerably longer to leave home, to finish their education, to marry and have children—the milestones traditionally associated with adulthood— than did those of thirty years ago. By 1980, the percentage of young adults who had completed the transitions traditionally associated with adulthood within four years after high school graduation had dropped by more than half from their peers a generation before, but that was only the beginning.[2] Ten years later a record number of twentysomethings were living in their parents' homes in a state of quasi-childlike dependence.[3] Today, as the workplace has begun to demand more highly skilled workers, the number of kids who have put off working in order to continue their education has skyrocketed. In 1959 about 3.5 million students attended an institution of higher education; by 1992, that number had climbed to 14.5 million. And many of these young adults are taking more time to complete their degrees. During the same period, the percentage of students who graduated within five years was declining to an all-time low.[4]

The age of first marriage, the most significant marker of adulthood, has also climbed to new records. In 1964 the median age of first marriage was 23 for men and 20 for women. By 1987 that age was at a record high of 23.6 for women and a near-record 25.8 for men. By 1994 it had climbed to close to 27 for men and 25 for women, and possibly even older for those with higher incomes. The most striking evidence of delayed adulthood is the 23 percent of never-married men between 30 and 34, up from 9 percent in 1970.[5] "It may be time to redefine the meaning of being 'grown-up,'" one psychologist has concluded. "If we continue to apply the same standards used to identify the transition from childhood to adulthood among baby boomers, we may discover that Gen X will never grow up."[6]

But merely redefining the term *grown-up* won't solve the puzzle of the postmodern postadolescent. The ill-defined limbo of this life stage is not merely a structural or demographic fact; it is the very essence of its identity. Postmodern postadolescents wear their aimlessness and uncertainty on their sleeves. Their condition is epitomized by one of their favored words—*whatever*. In an essay in the *New York Times Magazine*, Katie Roiphe captured the soul of this new life stage. She and her friends, she says, "exist in an ambiguous state of rented apartments, takeout dinners, and postponed futures. We all want babies, but we want them in the abstract way that children want to be ballerinas and firemen when they grow up . . . The biggest commitment that a surprising number of people I know have made is to a cat."[7]

The postadolescents' uncertainty and rootlessness has a number of causes, but one of them surely lies in the nature of their childhood experience. This is the first generation to feel the full brunt of anticulturalism. Pronounced competent, rational, and self-aware from an early age, they were given an unprecedented amount of information and the self-sovereignty to make sense of it all. To their parents, children were individuals worthy of full respect and dignity. What no one foresaw was that premature freedom could have the effect not of freeing human potential but of draining it of purpose. Without a deep connection to a way of life, a set of values, or a cultural framework, postadolescents hesitate to place themselves in the adult world. Moreover, their early freedom has exhausted the hopeful enthusiasm that a new generation needs to accompany its graduation into adulthood. In all too many cases, the postadolescent's premature maturity has blended into a tired oversophistication and, according to one marketing researcher, "disillusionment and alienation."[8]

One can trace this process by considering the political behavior of the postadolescent. Today's postadolescents are the first generation to benefit fully from the expansion of the constitutional rights to minors, which we examined in chapter 5, but their habits don't suggest that this expansion has done much to increase their sense of political engagement, much less their idealism. Late teens and twentysomethings vote in minuscule numbers; fewer than a third cast ballots in the 1996 presidential election despite intensive efforts to make politics entertaining. ("Vote baby vote/Vote baby vote/Are you registered baby?" went a "rock the vote" ad on MTV.) A longitudinal study begun in 1985 by the UCLA Higher Education Research Insitute found that though during their college years students tend to become more politically engaged, four years after graduation their interest in both politics and community work drops off substantially.[9] Since 1985 late teenagers and postadolescents have shown a steady decline in interest in public affairs. In the space of five years, between 1991 and 1996, the percentage of students who had never voted in an election increased by a third.[10] A Times Mirror study aptly entitled the "The Age of Indifference" found that regular newspaper reading dropped among eighteen-to-twenty-nine-year-olds from 70 percent in 1965 to 30 percent in 1990. Watching the television news also diminished from 52 to 41 percent.[11] The low levels of political involvement in the American public undoubtedly has many causes, but this generation appears to mark something new. For many people of previous generations, reaching voting age, the age of complete citizenship, was a thrill; after almost two decades of childhood, they could now finally have some say in the political process. Could it be that having known so much freedom from such an early age, today's new voters take these privileges for granted?

This same "early ripe, early rot" phenomenon seems to characterize the postadolescent love life as well. As we might have predicted from the previous chapter, the creed of sexuality has had a miserable impact on twentysomething romance, and even on sexual activity itself. For those who have had a lifelong education in the virtues of autonomy, sexuality seems to have hit a wall. Searching the words of postadolescents, it is difficult to find any of the heady thrill of charting unknown cultural waters that colored single life in the late sixties and seventies. The freedom available to today's postadolescent fails to evoke even the tacky erotic excitement of the Cosmo girl's sexy underwear or the Playboy bachelor's smoking jacket, much less the barebreasted ease of the "summer of love" generation. Doubtless, this is partly because of the threat of AIDS. An element of trepidation, even dread, is the grim chaperone for any casual encounter today, and even throughout all the early stages of a relationship.

But AIDS is not the only problem. Even as the blood tests come back negative and relationships grow beyond the tentative "will he call?" stage, postadolescents often find themselves weighed down by what Roiphe calls "the accumulated anonymity of it, the haphazardness."[12] When a twenty-four-year-old has already had eight lovers (a common situation today and perhaps even a modest number in some circles), encounters easily become dulled by a been-there-done-that jadedness. It's difficult for postmodern postadolescents to gather up the sense of hope, longing, or specialness that helps propel desire into love. Katie Roiphe offers two examples: A weary, oversophisticated thirty-year-old friend tells how he felt on meeting his girlfriend's parents: "I just couldn't summon up the energy to be charming. I've done it too many times before." Roiphe recalls how she herself once went out with a man who mused that he had slept with five Katies, not exactly the kind of comment to inspire joy in a young lover's heart.[13]

Tired, highly possessive of their personal freedoms, and fearful of emotional dependency, postadolescents are naturally wary of marriage. The steady rise in the number of cohabiting adults, the vast majority of whom are young, is one example of this wariness. To be sure, many of those relationships are merely short-term preludes to marriage, but an increasing number of young cohabiters see their arrangement as an alternative to marriage. These relationships are typically more tenuous, not to mention unhappier, than those of married couples. Hanging on to their independence as long as possible, cohabiting postadolescents are more likely to think in terms of splitting living expenses rather than pooling resources.[14] Rather than preparing them for adulthood, the experience of cohabitation often merely sours them on the possibilities of enduring bonds.[15] The postadolescent authors of *Late Bloomers* put it this way: "We've been preparing for marriage. But we've also been prepping for divorce, learning how to divide joint property, how to argue over owed money, how to close off your old love-response toward someone who you, officially anyway, no longer love."[16]

Indeed, many young people seem to carry around with them a bag loaded with disappointments collected over the years. "Self protection and closing the deal are paramount," writes Candace Bushnell in *Sex in the City,* detailing "The End of Love in Manhattan." "No one has breakfast at Tiffany's, and no one has affairs to remember—instead, we have breakfast at seven A.M. and affairs we try to forget as quickly as possible."[17] Young people adopt a tough, mistrustful exterior, which finds its outward form in some of the macho, heavy-booted fashions that have been popular over the past several years.

Low expectations about the possibilities for deep, enduring relationships lead some postadolescents to lower their sights to friendship. Some continue their campus habits of going out or meeting in bars in large groups. Others try a strange new brand of asexual coupling: "Gen X men and women," Barbara Dafoe Whitehead has found, "may share beds without ever having sex, or they may start out in a sexual relationship and then eventually shift to a comfy, asexual living-relationship for the sake of companionship and convenience."[18] "Relationships are too intense," a twenty-five-year-old male told Candace Bushnell, listing hassles like disease and pregnancy. "Why not just be with your friends and have real conversations and a good time?"[19]

To get a sense of just how recently postadolescence has elbowed a space for itself into American life and of how it has come to grapple with its loneliness, it's useful to look at its portrayal in popular culture.[20] In the 1950s, families reigned on television. The few singles were likely to be widowers, like the character played by Fred Mac-Murray in *My Three Sons,* whose single status, when combined with his curious prattling children, created opportunities for humorously romantic plotlines. Only in the late 1960s did the first signs of change come—with *That Girl,* starring Marlo Thomas. Although an aspiring career girl, the heroine was engaged, and her clean-cut fiancé dropped by often enough to assure us that all would turn out as it should, namely, with marriage. A few years later America was introduced to the prototype single, Mary Richards, the lead character of the *Mary Tyler Moore Show.*

Though *Mary Tyler Moore* foretold several of the prominent themes in the new genre, it also revealed some uncertainty about the new life stage. The main character was a young, single woman who lived in the city and whose life centered around her friends and her job in a television newsroom and not, like almost all sitcoms in the past, around her family. Mary's parting words to her colleagues in the series' final episode illustrated the enormity of the change from earlier shows: "What is a family? A family is people who make you feel less alone and really loved. Thank you for being my family."[21] In the post-sixties media home, friends and coworkers would often replace family and the workplace would become the locus of intimate life. Still, *The Mary Tyler Moore Show* hinted at the apprehensions inevitable at the early stages of profound social change. Mary's nervousness was a staple of the show; trembling her lip, she warbled, "Oh, Mr. Grant!" The strained optimism of the opening theme song—*You're gonna make it after all*—introduced a mild uneasiness about Mary's autonomy; it was always as if she were trying on a dress which didn't quite fit. Nevertheless, regardless of the uncertainty about her predicament and in spite of her nervousness, there was no question that she was a grown-up, one who, in fact, *had* to make it on her own.

In the mid and late nineties, as postadolescence has become a fact of American life, this maturity has disappeared. It is the childishness of twentysomethings that dominates contemporary shows. On *Friends,* two of the male leads play a game, popular among the ten-year-old set, called Foosball on the rare occasions when they're not watching TV. One of them, unaccountably dressed for this episode in a suit and tie, brags about the hard drive and RAM capacity of his new computer. "Nice," says one of the friends. "What will you do with it?" He looks blank for a minute before answering brightly, "Games 'n' stuff!" On *Seinfeld,* Kramer wants to be a fireman, George craves Bosco and milk, Elaine and Kramer fight over a Schwinn bicycle, and Jerry slips his girlfriend a mickey so he can play with her vintage toy collection. Many of these characters don't even appear to work; when not installed in front of the TV in their IKEA-furnished apartments, they drift in pleasurable vacancy around the city, going to movies and restaurants, hanging out in coffee shops or hip bars.

Even the careerists among them are big babies. The hit series *Ally McBeal* takes place in a law firm, but it is still a child's world. Ally herself may be ambivalent about her singleness, but her immaturity is the series' mainstay motif. She stutters and fumbles when she is embarrassed (which is nearly all the time), slow-dances with her pillow, wears funny little flannel pj's, and beats up on her Bobo doll when she's cranky. Many of the show's scenes occur in the firm's coed bathroom. This is supposedly a sign of the characters' sophistication and sexual ease, but the bathroom turns out more often than not to be the site of blushing embarrassment as these lawyers gossip and titter about each others' tics and fetishes, peer under stalls, and just hang out. The mid-eighties drama series *Thirtysomething* was once descibed as high school with money. *Ally McBeal* is junior high school with law degrees.

Yet the laughs and gossipy, easy sociability barely disguise the hollowness at the heart of postadolescence, a hollowness that has been gradually uncovered since the time of *The Mary Tyler Moore Show.* *Seinfeld's* characters go through partners faster than they go through Jerry's cereal boxes, but these relationships barely register on the emotional radar screen. Jerry and Elaine themselves, though they once dated, could be brother and sister for all the heat they generate. The creators of the show were quoted as saying it was a show about "nothing," and they meant the word to refer to more than banal plotlines.

Still, much of the appeal of these shows stems from the way they ward off the loneliness of single life with the fantasy of a caring, faithful postadolescent peer group. Though they date and have sex—and, even more, *talk* about dating and sex—friendships fill up their lives. What is portrayed is really not much different from the loving companionship that once tantalized viewers of family shows in the fifties and that lasted well into the seventies with *The Brady Bunch*. David Schwimmer, one of the stars of *Friends,* understood this when he speculated in an interview that the popularity of the show stems from the longings of children of divorce, who constitute much of the show's audience: "I think for some people it's a fantasy to have this close a group of people, to have a family really . . . So many people have grown up products of divorce or not ideal family situations. And to have this kind of solid support group is something . . . everyone wants in their lives."[22]

Several of the more sophisticated chroniclers of the current scene directly address the postadolescent's ambivalence about more enduring bonds. The best example is the 1992 movie *Singles.* Its title refers both to its characters' marital status and their one-bedroom Seattle apartments. The soft comedy begins on a determinedly upbeat note with a young woman standing in front of a house. "I was living in this duplex. For the first time, I was alone," she says, smiling to the camera. "No dorm. No roommates. My own place. I was so happy." But director Cameron Crowe is cleverly setting these ideals up for a fall. After an initially rocky love affair, which culminates happily when the young woman and her boyfriend move in together, *Singles* ends in an intentionally ambiguous mood. "Some people think living alone is a nasty hang," says Cliff, an aspiring though untalented rock musician. "Not me . . . I'm a self-contained unit." The self-contained residential unit becomes the movie's symbol of the autonomy of the postmodern postadolescent, an autonomy, with all its sad, self-deluded isolation, the sophisticated script gently mocks.

Finally, it is the autonomy, the value that postadolescents have learned throughout their childhood, that is to be prized above all others, that the more intelligent people working in the singles genre are trying to tackle. *Seinfeld*'s creators understood that its characters' inability to grow up and form lasting attachments—however eccentric and hilarious this made them—represents a serious moral failure. In the show's final episode all four of the main characters are arrested for "criminal indifference" (for failing to help the victim of a robbery) and convicted of "selfishness, self-absorption and greed." These same qualities had been on abundant display throughout the series' run; indeed, one season began with two of the main characters, George and Jerry, sitting in their favorite booth at the local coffee shop discussing Jerry's breakup with a girl for "shushing" him while she was watching TV. The dialogue that follows sits flat on paper but is humorous when it comes, as it does on *Seinfeld,* from the mouths of two such determinedly silly boy-men whose main preoccupations are sports, girls, and action-adventure movies:

"What are we doing?" demands Jerry suddenly. "What kind of lives are these? We're not men. Are we going to be sitting here when we're sixty?"

George begins to get excited: "We should be having dinner with our sons when we're sixty!" His voice rises: "We're kids. We're not men."

Jerry gets even more worked up. He will marry! he decides. "I want to be normal. I'm going to do something about my life!"

Of course, as any Seinfeld fan could have predicted, neither of these postadolescents will end up marrying. In fact, George will spend the entire season trying to get off the hook, something at which he succeeds only when his fiancée dies after licking the poisonous glue on the cheap wedding invitations he had insisted on buying. But as we'll see, *Seinfeld*'s creators were on to something when they hinted that marriage is the key to the ambiguity of the postmodern postadolescent.

Sociologists sometimes talk about a *life script,* the scenario for the way a culture structures the life course. For over a century, the American script meant an elongated, protected childhood; an annex called adolescence; an adulthood marked by entrance into the workplace, marriage, and childrearing; and then old age and, inevitably, death. There were always people who improvised, of course, especially among the poor: working-class kids who labored in coal mines or steel factories, adolescents who themselves had children, adults who didn't marry. But they were exceptions.

The psychologist Erik Erikson once described adulthood as the period of "generativity," a period whose primary task is "establishing and guiding the next generation."[23] In a society where marriage has become a "lifestyle choice" and childbearing is viewed as the expression of "individual reproductive goals" or, more generally, of self-fulfillment, it's difficult to recapture how universally human cultures have held to this view. Virtually all human societies have marked the individual's entrance into this "period of generativity" through the ceremony of the wedding. Indeed, marriage and adulthood were so intertwined that the wedded state said more about status than chronological age. In Korea a person's wedding day is sometimes referred to as Day One, the beginning of complete personhood. There, as in many cultures, young unmarrieds wear their hair loose while the married adults must pin their hair up. A story is told of an early-twentieth-century Western traveler who pointed at an eleven-year-old youngster with his hair knotted on top of his head and asked, "Is that little boy really married?" His interlocutor looked in the direction of his gaze. "Whom do you mean?" he puzzled, having located the little person in question. "That man?"[24] When the the feckless George on *Seinfeld* becomes engaged, even he announces, "I'm a *man*, Jerry! I'm a *man!*"

It is true that many cultures have had ways other than marriage to mark the arrival of maturity. In the ritual hazing that occurred at puberty in tribal cultures, boys were welcomed into the tribe as hunters and girls as fertile women. But in Europe and America the wedding was the only commonly recognized rite of initiation into adulthood. "Only with marriage has a person achieved his or her purpose in life," one historian has written. "Youth, by contrast, is a state of incompleteness."[25] In premodern France even a forty-year-old was sometimes called *garçon* ("boy") if he was unmarried and especially if he was in unsettled circumstances, such as working as a domestic or a journeyman or being in the army. After marriage, however, he became *homme* ("man"). In parts of Europe a deceased unmarried male was laid out for his funeral in his wedding clothes, his coffin accompanied by a "white bride" and a "black bride," a symbolic way of completing his foreshortened life span.[26] Psychiatric experts in the United States during the 1950s couched these common cultural attitudes in quasi-scientific language. The selection of a mate and "adjustment" to marriage were signs of healthy adulthood, and the bachelor was viewed as a kind of child—selfish, immature, and possibly suffering from a mother-fixation. Vestiges of the close kinship of marriage and adulthood appear even today in the postmodern United States in the form of state laws that automatically emancipate a minor upon marriage.

Marriage held such a position of honor not because it enshrined love and commitment, but because it signaled the individual's readiness to procreate and thereby ensure the continuation of the society. Among the Puritans, women could divorce their husbands for *coitus interruptus* and impotence, because they limited their chance for conception. In many cultures, childlessness has been considered a kind of tragedy, as it continues to be for numerous infertile couples in America today;[27] in a few societies, it is known to lead to suicide. Because marriage is so closely tied with procreation, societies have had little interest in recognizing unions that are not likely to result in children, for example, those of homosexuals or the elderly. In Korea, the elderly do not have weddings though they may officially register their relationship.[28] In early modern France and in parts of Italy, protesting bands of young peasant men carried an effigy of a dead spouse when a widower remarried—among widows, only the very rich who were outside the venue of peasant rule had such luck—and serenaded him with pots and pans. In Bali, men were once defined almost completely by their parental status. When they had children, they were renamed, for instance, "father of Sam." In *Kinship in Bali,* Clifford and Hildred Geertz, described the childless male Balinese as follows: "A man who has never had a child remains all his life a child terminologically. When all of his age-mates have become 'father of' and 'grandfather of,' he retains his childhood name, and the shame of this is often very deeply felt."[29]

It's worth lingering over these facts, because they serve as a reminder of the uniqueness of our own cultural moment. As people marry later into their twenties and even, especially among the elite, into their thirties, we find ourselves with a demographic group with no history and no social purpose. Late marriage is not simply a demographic quirk. The postadolescent is really a kind of freak of culture, an adult who is no adult, a child who is no child. His marriage anxiety reflects not merely an understandable human fear of making permanent choices or of committing oneself to one person; it constitutes a retreat from social rootedness in a much broader sense. It reflects an unwillingness to undertake the task of cultural continuance and renewal. This is not to say that marriage and procreation are the only way people do this. But poor voter turnout and community involvement among this age group suggests that the ambivalence towards marriage may well be part of a more general indifference to public and social life. It seems that *Seinfeld*'s writers were on to something when they condemned its characters for "self-absorption."

It could be argued that this stage, assuming that the postadolescent moves on to marriage—after all, the vast majority of young people want to marry and even *Seinfeld*'s do-nothings still considered it the "normal" thing to do—is really nothing new. With the exception of the period right after World War II, a long transitional period between childhood and adulthood, known as youth, was long part of the Western biography. In Western Europe, marriage in one's mid to late twenties has been the norm since premodern times, except among the nobility, who, assured of a home and dowry, sometimes wed in their teens.[30]

But there are two glaring differences between today's postmodern postadolescence and what used to be called youth, and both of them point to a problem in our current predicament. First, yesterday's youth lived in a condition scholars call semi-dependence. That is, they were part of a household and a community.[31] Today's version, however, are free to take up residence independent of their family, surrounded by others living just like them. With no communal ties or obligations, they can wander to the pleasure-filled city of their choice, where they might create small lifestyle enclaves. It's impossible to overstate the ramifications of this change; the twentieth century initiated, probably for the first time in human history, a new biographical possibility: young single life in an independent home, that is, complete, rootless autonomy for men *and* women.

The second key difference between the youth of yesterday and today is apparent in the aimlessness that the more insightful chroniclers of postadolescence, like the director and screenwriter Cameron Crowe and Jerry Seinfeld, seem to recognize. No matter how long it took, youth of the past knew they had a central task: to prepare themselves for a fixed state known as adulthood, a state communally defined by marriage. Not only do today's youth have no such clearly marked terminus, but their entire life script has become an indecipherable maze.

Once again, popular culture provides a helpful framework for discussing this stalemate. The postadolescent's reluctance to give up his status as a self-contained unit and his unwillingness to enter into adulthood are symbolized perfectly in what seems to have become the most popular ceremony in the singles entertainment genre: the interrupted wedding. In the interrupted wedding the couple never gets to say "I do" to each other—or to adulthood; there is a change of mind for either the bride or the groom just before the final moment. Several seasons ago viewers of the television series *Party of Five* could watch two failed weddings in one season. In the first, Charlie, the oldest of the five orphaned siblings alluded to in the series' title, has second thoughts as he poses for his prenuptial pictures, leaving his bride weeping to the camera. In another episode some months later, that same abandoned bride, about to take her vows with a more reliable man, turns the tables and walks out on *him* when Charlie abruptly reenters her life. Not that a completed wedding is now finally in the offing: "I can't promise you anything," Charlie explains to his jilted and jilting girlfriend after her near escape from marriage in a perfect expression of postadolescent ambivalence. "I don't know where this is going."

The interrupted wedding is not without honorable literary precedents. Yet the difference between the premodern and postmodern versions is revealing. In Shakespeare's *Much Ado About Nothing,* for instance, Claudio forestalls his marriage to Hero after hearing false rumors of her faithlessness. But this occurs in the *middle* of the play. The play ends (as comedy so often did in the past) with a marriage, in fact, a double marriage—Claudio and his vindicated betrothed and the prototypical "witty duo," Beatrice and Benedick.

The contemporary singles genre altogether abandons the wedding as a celebration of the passing of generations and, by extension, of the bride and groom's good-bye to childhood. Instead, it introduces the *nuptialis interruptus,* a ceremony that enshrines freedom, open-endedness, and the elongation of youth. A perfect contemporary counter-symbol to the traditional wedding and a truly postmodern rite of passage, the interrupted wedding invites the audience to celebrate the postadolescent's continuation as a self-contained unit. The ending of the 1995 season of *E.R.* is a particularly striking example: When one of the main characters is left at the altar, she cries briefly, shrugs her shoulders, and goes off to join the restless wedding party waiting under the caterer's tent. Viewers were left at the end of the season with the strange contemporary image of a joyful celebration, complete with family and friends, a banquet, a toast, and a radiant, dancing, though groomless, bride. "I guess I'm just lucky to be alive and have such wonderful friends," she says raising her glass in an echo of Mary Tyler Moore's parting statement. Her words are followed by misty Hallmark shots of friends laughing, embracing, and dancing. The ceremony marks the bride's passage not into a new familial group and adulthood but into a renewal of her vow to open-endedness and to her postadolescent peer group.

Though meant to be upbeat, moments like these speak volumes about the diminished expectations of contemporary young people. They have given up enough hope and idealism that they can no longer allow themselves to enjoy fully the traditional ending of the romantic comedy, the union of two lovers. Of course, romantic endings have not disappeared entirely, but it is increasingly difficult to find convincing examples from our storytellers in Hollywood. They seem to prefer anticlimactic climaxes like that in the 1997 *My Best Friend's Wedding.* In this movie, the heroine, played by Julia Roberts, engages in all sorts of chicanery to stop the marriage of her best friend, a man she has come to realize she actually loves. Throughout her travails, her close confidante is George, a handsome and single male friend. In any previous era, she would have come to realize that the devoted George was the more promising love anyway, but, alas, that cannot happen here because George is gay. Thus, the movie has only a lame and shallow climax to replace the archetype: a handsome young man leads a gorgeous young woman onto the dance floor during a wedding party to celebrate . . . well, to celebrate a party. "There may not be marriage," he says, "there may not be sex, but by God, there will be dancing!"

There is one more extremely important source of this hopelessness that we have not yet discussed: the high rate of marital breakdown. Postadolescents are the first generation to grow up in a world that takes for granted that marriages are just as likely to end in divorce as to endure. They have witnessed anger, betrayal, and pain in their own homes and in those of their friends and relatives. Before divorce became normal, many children grew up in unhappy homes marked by rage and coldness, but this was a private grief for those families to bear alone. Somehow this brand of lonely unhappiness did not murder hope. Now, however, marital misery is a public truth. In fact, it may be the most common piece of cultural wisdom the young receive. It is drilled into them young starting in the nursery. They hear it repeated throughout childhood, either as a consequence of personal experience or from the media's endless thematic repetition. Even educators are intent on passing down family rot as a central piece of cultural wisdom. In a study of textbooks on marriage and family for college students, Norval Glenn found "a determinedly pessimistic view of marriage," whose typical dangers are depicted as abuse, psychological stultification, and neurotic codependence.[32] Given this kind of training, postadolescent stalling seems almost healthy.

Clearly, postadolescence is a symptom of a profoundly changed life script in which traditional age boundaries shift and predictable roles implode, but it is not the only one. As we have seen throughout this book, childhood has lost its familiar contours too. And so, it seems, has adulthood.[33] The average age of first marriage for women today is near twenty-five, but this number disguises the huge variation in bridal age, a subject addressed in a *Bride's Magazine* feature entitled "Marriage at 20, 30, 40." Middle age has been lost somewhere in the swelling crowd of forty-five-year-old first-time mothers. The number of births to women over the age of forty has increased more than sixfold since 1970.[34] A woman today can easily find herself simultaneously mother and grandmother to newborn infants, a situation exploited in the movie *Father of the Bride 2,* whose climax has the hero running between wife and daughter in nearby delivery rooms. In one famous case a woman "loaned her womb" to her daughter and became both mother and grandmother simultaneously.

Thus, postmodern postadolescents have yet another reason to stall. Having just arrived from a childhood that was barely a childhood, they look around them and find an adulthood that is scarcely an adulthood. If postadolescents are reluctant adults, they are no less so than the people who reared them. In fact, a new definition of adulthood is the unspoken premise behind both postmodern postadolescence *and* anticultural childhood. Over the last thirty years—the time during which postadolescents grew up under anticultural ideas—adulthood underwent a radical redefinition that was a great departure from the conventional idea of "establishing and guiding the next generation." If the old adulthood was stable, finished, and prepared to pass on cultural ideals to the next generation, the new adulthood was fluid, explorative, and uncommitted to any fixed ideas. It could not possibly be a source of cultural wisdom, because such wisdom was in constant flux and subject to personal trial and error.

One of the most influential proponents of this quasi adulthood that was coming into focus in the seventies and eighties was Gail Sheehy. In her best-selling 1976 book *Passages: Predictable Crises of Adult Life,* which adapted the theories of humanistic psychologists Abraham Maslow and Carl Rogers, Sheehy celebrated what she saw as "the underlying impulse toward change" in the healthy adult's "lifelong pursuit of identity." "You are moving out of roles and into the self," she wrote. "If I could give a gift for the send-off on this journey, it would be a tent. A tent for tentativeness." In the book Sheehy refers disparagingly to "locked in" souls, those who resist tentativeness, seeking security and permanence. "Times of crisis," she continues, "of disruption or constructive change, are not only predictable but desirable. They mean growth."[35]

Change and growth, once the obligation of children, thus became the prerogative of adults. The seventies were the heyday for this language; magazines with titles like *Personal Growth* began to appear on newstands and in bookstores. But the makeover of adulthood into growth and tentativeness has continued to this day and has even found its way into academic psychology. Titles like *Growing Up Again: Parenting Ourselves, Parenting Our Children* still appear in book catalogues, as do more intellectually serious books like *The Protean Self,* whose author is as optimistic as Sheehy about the "self of many possibilities" and "the malleability of the self."[36] In this atmosphere, marriage has had to be redefined as well. By the seventies, "staying together for the sake of the children" came to seem an archaic and cruel refrain; it turned a cold shoulder to the needs of the ever-developing self. *Creative Divorce: A New Opportunity for Personal Growth,* the title of one self-help tract, is more in keeping with the new zeitgeist. According to Barbara Whitehead, modern divorce experts have often presented a picture of "emotionally fragile" adults and "emotionally resilient" children.[37]

These ideas took hold so quickly that it's easy to lose sight of the view that they replaced. Less than a generation before Sheehy, young people looked forward not to a lifetime of growth but to growing up. "Everything in the culture of the 1950's provoked one to grow up," the writer Joseph Epstein has explained. "The ideal, in the movies and in life, was adulthood." To grow up meant to be free, to have money and the objects it could buy, to drink, to smoke, and to have sex.[38] The sea change that took place in these years is captured in a 1981 essay in which A. Alvarez wrote, in some bewilderment, about his first marriage in the fifties: "I had this terrible lust for premature maturity, this irresponsible desire for responsibility, before I had any idea what maturity involved or had even tasted the pleasures of youthful irresponsibility."[39] Of course, Alvarez is criticizing what he believes to have been his personal delusions, but what's striking about this statement is its evocation of a profound cultural shift. A young man in the fifties longed to grow up and, presumably, to be married. By the Sheehyesque eighties, a middle-aged man could not conceive of such a dream.

These ideas remain a prominent theme in popular culture today. Hollywood has also sought to overthrow staid adulthood in favor of an even more pronounced childishness. In the 1991 film *Regarding Henry,* Harrison Ford plays a workaholic, combative lawyer who suffers brain damage after being shot in the head. Seeing his dog-eat-dog world with the fresh eyes of the innocent, he utters childlike indiscretions in the name of honesty. But it is boy wonder and director Steven Spielberg who is the greatest believer in this myth. His 1991 *Hook* is the story of Peter Banning, the adult alias of Peter Pan. As an adult he is, naturally, rigid, nasty, and ambitious; "All grown-ups are pirates," announces one of Spielberg's hip lost boys. Peter returns to Neverland, where he can regain the imaginative, vital childhood self that is his real essence. In James Barrie's original play of *Peter Pan,* Peter is the leader of the lost boys, older and wiser than they. In Spielberg's *Hook,* as in all anticultural texts, it is the lost boys who are the teachers. They instruct Peter, now an adult, in the lost arts of childhood. According to Spielberg, this is no mere conceit. "Neverland is not a cartoon world," the veteran director said, apparently with a straight face. "It is a real place."[40] No wonder postadolescents are confused!

Spielberg was echoing the sentiments of the recovery movement, the source of the most extreme rejection of adulthood's traditional meaning. Recovery gurus have gone so far as to announce that adulthood does not even exist. The "real" self, they say, is a child hiding inside, the "inner child"; the only hope for well-being is to recover the inner child, a spiritual and free creature untarnished by life's exigencies and, in particular, by "toxic" parents. During the workshops of John Bradshaw, best-selling author and star of a popular PBS television series, participants grasp teddy bears and weep uncontrollably. He suggests that you write letters both to "you as an infant" and "from your inner infant to you now," like the one he, a highly successful businessman in his fifties, wrote to himself with his nondominant hand so that it looked like the jagged scrawl of a five-year-old: "Dear

John, I want you to come and get me I want to matter to someone. I don't want to be alone. Love, Little John."[41] The authors of *The Courage to Heal* suggest a similar approach in their praise for a twenty-five-year-old woman who had suffered abuse as a child. This young woman sets herself a five-year timetable to heal and starts by celebrating her "fifth birthday." "I celebrated my 'fifth' over children's stories and chocolate cake," she explains. "I'll be celebrating my 'third' birthday . . . [by building] a tent out of bed sheets . . . and read[ing] stories by flashlight. There will be glow-in-the-dark stars on the tent ceiling too. Oh, I love being little!"[42]

A new breed of cyberprophets has also begun to appear, urging adults to become more like children. These thinkers maintain that kids are better than adults precisely because they are malleable and restless, qualities once viewed as deficits. They can accept chaos, discontinuity, and nonlinearity, according to Douglas Rushkoff, a techno-guru in *Playing the Future: How Kids' Culture Can Teach Us to Thrive in an Age of Chaos*. "Rather than being an adult child who wanders through life on faith, be a child-adult—a child of chaos."[43] Seymour Papert, the inventor of the computer language Logos, concurs. Papert is a great enthusiast of what he sees as children's remarkable inventiveness and openness. Of his own experience in working on computers he says, "I was playing like a child and experiencing a volcanic explosion of creativity." It was Papert who wrote a book on computers entitled *The Children's Machine*.[44]

All of this goes a long way toward explaining the popular theme of "cross-aging" in American popular culture. Beginning twenty years ago, America became enamoured of weird boy-men like Tiny Tim and Pee Wee Herman. More recently we have seen their more conventional counterparts, like Michael J. Fox, whose most famous movies, the *Back to the Future* series, cast him as both teenager and middle-aged father, as both child of and peer to his own parents. Tom Hanks was a similarly ageless hero in two major hits, *Big* (a boy magically takes on a man's body) and *Forrest Gump* (a childlike retarded man as American picaresque hero). In *Billy Madison* the main character, the twenty-year-old son of a wealthy businessman, spends his days either drinking beer and reading girlie magazines while he drifts around in the swimming pool or playing third-grade-style practical jokes and practicing Nintendo, thus lending a contemporary twist to the word *playboy*. Finally, his father can stand it no longer and sends him back to school—elementary school, that is. In *Big,* Josh, played by Tom Hanks, tells his friend, the only one who knows he is really a child, that the adult world "is a lot like camp." When Josh tries to explain to his girlfriend why he is unable to be more committed to their relationship, he says, "I'm a thirteen-year-old kid!" "Oh yeah," she sneers in a humorously resonant comeback. "And who isn't?"

But the childlike adult is not simply an invention of New Age flim-flam men and faddish experts, popular journalists, and filmmakers. Like his mirror image, the adultlike child that we've been looking at throughout this book, he has deep roots in contemporary society. One of those roots lies in the changes taking place in our postindustrial economy since the 1960s. At one time, though it might have taken many years, individuals could usually expect to complete their education and training and enter into a career. The first two-thirds of the twentieth century was a time of relative stability in technology and industry, but by the late sixties America was entering what Peter Drucker called the "Age of Discontinuity."[45] With innovations coming at a rapid pace and a constantly shifting marketplace, workers began to find that they had to modify their jobs or even enter entirely new professions. "Continuing change is now a fact of life," concurred management theorist Rosabeth Moss Kanter. "There will be increasing uncertainty and instability of corporate careers."[46] Already in 1968 Drucker was predicting a life span that would include several occupations. The explosive growth of temporary agencies and in the number of "contingent workers"—it's been estimated that they constitute between a quarter and a third of the U.S. workforce[47]—is another symptom of the same discontinuity.

All of this could not help but shake up adulthood. For one thing, adults in need of retraining are now forced to be students, formerly the occupation of the young. Educators and politicians have begun to speak of "the ideal of lifelong learning." Individuals once considered finished adults are now going back to school, and college has become a chronological melting pot. "Higher education is no longer something one does only between 18 and 22," says the executive director of the National University Continuing Education Association. "Education today is on-going—whether you're doing it just for self-improvement or to remain employable."[48] Fewer than one in six undergraduates fit the traditional idea of a full-time college student living on campus. In 1980 only one in four college students was over twenty-five years old; by 1990 the percentage had almost doubled, to four in ten. In fact, 18 percent of college students were over thirty-five. The fastest-growing age group on college campuses, now 11 percent of the student population, is composed of those who are over forty.[49]

Another setback for old-fashioned adulthood has been the redefinition of the worker. Yesterday's organization man needed loyalty, steadiness, and moderation in his slow but steady climb up the corporate ladder. Today's men and women of the globalized economy must be quick and supple "business athletes." Kanter cites the "four f's" of today's sought-after worker: "focused, fast, friendly, flexible."[50] In a knowledge economy where skill is based on knowledge and where technology and economy are likely to change fast," writes Drucker in the same vein, ". . . the only meaningful job security is the capacity to learn fast. The only real security in an economy and society at flux is to know enough to be able to move."[51] The paradox of the new work order is that security is founded on mobility and that stability is built on the ability to change.

Marketers sensed these transformations almost immediately. Seeking images to reflect the up-to-date values of flexibility, mobility, and change, they promoted the idea of youth, meaning not simply young people—who, after all, had limited resources—but "those who think young." In words that anticipated *Passages,* which would be published six years later, *Business Week* wrote in 1970 that this would be the decade "when youth becomes a state of mind and overflows all traditional age boundaries."[52] Throughout the sixties, in hugely successful and groundbreaking campaigns that set the tone for the advertising future, the upstart Pepsi had been challenging the tried-and-true Coca-Cola with fast-paced, lavishly colored ads portraying young people riding motorbikes, surfing, skiing; as the late-sixties counter-culture evolved, Pepsi began including in its ads images of longhaired men carrying flowers and shoeless women walking in the rain. Marketers began to look to youth to determine fashion in music, clothes, movies, television, even cars. The Pontiac GTO was the Pepsi of the auto industry, symbolizing on-the-go, fast-moving youthful verve. Hollywood too had begun to see youth as the key to its future. By the late fifties, producers began to use more teen heroes, rock-and-roll sound tracks and themes. This "juvenilization of movies"[53] continued apace for decades, until blockblusters like *Star Wars* and *Indiana Jones* established once and for all that grown-ups could be appealed to not just as youthful but as juvenile.

Thus, the baby boomer generation, whose older members are the parents of postadolescents, exploded conventional definitions of adulthood and childhood. Now settled into middle age (or "mid-youth," as Judy Ernest, executive director of the Boomer Institute in Cleveland, has taken to calling it),[54] they dress in the same jeans and sneakers as prepubescent kids, sometimes even at the office; they carry backpacks; they watch cartoons on television, they go to the same movies as their younger children, including action-packed extravaganzas about dinosaurs, creatures from outer space, and shoot-'em-up revenge fantasies; they noodle around on what Seymour Papert calls "the children's machine"; they take up "boxercise," bicycling, and roller-skating; they give themselves Halloween parties, where they dress up in funny costumes; and they whoop it up at big birthday parties, where they receive lots of presents. And, as Judith Martin (aka Miss Manners) has observed, they fuss endlessly over their food.[55]

Without question, smashing the life script has a certain appeal. Under the old regime, there was, for example, something deeply onerous for women about facing a twenty-fifth birthday without a ring. Getting rid of a script reveals yet another arena of expanded personal choice. Americans have always attempted to escape from contingent identity: they wanted to choose their own nation, their own communities, their own churches, their own names. Now we can demonstrate "our willingness, at last, to break free from the notion that chronology is destiny," in the words of Mary Hatwood Futrell, past president of the National Education Association.[56]

But it's important to understand that people have always gone along with the conventional life script—childhood, marriage and childbearing, old age, death—not because they were timid conformists afraid to break the mold but because this was the plotline that held the best chance for success in American society. At the same time, this life script mirrored in its broad outlines the rhythms of biology: birth and growth, puberty and reproduction, decreasing fertility and death. The traditional life script could never make everyone happy, but it went some way toward satisfying both cultural and biological needs. It should be clear by now, however, that an adulthood defined by change, growth, and youthfulness can do neither. It disorders the life of the young in serious ways. Growing is supposed to be something the young do. If adults are fluid and unsure, why should adolescents or young adults aspire to be like them? If adults are supposed to be tentative and changeable, how can they successfully rear children, who appear to thrive on stability and regularity? Americans have tried a convenient anticultural philosophy that says they are not required to shape their children or to pass on any cultural wisdom to them. But we have seen that this philosophy limits children's individuality and happiness.

Postadolescents must sense that they have been failed by a society that refused to guide them through childhood. Phrases like "self-care" or "self-esteem" or "child empowerment" wear thin after a while for those whose world seems incoherent. Their discontent with feckless adults is becoming a familiar theme in popular culture. In one episode of *Buffy the Vampire Slayer,* for example, the adults turn into sixties teenagers, making out on the dance floor, singing "Louie Louie" into the microphone, and just generally goofing off. In what she calls this "land of the irresponsible," Buffy's miniskirted mother, who is blowing bubble gum and carrying sex-toy handcuffs, looks soulfully into the eyes of her T-shirted boyfriend and says, "Getting married and having a kid was just a dream. And now everything's back to the way it's supposed to be." As things get out of control, Buffy wails, "I need help. I need grown-ups. . . . This is not normal." Though far less coherently, the movie *Pleasantville* also presents the kid's-eye view of the failed adult. In one of the first scenes, the self-absorbed mother of the teenaged characters, David and Jennifer, has a screaming fight over the telephone with her ex-husband over who is in charge of these teenagers that weekend. "It's your problem," she yells so that her children can hear. "If I want to take a mud bath with my boyfriend, then I'll take a mud bath with my boyfriend." David has to play mommy to the little-girl adults; in the course of the movie, he dries the tears of two different mother figures and reassures them that everything will be all right.

Gloria Steinem, alluding to the ever-growing adult, once said, "We can choose not to give birth to a child in order to give birth to ourselves."[57] Though few people are willing to make her either/or choice, at least Steinem recognized the unresolvable conflict of interest between nurturing the fragile and unknowable potential of young life and devotion to the full self-expression of adulthood. It is this conflict that anticulturalism's myth of the rational, self-sufficient child has tried to wish away. The first generation to come of age during the reign of anticulturalism proves that it was a vain and naive vision. Something's got to give, and unfortunately that something will likely be the kids themselves. Once experts working in child custody cases talked about "the best interests of the child"; now it's been suggested that they think instead in terms of "the least detrimental alternative." This change in language provides a perfect symbol of how in the last thirty years Americans have become disillusioned about childhood.

And yet this may be just the moment in which we can learn the lesson of anticulturalism's failures. Perhaps postadolescents' uneasiness with the incoherence they experienced as children will provoke them to define a more stable and rooted world for their own progeny. Disillusioned though they may be, hopeless they are not. In fact, their disillusionment speaks of a lingering cultural memory of a world that could still talk about a child's best interests, a world with a more mature understanding of the meaning of childhood. Postadolescents know things weren't always like this. The question is, Without giving into either glib nostalgia or naive visions of progress, can postadolescents redefine a genuine childhood to suit the next century? One thing remains certain: such a redefinition will take some real grown-ups.

Refilling
the Nest

At a recent discussion group for parents at my daughter's school, a mother worried out loud about her sixth grade son standing at the edge of the Darwinian teen jungle. "The best thing I can do is to be his ally," she concluded to the nods of many in the room. "As he goes through all of it, I can be there to support his self-esteem." Such sentiments are commonplace today. Adults define themselves as children's allies, trainers, partners, friends, facilitators, co-learners, and advocates. Their role is to empower children, advocate for them, boost their self-esteem, respect their rights, and provide them with information with which they can make their own decisions.

But is this really what children need? The truth is, children are ignorant. They look to those who have been here awhile to tell them what they should do and how to make sense of the world around them. All cultures have accepted that it is the natural state of things for adults to do these things for children. To be sure, this process has never been simple for Americans. To nurture a democratic and entrepreneurial spirit in their children, Americans have had to temper and soften these messages, to make their authority intelligible and flexible. Yet over the last thirty years, scientists, experts, teachers, advocates, the media—all of whom are supposed to give us information about what kids are really like—have been giving us a very different kind of message about what we owe our children. We should love them, they all tell us, but we shouldn't think we have much to teach them. Kids are rational, autonomous creatures. We should tell them from their earliest days, "We will give you information; you do with it as you see fit. You are a free and self-determining individual—ready or not."

Throughout the previous chapters, we have seen just how embedded these assumptions are in American culture today. Yet there is also plenty of evidence that Americans are not entirely satisfied with them. Parents are profoundly worried about their children. The sociologist Alan Wolfe found that middle-class suburbanites speak about their children and their future in terms we might expect from parents in Bosnia or Watts. Discussions about their children, who are growing up in conditions of extraordinary prosperity and safety, nevertheless "tended to bring out the language of doom-and-gloom: stress, despair, pressure, exposure—these are the words middle-class Americans use when they talk about the lives of their children."[1] This anxiety has permeated our political landscape. Politicians can barely utter a sentence without using the word *children*. For the first time in our nation's history, education has been lifted out of the domain of local politics and propelled into the national spotlight. In surveys, people reveal a deep-seated sense that their neighbors and friends are not doing well by their children. Americans may be uncertain about their role as adults, parents, and teachers, but clearly their nuturing instincts have not atrophied.

Children too appear to know something is amiss in their relationships with adults. In a variety of ways, they are sending the message that they are *not* ready—not ready for the chilly independence that is prematurely theirs, not ready to be treated as knowing peers. Surveys and anecdotal evidence alike point to their feelings of isolation and loneliness. Children speak about wanting more time from parents, and some even suggest that they need more rules. In focus groups run by children's television networks, for instance, researchers have been struck by how much today's children want to talk about their parents. When asking kids to suggest contest prizes, Betty Cohen, the president of Cartoon Network, was amazed at the number who spoke not of Disneyland or of meetings with Michael Jordan but of "spending a whole day with my Mom or Dad." When a group of children were asked about their favorite activities, some answered "quality time" with a parent—by which they meant nothing more than going to the dry cleaners or the grocery store with their mother or father. Some TV producers have begun to bring adults back into the world of children's television. Ads now show parents and children together, a longtime no-no in the children's market, and producers no longer reflexively use parents as comic buffoons and dupes. Kids are now saying that they don't like seeing their parents mocked.[2]

Even college students express longings for adult care and guidance. When she was in college in the late eighties and early nineties, Katie Roiphe noticed the butter pats stuck to the ceiling of the cafeteria and realized that she "had entered a world utterly devoid of adults." Ambivalent about "the liberating knowledge that no one cared what we did," she was startled—and comforted—when a professor noticed the circles under her eyes and suggested she might need some sleep.[3] Indeed, Roiphe was right in suspecting she had entered "a world utterly devoid of adults". After the campus upheavals of the sixties and seventies, the universities got out of the business of playing parent substitute: dorms and campus events began to go unsupervised, core curricula (and, indeed, in many places all required courses) were abandoned, and faculty cut down on their office hours. Today's students are asking that more adults take notice of the circles under their eyes. The *New York Times* recently reported that colleges are instituting "an updated and subtler version of 'in loco parentis'" in response to the new climate.[4] At the University of Wisconsin, students are clamoring to join a new residential college that integrates faculty and other adult staff and students and offers the kind of wholesome fare (such as bicycle trips, pumpkin carvings, and special dinners) that would have sent baby boomers into fits of jeering laughter. Some schools are insisting that staff members attend parties and spend time in the student dorms.

Children and teenagers unwilling or unable to tug on the sleeves of distracted and uncertain adults when they want more attention have other ways of announcing that something is missing. Educators, camp directors, and counselors talk about growing numbers of children who have difficulty getting along with their peers. Spared the nudging, consistent reminders from their caretakers to speak nicely, refrain from grabbing, or sit still, they have more difficulty controlling their impulses, becoming part of a group, and accepting limitations and rules. Educators find that an increasing number of children fail to notice other people in the most ordinary encounters. "Kids will walk right in front of you while you're talking to someone," one principal of a New York suburban middle school told me. "That's not new. What is new is that when you point it out to them, they don't know what you're talking about."[5] Struck by their students' blank insensitivity to other people's feelings, some educators have instituted courses in "emotional literacy," though these skills-oriented classes cannot offer kids the kind of marriage of love and discipline that republican theorists understood gives birth to the self-governing conscience.[6]

Many older kids, too, are expressing their neediness in destructive ways. The early autonomy granted to teenagers explains much of the increase in school discipline problems and juvenile crime; in general, such teenagers exhibit lower levels of self-restraint than their more supervised peers.[7] According to a 1996 study by Fordham University, the teen suicide rate has risen 95 percent since the early 1970s.[8] Halfway houses for more and more students with, in Arthur Levine's words, "no roots, no sense of place, and no strong relationships," college campuses are experiencing a leap in demand for their counseling services.[9] If some students are seeking out faculty-supervised dorms and campus centers, others merely give in to their untamed demons. Classroom disruption, drug abuse, binge drinking and suicide attempts on college and university campuses have all risen so much that one dean of students says his administration has turned into "a secondary social service agency." You can't send them home, another added, because "home is the problem."[10]

In a young and open society like America, however, confusion and unhappiness of this sort is not merely bad news. It is fuel for change.

The nation's optimistic faith in reason and progress may have helped launch the competent infant, the sophisticated tween, and the four-teen-year-old woman, but, paradoxically, these qualities can also help to dismantle them. It is precisely because of their own hollow experi-ence that this upcoming generation may be willing to come to a more sober understanding of American childhood. This particular genera-tion can bring to bear on their future the lesson that their own par-ents, protected and safely anchored within a stable if flawed social or-der, never had a chance to find out: that children are needy, chaotic, and confused, that they rely on adults not only to prevent them from throwing butter pats at the ceiling but to help them make meaning of the whirring events around them. In a number of recent precocious memoirs, we are beginning to hear these messages rescued from the anticultural wilderness. Though vastly different in tone, books like Elizabeth Wurtzel's *Prozac Nation,* Mayra Hornbacher's *Wasted,* and Wendy Shalit's *A Return to Modesty,* to name just a few, are all part reminiscences, part cautionary tales about growing up in a world that refuses to make order and meaning for children.

Despite their consciousness of "a culture in which adult irresponsi-bility is a fact of life,"[11] to quote Elizabeth Wurtzel, despite their wari-ness of marriage and adulthood, the emerging generation of young adults longs to bear children and to do well by them. Teenagers and postadolescents continue to cite marriage and children as their chief goal in life.[12] Those who as children suffered through their parents' divorce are known to be especially determined to protect their own children from going through the same. For the many young adults who are so frequently cynical about love, children appear to ignite the very feelings of idealistic, romantic intensity they had given up on. Even rock-and-roll artists, once the Pied Pipers of youth rebellion, have begun to sing of their babies. "Just the Two of Us," raps Will Smith, retrofitting an old love song for his five-year-old son, Justin. "I've been such a fool. I love you more than anything else in the world," says the feckless lover played by Jim Carrey in the movie *Liar Liar* after a just-in-the-nick-of-time airport reunion scene so common in romantic comedies. The surprising thing is that he is talking not to a woman but to his six-year-old son.

The persistent longing and love for children, despite diminished expectations for the permanence of marriage, exposes the crucial flaw of anticulturalism. Assured of our inviolate self-sufficiency, Americans may guard their autonomy like jealous lovers, but their desire for children suggests that human nature can be stretched only so far. The human need for deep connection and the desire to place oneself in relation to the past and the future, with all the sacrifices these entail, are bound to triumph.

Yet hopeful as this is, the longing for children and the desire to rear them well should not leave us entirely sanguine. Recapturing the purpose and meaning of childhood will not be an easy task. Rather than correcting the errors of the past, backlashes have a tendency to create new errors of their own. In the past, parents who have projected onto their young the burdensome weight of their own disappointments in love have been prone to misread the needs of their children. The next generation of children will possess their own temperaments and face a new set of social conditions, and this is likely to present a problem for those who place all their romantic hopes on them. Another danger is that parents with no cultural memory of the informal customs and manners that once restrained children's darker urges might be tempted to revert to harsher measures out of keeping with the best American traditions. There are already signs of a greater societal acceptance of such approaches. A new breed of advice givers has endorsed spanking, though freedom from physical force has always been a defining quality of republican childhood.[13] Schools have resorted to the use of guard dogs, policemen, and metal detectors. Some inner-city schools have reinstated military-style teaching methods strongly reminiscent of those used by strict turn-of-the-century schoolmarms. And the use of psychotropic drugs and Ritalin, another means of forceful control, have become commonplace. These drugs may make temperamentally impulsive or needy children behave, but they will never mold them into self-regulating, free adults.

The far greater danger for the next generation of parents is not that it will resort to a crude use of power over the young but the opposite: that it will be as uncertain about authority as its baby boomer predecessor. In fact, contriving some image of authority that will satisfy both our modern democratic sensibilities and children's needs is the greatest challenge facing future American parents. Child liberationists of the sixties and seventies were not entirely wrong when they railed against adult authority; they understood that childhood in any meaningful sense cannot exist without it. Adults must use their authority to represent a moral universe and a way of life, no matter how flexible its outlines. Today more than ever, adults will have to constrain children's fleeting urges in deference to this way of life. The task for young American parents is to recall clearly the purposes of adult authority, for, though children long for order and meaning, they also rebel against them. Such authority, it might help to remember, is only provisional. Childhood by its very nature is ephemeral. Even children know that.

The passion for equality is not the only roadblock to developing a more mature understanding of childhood. The stressful conditions of postmodern family life, which are unlikely to change any time soon, will make it hard to resist thinking of children as rational and autonomous decision makers and will reinforce an image of childhood wherein adult devotion can be purged of authority. Women are going to remain in the workforce, and many homes and neighborhoods will be empty during the day. Despite the determination of children of divorce to spare their own children, past experience suggests that they will not succeed in great numbers and that the divorce rate will remain high. The consumer ethos will urge parents to endow the opportunity to choose in matters of style and taste—what movies to watch, what books to read, what to have for dinner—with the air of high, moral principle and will make parents want to extend its privileges to young children. A highly competitive social environment will inspire parents to be overly impressed by precocious success, whether on the athletic field, at the computer, or simply on the play-date or party circuit. And, as always, children will demand to grow up fast.

Furthermore, satisfying models of authority are hard to find in our society. Popular culture continues to fill our imaginations with authority's dangers: the beer-bellied fascist cop, the nerdy, buttoned-up teacher, the buffoonish governor, the heartless CEO. Our real-life political leaders, artists, and intellectuals seem hardly better. Certainly, given their recent history, experts are more a part of the problem than the solution. And this in itself demonstrates how the problem of authority in America is in fact deeply cultural.

If we are to find any resolution to the problem of adult authority, it too must be cultural. As it happens, we do possess a cultural tradition that, while it cannot give us an exact recipe for how to behave as parents, can at the very least enrich our ongoing discussion about it. Our republican ideals remind us of the need to find a balance between our children's desires and the communal good. They allow us to recall that a sheltered childhood, protected not just from R-rated images but from the forces of the market, gives space for the individual spirit to breathe and thrive.

In other words, the republican tradition teaches the lesson that childhood can only slowly and gradually prepare the young for freedom and individual fulfillment, that freedom and individual fulfillment are a gift of cultural learning rather than of natural inheritance. And that lesson brings us face-to-face with the humbling fact that the way we love our children is never merely personal. Indeed, it is the most profoundly social thing we do.

Acknowledgments

. . . .

During these past years I've often re-
marked upon the isolation and loneliness of the writer's life. But on
looking back on what Samuel Beckett once referred to as "the siege in
the room," I realize I have been surrounded by many thoughtful and
generous allies.

Over the years many people—some mere acquaintances who didn't
deserve it—have been forced to listen to my speculations, ruminations,
and qualifications about childrearing today. It is to their forebearance
and good humor that I owe my first debt. In particular, I want to thank
my good friends Mary Claire Barton and Lillian Bayer. They listened,
but more important, with their instinctive good sense on many of the
themes of *Ready or Not,* they taught me. Cynthia Cohen-Congress has
also been an acutely intelligent listener, practical adviser, and loyal
friend.

When my older children were quite young, Ben Gerson, then an
editor at *Newsday,* suggested that some of the issues preoccupying me
were worthy of exploration in print. Little did he know what he had
unleashed! It is no exaggeration to say that this book could never have
been written had Ben not provided me with both his friendship and a
model of intellectual depth and courage. I am grateful to other friends
as well: Andy Zimbalist, Willa Appel, Barbara Iwler, Mark

Mellinger, Margaret Snow, and Lois Greenfield, who, in addition to offering support, has done the impossible by taking a photograph I can look at without wincing. I also want to thank others for more practical help: Stacey Caplow, Caroline Payson, Maggie Gallagher, Ed Craig, Gabriel Schoenfeld, Susan Arellano, Christopher Edgar, Amy Holmes, and Holly Ruff.

A number of people were kind enough to read chapters of *Ready or Not* at various stages along the way and to offer useful suggestions. Thanks to Silke Weineck, Peter Reinharz, Dennis Saffran, Gary Rosen, Myron Magnet, and James Taranto. David Blankenhorn has provided much information and help. In his position as president of the Institute for American Values, he commissioned and championed the paper that ultimately turned into chapter 7. Sections of chapter 4 also appeared in *Tikkun*.

The Manhattan Institute has given me the kind of financial support and intellectual freedom of which most writers can only dream. Larry Mone was willing to stretch the institute's usual areas of concern to accommodate my obsessions; I am enormously grateful to him for his flexibility and patience. I am also thankful to Myron Magnet for allowing me to pursue my interests in articles in *City Journal,* several of which appear in altered form in this book, as well as for his patient understanding and intelligent support when this project dragged on—and on. Mabel Weil always had an encouraging word. Andrew Hazlett and Lindsey Young have already been cheerful and insightful advocates; I look forward to working with them as this book reaches print.

My editor at The Free Press, Paul Golob, must have looked on the first draft of *Ready or Not* with a sinking heart as he realized he was going to have to teach this aging novice how to write a book. I believe he somehow managed to do that, and I am forever grateful. He has proved that his sterling reputation is well earned. His assistant, Alys Yablon, improved the book greatly by showing me how to tighten its argument and by correcting awkward and imprecise wording. Edith Lewis and her copyediting staff did a meticulous job.

My greatest blessing has been my family. Throughout a difficult time, my mother, Emily Sunstein, never failed to wield her signature—and for me, inspirational—intellect. My father, Leon Sunstein's, unquestioning support has been no less important. Paul Sunstein's enthusiasm and advice have been a very welcome source of help, especially as my energy threatened to flag. With her penetrating and wide-ranging intelligence, Silke Weineck made me think harder. Lauren Sunstein's cheerful concern always came at the right moment.

Paul Hymowitz has been the most loving, forebearing, and thoughtful of husbands. He did not ask to have this demon child of a book mess up our vacations, turn dinners into hurried leftovers, ravage our house with scribbled note cards and torn newspaper clippings, and in general leave me so distracted that I would throw out his passport with the garbage, but he never—well, almost never—complained. A psychologist by training and a comic by instinct, he kept me laughing through the stress, especially when he compared the states of mind that accompany the writing of a book to various mental impairments found in the *DSM*. I fear I gave him plenty of material.

This book is dedicated to our children, Danny, Nora, and Anna Hymowitz. I know it is not easy to live in a home where your most offhand comment, not to mention a thought that appears to arrive in your mother's brain direct from some alien commander, can send her rushing for her notebook and pencil while muttering strangely. Several years ago, Anna wrote a short story that began, "Once there was a girl and her father. Her father was not very dependable. He was a writer and was always dreaming about his book." It should go without saying that when she wrote these words, it wasn't her father who was writing a book.

Yet I hope that Anna's own loving, lively, and curious nature, like those of her older siblings, Danny and Nora, offers some proof that dreaming about my book was very much tied up with dreaming about my children. In truth, *Ready or Not* was inspired by my love for them.

N otes

Introduction: Empty Nests

1. Ellen Key, *The Century of the Child* (New York: Putnam, 1909), p. 183.
2. See, for example, Barry C. Feld, "The Transformation of the Juvenile Court," *Minnesota Law Review,* vol. 75, 1991, pp. 722–25; Janet E. Ainsworth, "Re-Imagining Childhood: Abolishing the Juvenile Court," in *Child, Parent, and State: Law and Policy Reader,* ed. Randall Humm (Philadelphia: Temple University Press, 1993).
3. "Indianapolis Student Searches Are Widened," *New York Times,* April 9, 1998, p. A18.
4. According to Ronald D. Stephens, Director of the National School Safety Center, close to 2,000 copycat attempts or threats followed the events in Littleton.
5. Joyce Abma and Freya L. Sonenstein, *Teenage Sexual Behavior and Contraceptive Use: An Update,* National Center for Health Statistics, Centers for Disease Control, and the Urban Institute, 1998. For more anecdotal evidence, see DeNeen L. Brown, "Children and Sexual Behavior," *Washington Post,* April 27, 1997, pp. B1, B8. For the prevalence of oral sex among teens, see Tamar Lewin, "Teenagers Alter Sexual Practices Thinking Risks Will Be Avoided," *New York Times,* April 5, 1997, p. 8.
6. Clifford J. Levy, "Fifth Graders Get Condoms in New Haven," *New York Times,* July 28, 1993, p. B1.

7. Jane E. Brody, "Teen-Agers and Sex: Younger and More at Risk," *New York Times,* September 15, 1998, p. F7.

8. Gina Kolata, "A Parent's Guide to Kids' Sports," *New York Times Magazine,* Part 2, April 26, 1992, pp. 12ff.

9. Dirk Johnson, "Many Schools Putting an End to Child's Play," *New York Times,* April 7, 1998, pp. A1, 18. For homework, see Michael Winerip, "Homework Bound," *New York Times,* Education Life, January 3, 1999, pp. 28ff. Winerip quotes a survey from the Institute for Social Research at the University of Michigan, which cites a tripling of time spent on homework in the elementary schools.

10. Trish Hall, "Battle of Bedtime: The Children Won," *New York Times,* March 1, 1990, p. C1.

11. Laura R. Petovello, *The Spirit That Moves Us: A Literature-Based Resource Guide: Teaching About Diversity, Prejudice, Human Rights, and the Holocaust* (Gardner, Maine: Tilbury House, 1998). Volume 1 recommends literature, including illustrated picture books about the Holocaust, for kindergarten through grade four.

12. Quoted in Jerry Adler, "Tomorrow's Child," *Newsweek,* November 2, 1998, p. 64.

13. From an interview by the author, July 1998.

14. Toy Industry Manufacturer's Factbook; Web site: www.toy-tma.com/PUBLICATIONS/factbook98/economics.html.

15. David Elkind, *The Hurried Child: Growing Up Too Fast, Too Soon* (Reading, Mass.: Addison-Wesley, 1981); Marie Winn, *Children Without Childhood* (New York: Pantheon, 1983); Neil Postman, *The Disappearance of Childhood* (New York: Delacorte Press, 1982). See also Joshua Meyerowitz, *No Sense of Place: The Impact of the Electronic Media on Social Behavior* (New York: Oxford University Press, 1985), especially the section entitled "There's No Such Thing As Children's Television."

16. Patricia Hersch, *A Tribe Apart: A Journey into the Heart of American Adolescence* (New York: Fawcett Columbine, 1998), p. 103.

17. Lyn Mikel Brown and Carol Gilligan, *Meeting at the Crossroads: Women's Psychology and Girls' Development* (New York: Ballantine Books, 1992), p. 43.

18. Carol Gilligan and Grant Wiggins, "The Origins of Morality in Early Childhood," in *The Emergence of Morality in Young Children,* ed. Jerome Kagan and Sharon Lamb (Chicago: University of Chicago Press, 1987), pp. 296–97.

19. Brown and Gilligan, pp. 86, 56.

20. Robert Coles, *The Moral Intelligence of Children* (New York: Random House, 1997), pp. 4, 172, 173. For a similarly ambivalent expert, see William Damon, *Greater Expectations: Overcoming the Culture of Indulgence in America's Homes and Schools* (New York: Free Press, 1995). The recent works of disciplinarians like James Dobson and John Rosemond are obvious exceptions.

21. James Q. Wilson, *The Moral Sense* (New York: Free Press, 1995), p. 85.

22. Peter N. Stearns, "The Role of Fear: Transitions in American Emotional Standards for Children, 1850–1950," *American Historical Review,* vol. 96, 1991, p. 71. Though it has been minimized recently, fear is the one irrationality that remains visible in contemporary American childrearing texts.

23. Anne Scott MacLeod, *American Childhood: Essays on Children's Literature of the Nineteenth and Twentieth Centuries* (Athens, Ga.: University of Georgia Press, 1994), p. 204. On Blume, see also Michelle Landsberg, *Reading for the Love of It* (Englewood Cliffs, N.J.: Prentice-Hall, 1987), pp. 210ff.

24. Donna Gelfand and Sigurdur J. Gretarsson, "Mother's Attributions Regarding Their Children's Social Behavior and Personality Characteristics," *Developmental Psychology,* vol. 24, 1988, p. 267.

25. Elkind, *The Hurried Child,* revised preface, 1988, p. xiv. For another interesting example of overcredulousness about children's understanding, see Joseph Adelson, "The Political Imagination of the Young Adolescent," in Adelson, *Inventing Adolescence: The Political Psychology of Everyday Schooling* (New Brunswick, N.J.: Transaction, 1980).

26. Jonathan Kozol, *Amazing Grace: The Lives of Children and the Conscience of a Nation* (New York: Crown, 1995), p. 84.

27. Coles, pp. 175–76.

28. "Giving Your Child a Good Start," *Newsweek* Special Edition, Spring/Summer 1997, p. 8.

29. Quoted in Jesus Sanchez, "Children's Advertising Grows Up," *Los Angeles Times,* May 29, 1990, p. 6.

30. Susan Antilla, "'I Want' Now Gets," *New York Times,* Education Supplement, April 4, 1993, p. 17.

31. Steven Shiffrin, "Government Speech," *UCLA Law Review,* vol. 27, 1980, p. 647.

32. Robert Bellah et al., *Habits of the Heart: Individualism and Commitment in American Life* (New York: Harper & Row, 1986), p. 82.

33. Kenneth J. Gergen, *The Saturated Self* (New York: Basic Books, 1991), p. 66. The number of stay-at-home mothers in 1960 comes from U.S. De-

partment of Labor, Labor Force statistics derived from *Current Population Survey,* 1948–1987, Bureau of Labor Statistics, Washington, D.C., 1988, pp. 804–5. The current figures come from unpublished Bureau of Labor statistics from the *Current Population Survey,* March 1998.

34. Hersch, p. 11.

35. Jane Gross, "After School and Before Home," *New York Times,* May 26, 1998, pp. B1, 4.

36. Figures cited in Sylvia Anne Hewlett and Cornel West, *The War Against Parents* (New York: Houghton Mifflin, 1998), pp. 49–50.

37. Victor R. Fuchs, *Women's Quest for Equality* (Cambridge: Harvard University Press, 1988), p. 111.

38. Laurence Steinberg, *Beyond the Classroom: Why School Reform Has Failed and What Parents Need to Do* (New York: Simon & Schuster, 1996).

39. Jane Jacobs, *The Death and Life of Great American Cities* (New York: Vintage, 1961), p. 82. Alan Ehrenhalt's *Lost City* (New York: Basic Books, 1995), p. 95, also nicely evokes this communal adult responsibility for children.

40. Public Agenda, *Kids These Days: What Americans Really Think About the Next Generation* (New York: Public Agenda, 1997), p. 26.

41. Ibid, p. 15.

42. Evelyn Bassoff, *Cherishing Our Daughters: How Parents Can Raise Girls to Become Strong and Loving Women* (New York: Dutton, 1998), p. 92.

43. Jane Gross, "Wall Street's Frenetic? Try Eighth Grade," *New York Times,* October 5, 1997, p. 38.

44. Interviews by the author, July 1998.

45. Jeffrey A. Butts and Howard N. Snyder, *The Youngest Delinquents: Offenders Under Age 15,* Juvenile Justice Bulletin of the Office of Juvenile Justice and Delinquency Prevention (Washington, D.C.: Department of Justice, September 1997).

46. Edward Humes, *No Matter How Loud I Shout* (New York: Simon & Schuster, 1996), p. 361.

47. Quoted in Anne Matthews, *Bright College Years: Inside the American Campus Today* (New York: Simon & Schuster, 1997), p. 91.

48. The term "emotional downsizing" comes from Arlie Hochschild, *The Time Bind: When Work Becomes Home and Home Becomes Work* (New York: Metropolitan Books/Henry Holt, 1997).

49. NICHD Network, "Child Care in the First Year," *Merrill-Palmer Quarterly,* vol. 43, July 1997, p. 355.

50. Hochschild, p. 227.

51. Children of divorced parents tend to lose a good deal of parental atten-

tion. See Judith S. Wallerstein and Sandra Blakeslee, *Second Chances: Men, Women and Children a Decade After Divorce* (New York: Ticknor & Fields, 1989). In general, single parents supervise their children less than their married counterparts. See Sara McLanahan and Gary Sandefur, *Growing Up with a Single Parent: What Hurts, What Helps* (Cambridge: Harvard University Press, 1994), especially pp. 103ff.

52. Barbara Dafoe Whitehead, *The Divorce Culture* (New York: Knopf, 1997), p. 177.

53. The numbers from 1962 come from *Current Population Reports,* pp. 20–125, U.S. Bureau of the Census, Washington, D.C., March 1962. The numbers from 1994 come from "Marital Status and Living Arrangements, 1994," *Current Population Survey,* U.S. Bureau of the Census, Washington, D.C., 1994. The number of surviving grandparents comes from "Marital Status and Living Arrangements, 1990," *Current Population Reports,* U.S. Bureau of the Census, Washington, D.C., June 1990, p. 3.

54. Cited in Hochschild, pp. 226–27.

55. Quoted in Elaine Yaffe, "Expensive, Illegal, and Wrong: Sexual Harassment in Our Schools," *Phi Delta Kappan,* vol. 77, November 1995, p. K10. See also Maria Newman, "Cautious Teachers Reluctantly Touch Less," *New York Times,* June 24, 1998, pp. B1, B9, and Bettijane Levine, "The Forbidden Touch," *Los Angeles Times,* November 18, 1993, p. E1.

56. Carin Rubenstein, "Worries About Abuse Change Camps," *New York Times,* June 9, 1994, p. C1.

57. See, for instance, Rebecca Staples New, "Parental Goals and Italian Infant Care," pp. 51–64, and Amy L. Richman, Patrice M. Miller, and Margaret Johnson Solomon, "Socialization of Infants in Suburban Boston," pp. 65–74, in *Parental Behavior in Diverse Societies,* ed. Robert A. LeVine, Patrice M. Miller, and Mary Maxwell West (San Francisco: Jossey-Bass, 1988). See also Duane Alwin, "From Childbearing to Childrearing: The Links Between Declines in Fertility and Changes in Socialization," *Population and Development Review,* Supplement, 1996, no. 22, pp. 176–96.

58. Hochschild, pp. 224, 228.

59. Peter N. Stearns, *American Cool: Constructing a Twentieth Century Emotional Style* (New York: New York University Press, 1994).

60. Sandra L. Hofferth, "Healthy Environments, Healthy Children: Children in Families," Panel Study of Income Dynamics, 1997. Web site: www.isr.umic.edu/src/child-development/timerep.html.

61. Beatrice Blyth Whiting, *Children of Different Worlds: The Formation of Social Behavior* (Cambridge: Harvard University Press, 1988), p. 274. Judith Rich Harris (*The Nurture Assumption* [New York: Free Press, 1998]), who argues that it is peer groups rather than parents who socialize kids, neglects to deal with the point that some cultures modify the power and influence of peer groups. She describes a transformation in her own personality occurring only after she moved to an unfamiliar place and spent "years of solitude, of seeking solace in books." In other words, it was only by escaping the peer group that she was able to become the inventive and ambitious girl who would go on to write a headline-grabbing book.

62. See Patricia A. Adler and Peter Adler, *Peer Power: Preadolescent Culture and Identity* (New Brunswick, N.J.: Rutgers University Press, 1998).

63. Study cited in Jacqueline L. Salmon, "Finding Time to Be a Family," *Washington Post,* National Weekly Edition, May 12, 1997, p. 31.

64. Stanley I. Greenspan with Beryl Lieff Benderly, "How Love Boosts Brainpower," *Parents,* February 1997, pp. 84–90.

65. Christopher Lasch, *The Culture of Narcissism* (New York: Warner Books, 1979), p. 30.

66. Robert D. Putnam, "Bowling Alone: America's Declining Social Capital," *Journal of Democracy,* January 1995, pp. 65–78.

67. Alan Wolfe, *One Nation After All* (New York: Viking, 1998), p. 251.

Chapter 1: The Nature Assumption

1. Rebecca Staples New, "Parental Goals and Italian Infant Care," pp. 51–64, Amy L. Richman, Patrice M. Miller, and Margaret Johnson Solomon, "Socialization of Infants in Suburban Boston," pp. 65–74, and Lois Wladis Hoffman, "Cross Cultural Differences in Childrearing Goals," pp. 99–122, in *Parental Behavior in Diverse Societies,* ed. Robert A. LeVine, Patrice M. Miller, and Mary Maxwell West (San Francisco: Jossey-Bass, 1988); Mary Ellen Goodman, *The Culture of Childhood: Child's-Eye Views of Society and Culture* (New York: Teachers College Press, 1970); Richard A. Shweder, Lene Arnett Jensen, and William M. Goldstein, "Who Sleeps by Whom Revisited: A Method for Extracting Moral Goods Implicit in Practice," in *Cultural Practices as Contexts for Development,* ed. Jacqueline J. Goodnow, Peggy J. Miller, and Frank Kessel (San Francisco: Jossey-Bass, 1995); Meredith F. Small, *Our Babies, Ourselves: How Biology and Culture Shape the Way We Par-*

ent (New York: Anchor, 1998); Robert A. Levine, "Infant Environment in Psychoanalysis: A Cross-Cultural View," in *Cultural Psychology: Essays on Comparative Human Development,* ed. James W. Stigler, Richard A. Shweder, and Gilbert Herdt (Cambridge, Cambridge University Press, 1990); Charles M. Super, Sara Harkness, Nathalie van Tijen, Ellen vander Vlugt, Marinka Fintelman, and Jarissa Dijkstra, "The Three R's of Dutch Childrearing: Socialization of Infant Arousal," and Abraham W. Wolf, Betsy Lozoff, Sara Latz, and Robert Paludetto, "Parental Theories in the Management of Young Children's Sleep in Japan, Italy, and the United States," in *Parents' Cultural Belief Systems,* ed. Sara Harkness and Charles M. Super (New York: Guilford Press, 1996). The study on touch is cited in Lawrence Kutner, "Parent and Child," *New York Times,* December 12, 1991, p. C12.

2. Suzanne Dixon, Edward Tronick, Constance Keefer, and T. Berry Brazelton, "Mother–Infant Interaction Among the Gusii of Kenya," in *Culture and Early Interactions,* ed. Tiffany M. Field, Anita M. Sostek, Peter Vietze, and P. Herbert Leiderman (Hillsdale, N.J.: Erlbaum, 1981), pp. 149–68.

3. New, pp. 51–64.

4. Quoted in Richard Rapson, "The American Child As Seen by British Travellers 1845–1935," in *The American Family in Social Historical Perspective,* ed. Michael Gordon (New York: St. Martin's Press, 1973), p. 197.

5. David Hunt, *Parents and Children in History: The Psychology of Family Life in Early Modern France* (New York: Basic Books, 1970). Hunt points out (p. 138) that Louis may have been lucky; his father, Henri IX, was known at the time as an easygoing parent.

6. Quoted in Daniel Beekman, *Mechanical Babies: A Popular History of the Theory and Practice of Childrearing* (Westport, Conn.: L. Hill, 1977), p. 56. See also Philip J. Greven, *The Protestant Temperament* (New York: Knopf, 1977).

7. Quoted in Jacqueline S. Reinier, *From Virtue to Character: American Childhood 1775–1850* (New York: Twayne, 1996), p. 43.

8. Though my description of republican childhood differs in emphasis from theirs, I have relied largely on the following: Jacqueline S. Reinier; Bernard Wishy, *The Child and the Republic: The Dawn of Modern American Child Nurture* (Philadelphia: University of Pennsylvania Press, 1968); Mary P. Ryan, *Cradle of the Middle Class: The Family in Oneida County, New York 1790–1865* (Cambridge, Mass.: Cambridge University Press, 1981); Steven Mintz, "The Family as Educator," in *Education and the American Family: Historical Trends in the So-*

cialization and the Transmission of Content Within the Home: A Research Synthesis, ed. William J. Weston (New York: New York University Press, 1989); Carl N. Degler, *At Odds: Women and the Family from the Revolution to the Present* (New York: Oxford University Press, 1980); Peter Gregg Slater, *Children in the New England Mind: In Death and in Life* (New York: Archon Books, 1977); Nancy Cott, *Bonds of Womanhood: 'Women's Sphere' in New England 1780–1835* (New Haven, Conn.: Yale University Press, 1977). For more general background on the change from old regime to modern European childrearing, I relied mostly on Edward Shorter, *The Making of the Modern Family* (New York: Basic Books, 1975), and Lawrence Stone, *Family, Sex and Marriage in England 1500–1800* (New York: Harper & Row, 1979).

9. Herman Humphrey, "Domestic Education," quoted in Degler, p. 89.

10. Horace Mann, *The Republic and the School: On the Education of Free Minds,* ed. Lawrence A. Cremin (New York: Teachers College Press, 1957), p. 50.

11. This is the mistake made by many modern academics. See especially David J. Rothman, *The Discovery of the Asylum: Social Order and Disorder in the New Republic* (Boston: Little, Brown, 1971). A more ambivalent portrait comes from Elizabeth Pleck, *Domestic Tyranny: The Making of Social Policy Against Family Violence from Colonial Times to the Present* (New York: Oxford University Press, 1987).

12. Peter Berger, Brigette Berger, and Hansfried Kellner, *The Homeless Mind: Modernization and Consciousness* (New York: Vintage, 1974), pp. 192–3.

13. Mann, p. 58.

14. Lydia Child, *The Mother's Book* (New York: Arno Press, 1972), p. 19. First published 1831.

15. Quoted in Charles Strickland, "A Transcendentalist Father: The Child-Rearing Practices of Bronson Alcott," in *Perspectives in American History,* vol. 3, 1969, p. 22.

16. Mann, p. 37.

17. John Demos, *Little Commonwealth: Family Life in Plymouth Colony* (New York: Oxford University Press, 1970), p. 133. See also Christina Hardyment, *Dream Babies: Three Centuries of Good Advice on Babies* (New York: Harper & Row, 1983), pp. 9–10. More generally, Edmund S. Morgan, *The Puritan Family: Religion and Domestic Relations in Seventeenth Century New England* (Westport, Conn.: Greenwood Press, 1986). First published 1966.

18. Small, p. 204 (see chap. 1, n. 1). By contrast, Small reports that today

only about a half of all infants are breast-fed and most of them only for about four months.

19. Quoted in *Preschool Education in America: The Culture of Young Children From the Colonial Era to the Present* (New Haven, Conn.: Yale University Press, 1995), p. 33.

20. The same tendency to limit family size is becoming apparent among middle-class married black couples today. Steven A. Holmes, "In Climb Up the Ladder, Married Blacks Are Choosing Small Families," *New York Times,* July 21, 1998, p. A10.

21. Charles Taylor, *The Ethics of Authenticity* (Cambridge: Harvard University Press, 1992), p. 26.

22. J. S. C. Abbott, "On the Mother's Role in Education," in *Child Rearing Concepts: 1628–1861,* ed. Philip Greven (Itasca, Ill.: F. E. Peacock, 1973), p. 127.

23. Jane Addams, *Twenty Years at Hull House* (New York: New American Library, 1981), p. 28. First published 1910.

24. Anne Scott MacLeod, *American Childhood: Essays on Children's Literature of the Nineteenth and Twentieth Century* (Athens, Ga.: University of Georgia Press, 1994), p. 29.

25. Quoted in MacLeod, p. 10–11. See also Elliott West, "Children on the Plains Frontier," *Small Worlds: Children and Adolescents in America 1850–1950,* ed. Elliott West and Paula Petik (Lawrence, Kans.: University of Kansas Press, 1992), pp. 26–41.

26. Catherine Beecher's *Treatise on Domestic Economy,* published in 1834, was a popular example of this harsher side.

27. Child, pp. 109, 112.

28. Ron Chernow, *Titan: The Life of John D. Rockefeller Sr.* (New York: Random House, 1998), p. 22.

29. Strickland, p. 51. It needs to be noted that even today some researchers report that American children are frequently spanked: George W. Holden and Robert J. Zambarano, "Passing the Rod: Similarities Between Parents and Their Young Children in Orientations," in *Parental Belief Systems,* ed. Irving E. Sigel, Ann V. McGillicuddy DeLisi, and Jacqueline J. Goodnow (Hillsdale, N.J.: Erlbaum, 1992), pp. 143–73.

30. Anne Scott MacLeod, pp. 131–32. Also David I. Macleod, *Building Character in the American Boy: The Boy Scouts, YMCA, and Their Forerunners 1870–1920* (Madison, Wis.: University of Wisconsin Press, 1983), pp. 4–5.

31. Emily E. Werner, *Reluctant Witnesses: Children's Voices from the Civil*

War (Boulder, Colo.: Westview Press, 1998). This continued until World War I.

32. Quoted in Joseph F. Kett, *Rites of Passage: Adolescence in America 1790 to the Present* (New York: Basic Books, 1977), p. 169.

33. Mary Ann Mason, *From Father's Property to Children's Rights: The History of Child Custody in the United States* (New York: Columbia University Press, 1994), p. 78. See also David Stern, Sandra Smith, and Fred Doolittle, "How Children Used to Work," *Law and Contemporary Problems,* vol. 39, Summer 1975, pp. 93–117.

34. William Kessen, "Discussion of Wolfgang Edelstein's Cultural Constraints on Development and the Vicissitudes of Progress," *The Child and Other Cultural Inventions,* ed. Frank S. Kessel and Alexander W. Siegel (New York: Praeger, 1983), p. 83.

35. Chernow, p. 188.

36. Beekman, p. 121 (see chap. 1, n. 6). Martha Wolfenstein, "Fun Morality: An Analysis of Recent American Child-Training Literature," in *Childhood in Contemporary Cultures,* ed. Margaret Mead and Martha Wolfenstein (Chicago: University of Chicago Press, 1955).

37. Christopher Lasch, *Haven in a Heartless World: The Family Beseiged* (New York: Basic Books, 1977), p. 6.

38. Rapson, pp. 199, 198 (see chap. 1, n. 4). Also see Alexis de Tocqueville, *Democracy in America* (New York: Vintage Classics, 1990), vol. 2, chapters 8–9; Seymour Martin Lipset, *First New Nation: The United States in Historical and Comparative Perspective* (New York: Basic Books, 1963), pp. 119ff, and Frank Furstenberg, "Industrialization and American Family: A Look Backward," *American Sociological Review,* vol. 31, June 1966, pp. 334–35.

39. Harriet Martineau, *Society in America,* ed. Seymour Martin Lipset (New Brunswick, N.J.: Transaction Press, 1968), p. 311.

40. Charlotte Gilman, *The Home: Its Work and Influence,* 1903, quoted in Lasch, p. 14. See also Miriam Van Waters, *Parents on Probation* (New York: New Republic, 1927).

41. Julian W. Mack, "The Chancery Procedure in the Juvenile Court" in *The Child, the Clinic, and the Court* (New York: New Republic, 1925; reprint, Johnson Reprint Corp., 1970), pp. 315–16.

42. John B. Watson, *The Psychological Care of Infant and Child* (New York: Norton, 1928), pp. 5, 81, 87. See also Celia B. Stendler, "Sixty Years of Child Training Practices: Revolution in the Nursery," *Pediatrics,* vol. 36, 1950, pp. 122–34.

43. There was a 650 percent increase in high school enrollment between 1900

and 1930. By that later date, 60 percent of the high-school-age population was in school. Paula S. Fass, *The Damned and the Beautiful: American Youth in the 1920s* (New York: Oxford University Press, 1977), p. 124.

44. See Steven Mintz and Susan Kellogg, *Domestic Revolutions: A Social History of American Family Life* (New York: Free Press, 1988), p. 167.

45. James Coleman's *The Adolescent Society: The Social Life of the Teenager and Its Impact on Education* (New York: Free Press, 1961) was the most prominent example.

46. See, for instance, Paul Goodman, *Growing Up Absurd* (New York: Random House, 1956); Edward Friedenberg, *The Vanishing Adolescent* (Boston: Beacon, 1959); Friedenberg, *Coming of Age in America: Growth and Acquiescence* (New York: Random House, 1965). More recently some of the same criticisms have been levied on behalf of girls; see Wini Breines, *Young, White, Miserable: Growing Up Female in the Nineteen Fifties* (Boston: Beacon, 1992).

47. Erik H. Erikson, *Identity, Youth and Crisis* (New York: Norton, 1968), especially p. 128.

48. With fewer opportunities available to them, lower-class children continued to enter the labor force and marry earlier than their middle-class counterparts. Adolescence is both a middle-class creation and a middle-class necessity. See John R. Gillis, *Youth and History: Tradition and Change in European Age Relations: 1779–Present* (New York: Academic Press, 1974); John Modell and Madeline Goodman, "Historical Perspectives," in *At the Threshold: The Developing Adolescent,* ed. S. Shirley Feldman and Glen R. Elliott (Cambridge: Harvard University Press, 1993), pp. 93–122.

49. Anthony M. Platt, *Child Savers: The Invention of Delinquency* (Chicago: University of Chicago Press, 1969), pp. 176–77. See also Steven Schlossman, *Love and the American Delinquent: The Theory and Pactice of 'Progressive' Juvenile Justice* (Chicago: University of Chicago Press, 1977); Robert M. Mennel, *Thorns and Thistles: Juvenile Delinquency in the United States 1825–1940* (Hanover, N.H.: University of New England Press, 1973).

50. F. Raymond Marks, "Detours on the Road to Maturity: A View of the Legal Conception of Growing Up and Letting Go," *Law and Contemporary Problems,* vol. 39, Summer 1975, p. 89.

51. Phillipe Ariès, *Centuries of Childhood: A Social History of Family Life,* trans. Robert Baldick (New York: Random House, 1962), p. 128. See also Ariès' "The Family and the City," *Daedalus,* Spring 1977, pp. 227–35.

52. Ariès, p. 412.

53. Ariès, pp. 328, 406.

54. See, in particular, Elizabeth Badinter, *Mother Love: Myth and Reality: Motherhood in Modern History* (New York: Macmillan, 1981), pp. 97–98, 171–73.

55. Two exceptions, both of which tend to cast doubt on Ariès' thesis, are James A. Schultz, *The Knowledge of Childhood in the German Middle Ages 1100–1350* (Philadelphia: University of Pennsylvania Press, 1995); Shulamith Shahar, *Children in the Middle Ages* (New York: Routledge, 1990).

56. Margaret Mead, *Coming of Age in Samoa: A Psychological Study of Primitive Youth for Western Civilization* (New York: New American Library, 1963), p. 23. For the dispute over Mead's optimistic findings about the easy life of Samoan adolescents, see Derek Freeman, *Margaret Mead and Samoa: The Making and Unmaking of an Anthropological Myth* (Cambridge: Harvard University Press, 1983); Lowell D. Holmes, *Quest for the Real Samoa: The Mead/Freeman Controversy and Beyond* (South Hadley, Mass.: Bergin and Garvey, 1987); Donald Brown, *Human Universals* (Philadelphia: Temple University Press, 1991).

57. Hunt, pp. 162ff. (See chap. 1, n. 5).

58. Richard Farson, *Birthrights* (New York: Macmillian, 1974), p. 146; Shulamith Firestone, *The Dialectic of Sex: The Case for Feminist Revolution* (New York: Morrow, 1970), p. 222.

59. Jenny Kitzinger, "Defending Innocence: Ideologies of Childhood," *Feminist Review,* vol. 28, January 1988, pp. 77–87.

60. David Gottlieb, "Children as Victims," in *Children's Liberation,* ed. David Gottlieb (Englewood Cliffs, N.J.: Prentice-Hall, 1973), p. 29.

61. Tocqueville, p. 195.

62. Paul Adams, "The Infant, the Family and Society," *Children's Rights,* ed. Paul Adams et al. (New York: Praeger, 1971), p. 52.

63. R. D. Laing, *The Politics of Experience* (New York: Ballantine Books, 1967), p. 58.

64. See, for instance, Arlene Skolnick and Jerome H. Skolnick, "Rethinking the Family," in *Family in Transition: Rethinking Marriage, Sexuality, Childrearing, and Family Organization,* ed. Arlene Skolnick and Jerome H. Skolnick (Boston: Little, Brown, 1971), who argue that the nuclear family's isolation enhances parental power and is therefore responsible for an increase in the incidence of abuse. As should be clear from the preceding discussion, the way parental power is wielded is less a function of family structure than of cultural attitudes toward children. Still, recent evidence in our own society suggests that the nuclear family, in

contrast to stepfamilies and single-parent families, is the safest for children (although a certain amount of abuse is inevitable), the exact opposite of what liberationists of the sixties and seventies promised. See a summary of the literature in David Popenoe, *Life Without Father* (New York: Martin Kessler Books/Free Press, 1996), pp. 65–74.

65. Firestone, p. 117.

66. From a pamphlet by the organization Women Against Rape (WAR), quoted in Jill Duerr Berrick and Neil Gilbert, *With the Best of Intentions: The Child Sexual Abuse Prevention Movement* (New York: Guilford Press, 1991), pp. 10–11.

67. Kitzinger, p. 82. See also Howard Cohen, *Equal Rights for Children* (New York: Littlefield, Adams, 1980), p. 151, where he refers to the "ideology of child protection."

68. Christopher Lasch, *The Revolt of the Elites and the Betrayal of Democracy* (New York: Norton, 1995), p. 155. For the critique of the common school movement, see, among others, Raymond E. Callahan, *Education and the Cult of Efficiency* (Chicago: University of Chicago Press, 1962); Michael J. Katz, *The Irony of Early School Reform: Class, Bureaucracy and Schools* (Cambridge: Harvard University Press, 1968); Colin Greer, *The Great School Legend* (New York: Basic Books, 1972); Joel H. Spring, *Education and the Rise of the Corporate State* (Boston: Beacon Press, 1972).

69. Farson, p. 96. Using Ariès to bolster his argument, Ivan Illich in *Deschooling Society* (New York: Harper & Row, 1971) argues that no matter how progressive the classroom, it is still unsatisfactory because still compulsory.

70. Craig Haney and Philip G. Zimbardo, "The Blackboard Pentitentiary: It's Tough to Tell a High School from a Prison," *Psychology Today,* June 1975, pp. 26ff.

71. Gary B. Melton, "The Clashing of Symbols: Prelude to Child and Family Policy," *American Psychologist,* vol. 42, April 1987, p. 345.

72. Hillary Rodham, "Children Under the Law," *Harvard Education Review,* vol. 43, November 1973, p. 507; Rodham, "Children's Rights: A Legal Perspective," in *Children's Rights: Contemporary Perspectives,* ed. Patricia A. Vardin and Ilene N. Brody (New York: Teachers College Press, 1979), p. 26.

73. Lawrence H. Tribe, "Childhood, Suspect Classifications and Conclusive Presumptions: Three Linked Riddles," *Law and Contemporary Problems,* vol. 39, Summer 1975, pp. 8–37.

74. Quoted in Bruce C. Hafen, "Exploring Test Cases in Child Advo-

cacy," *Harvard Law Review,* vol. 100, 1986, p. 447. In the same spirit, Justice William O. Douglas in his 1967 dissent in *Ginsberg v. New York,* 390 U.S. 654, concerning the legality of selling pornography to minors, did not merely reject the constitutionality of blocking such sales but scoffed at the very idea, condemning the word "protection" to mocking quotation marks. For other examples, see Bruce C. Hafen, "Children's Liberation and the New Egalitarianism," *Brigham Young Law Review,* vol. 1976, pp. 605, 651, nn. 146–47.

75. See some of the essays in *Kinderculture: The Corporate Construction of Childhood,* ed. Shirley R. Steinberg and Joe L. Kincheloe (Boulder, Colo.: Westview Press, 1997) and Kieran Bonner, *Power and Parenting: A Hermeneutic of the Human Condition* (New York: St. Martin's Press, 1998).

76. Dominick Cavallo, *Muscles and Morals: Organized Playgrounds and Urban Reform 1880–1920* (Philadelphia: University of Pennsylvania Press, 1981).

77. See, for instance, Diana M. Pearce, "Children Having Children: Teenage Pregnancy and Public Policy from the Women's Perspective," in *The Politics of Pregnancy: Adolescent Sexuality and Public Policy,* ed. Annette Lawson and Deborah L. Rhode (New Haven, Conn.: Yale University Press, 1993), who calls for "affirming women who have chosen to be sexually active, an implicit acknowledgement of their status as adults in this sphere" (pp. 55–56), and Anne Murcott, "The Social Construction of Teenage Pregnancy: A Problem in the Ideologies of Childhood and Reproduction," in *Sociology of Health and Illness,* vol. 2, 1986, pp. 1–19. On incest, see Farson, p. 148, and Benjamin deMott, "The Pro-Incest Lobby," *Psychology Today,* March 13, 1980, pp. 11–16.

78. Maria Tatar, *Off with Their Heads: Fairy Tales and the Culture of Childhood* (Princeton, N.J.: Princeton University Press, 1992), p. 236. See also Jack Zipes, *Happily Ever After: Fairy Tales, Children, and the Culture Industry* (New York: Routledge Press, 1997).

79. Thomas Sowell, "Abolish Adolescence," *New York Post,* May 1, 1998. For the corresponding liberal position, see James E. Coté and Anton L. Allahar, *Generation on Hold: Coming of Age in the Late Twentieth Century* (New York: New York University Press, 1994).

80. Alfred Regnery, "Getting Away with Murder: Why the Juvenile Justice System Needs an Overhaul," *Policy Review,* vol. 34, Fall 1985, pp. 65–69. Janet E. Ainsworth, in "Re-Imagining Childhood: Abolishing the Juvenile Court," in *Child, Parent, and State: Law and Policy Reader,* ed. Randall Humm (Philadelphia: Temple University Press, 1994), and

Marvin E. Wolfgang, in "Abolish the Juvenile Court System," *California Lawyer,* vol. 2, November, 1982, pp. 12ff., argue the point from a different perspective. See also Victor L. Streib, "Perspectives on the Juvenile Death Penalty in the 1990's," also in *Child, Parent, and State.*

81. Laura Mansnerus, "Treating Teen-Agers as Adults in Court: A Trend Born of Revulsion," *New York Times,* December 3, 1993, p. B7. Illinois data from *Justice for Youth: Guide to the Juvenile Justice System,* cited in William Ayers, *A Kind and Just Parent: The Children of the Juvenile Court* (Boston: Beacon Press, 1997), p. 32.

82. Sam Howe Verhovek, "Texas Legislator Proposes the Death Penalty for Murderer as Young as 11," *New York Times,* April 18, 1998, p. A7.

83. Lisa Vickery, "Playpens Are Out, and Junior Is, Too," *Wall Street Journal,* October 10, 1996, pp. B1, 13.

Chapter 2: Baby Geniuses

1. Kevin Sack, "Georgia's Governor Seeks Musical Start for Babies," *New York Times,* January 15, 1998, p. A12. Apparently, the state of Michigan has also mandated the distribution of classical CDs to all families of newborn babies. See Ellen Winner and Lois Hetland, "Mozart and the S.A.T.'s," *New York Times,* March 4, 1999, p. A25.

2. Mark Singer, "Mom Overboard!" *New Yorker,* February 26 and March 4, 1996, p. 68. Also see Stephen S. Hall, "Test-Tube Moms," *New York Times Magazine,* April 5, 1998, p. 22.

3. William Kessen, "The Child and Other Cultural Inventions," in *The Child and Other Cultural Inventions,* ed. Frank S. Kessel and Alexander W. Siegel (New York: Praeger, 1983), p. 28. This volume contains a number of provocative articles on the cultural bias of developmental psychologists, several of them recounted in this chapter. I was also influenced by Ben S. Bradley, "Infancy as Paradise," *Human Development,* vol. 34, 1991, pp. 35–54; Cathy Unwin, "Developmental Psychology and Psychoanalysis: Splitting the Difference," in *Children of Social Worlds,* ed. Martin Richards and Paul Light (Cambridge: Harvard University Press, 1986); Stanley I. Greenspan, *The Growth of the Mind: The Endangered Origins of Intelligence* (Reading, Mass.: Addison-Wesley, 1997); Erica Burman, "Developmental Psychology and the Postmodern Child," in *Postmodernism and the Social Sciences,* ed. Joe Doherty, Espeth Graham, and Mo Malek (New York: St. Martin's Press, 1992); Jerome Bruner, *Acts of Meaning* (Cambridge: Harvard University Press, 1990); Adrienne E. Harris, "The Rationalization of

Infancy," in *Critical Theories of Psychological Development,* ed. John M. Broughton (New York: Plenum Press, 1987).

4. Quoted in Willard Gaylin and Bruce Jennings, *The Perversion of Autonomy* (New York: Free Press, 1996), p. 111.

5. Stephen Jay Gould, "Human Babies as Embryos," in *In the Beginning: Readings on Infancy,* ed. Jay Belsky (New York: Columbia University Press, 1982), p. 10.

6. Mary Ann Pulaski, *Your Baby's Mind: Piaget for Parents,* quoted in Christina Hardyment, *Dream Babies: Child Care from Locke to Spock* (London: Jonathan Cape, 1983), p. 273.

7. R. Baillargeon, "Object Permanence in 3½- to 4½-Months-Old Infants," *Developmental Psychology,* vol. 23, 1987, pp. 655–64. A more recent study—Susan M. Rivera, Ann Wakeley, and Jonas Langer, "The Drawbridge Phenomenon: Representational Reasoning or Perceptual Preference?" *Developmental Psychology,* vol. 35, 1999, pp. 427–35—illustrates the haste with which some scientists have attributed unrealistic powers to infants. Baillargeon had placed his infant subjects in front of a movable screen with an object behind it; when he moved the screen, it was stopped by the object. The babies sucked more vigorously on their pacifiers when the object was removed and the screen kept going, thus, he believed, demonstrating surprise that the object was no longer there. Rivera, Wakeley, and Langer make the more reasonable suggestion that the babies were merely stimulated by the continuing movement of the screen.

8. Michael Lewis and Jeanne Brooks, "Infants' Social Perception: A Constructivist View," *Infant Perception: From Sensation to Cognition: Vol 2. Perception of Space, Speech and Sound* (New York: Academic Press, 1975), pp. 101–48.

9. A. N. Meltzoff, M. K. Moore, "Imitation of Facial and Manual Gestures by Human Neonates," *Science,* vol. 198, 1977, pp. 75–78.

10. Study cited in Maya Pines, "Baby You're Incredible!" *Psychology Today,* February 1982, p. 50.

11. R. N. Aslin, D. B. Pisoni, and P. W. Jusezyk, "Auditory Development and Speech Perception in Infancy," in *Handbook of Child Psychology: Vol 2. Infancy and Developmental Psychobiology,* ed. M. M. Haith and J. J. Campos (New York: Wiley, 1983).

12. L. Joseph Stone, Henrietta T. Smith, and Lois B. Murphy, eds., *The Competent Infant: Research and Commentary* (New York: Basic Books, 1973), pp. 3, 4.

13. Daniel Goleman, "Study Finds Babies at Five Months Grasp Simple Mathematics," *New York Times,* August 27, 1992, p. A1.

14. Tiffany Field, *Infancy* (Cambridge: Harvard University Press, 1990).

15. A. J. DeCasper and M. J. Spence, "Prenatal Maternal Speech Influences Newborns' Perception of Speech Sounds," *Infant Behavior and Development,* vol. 9, 1986, pp. 135–50.

16. T. G. R. Bower, *The Rational Infant* (New York: Freeman, 1989), pp. 93–94, 152.

17. Alison Gopnik and Andrew N. Meltzoff, *Words, Thoughts, and Theories* (Cambridge: MIT Press, 1997), p. 23.

18. Pines.

19. Lewis P. Lipsitt, "Babies: They're a Lot Smarter Than They Look," *Psychology Today,* December 1971, p. 71.

20. Peggy Estman, *Your Child Is Smarter Than You Think* (New York: Morrow, 1985), p. 3.

21. Steven Pinker, *The Language Instinct* (New York: Harper Perennial, 1995), p. 276. See also Lisa Grunwald, "The Amazing Minds of Infants," *Life,* July 1993, pp. 46–58.

22. Art Ulene and Steven Shelov, *Discovery Play: Loving and Learning with Your Baby* (Berkeley, Calif.: Ulysses Press, 1994), p. 16.

23. Meredith F. Small, *Our Babies, Ourselves: How Biology and Culture Shape the Way We Parent* (New York: Anchor Books, 1998), p. 166.

24. Quoted in Bower, p. 15.

25. Pines, p. 50.

26. Kenneth Kaye, *Mental and Social Life of Babies: How Parents Create Persons* (Chicago: University of Chicago Press, 1982), pp. 80–81. See also Barbara Rogoff, *Apprenticeship in Thinking: Cognitive Development in a Social Context* (New York: Oxford University Press, 1990).

27. Lev Vygotsky, *Mind in Society: The Development of Higher Psychological Processes,* ed. Michael Cole et al. (Cambridge: Harvard University Press, 1978), p. 56.

28. Bruner, p. 71 (see chap. 2, n. 3). See also the essays in Bambi B. Schieffelin and Eleanor Ochs, eds., *Language Socialization Across Cultures,* (New York: Cambridge University Press, 1986).

29. H. J. Cummins, "What's on a Baby's Mind?" *Minneapolis Star Tribune,* August 27, 1997, p. 6A.

30. Bradley, p. 37 (see chap. 3, n. 3).

31. Alice H. Putnam, "What Should Our Children See?" *Kindergarten Review,* 1888, quoted in Alexander W. Siegel and Sheldon White, *Ad-*

vances in Child Development and Psychology, Vol. 17, ed. Hayne W. Reese (New York: Academic Press, 1987), p. 275.

32. Benjamin Spock and Michael B. Rothenberg, *Dr. Spock's Baby and Child Care,* rev. ed. (New York: Pocket Books, 1992), p. 11.

33. Michael Zuckerman, "Dr. Spock: The Confidence Man," in *The Family in History,* ed. Charles Rosenberg (Philadelphia: University of Pennsylvania Press, 1975), pp. 179–207.

34. Donald E. Brown, *Human Universals* (Philadelphia: Temple University Press, 1991), p. 136.

35. Spock, p. 182. Also see Judith Modell, "Adoption Literature and Dr. Spock," in *Emotion and Social Change: Towards a New Psychohistory,* ed. Carol Z. Stearns and Peter N. Stearns (New York: Holmes and Meier, 1988), pp. 151–91.

36. Penelope Leach, *Your Baby and Child: From Birth to Age Five* (New York: Knopf, 1977), p. 288. Spock (pp. 395–97) made famous an experiment by the nutritionist Clara Davis which purported to prove that babies would choose a well-balanced diet over time if given a range of healthy foods.

37. Spock, p. 11.

38. Luther Emmett Holt, *Care and Feeding of Children* (New York: D. Appleton, 1923), p. 156. For a general discussion of ideas about toilet training, see Nancy Pottisham Weiss, "Mother–Child Dyad Revisited," *Journal of Social Issues,* vol. 34, 1978, pp. 29–45.

39. Quoted in Celia B. Stendler, "Sixty Years of Child Training Practices: Revolution in the Nursery," *Pediatrics,* vol. 36, January 1950, pp. 132–33. The government pamphlet *Infant Care,* distributed by the Children's Bureau in the 1910s, also recommended this approach; see Molly Ladd-Taylor, ed., *Raising a Baby the Government Way* (Brunswick, N.J.: Rutgers University Press, 1986), p. 39. For the mother's view, see Anna G. Noyles, *How I Kept My Baby Well* (Baltimore: Warwick and York, 1913).

40. Erik H. Erikson, *Childhood and Society,* 2nd ed. (New York: Norton, 1963), p. 81.

41. Selma Fraiberg, *The Magic Years: Understanding and Handling the Problems of Early Childhood* (New York: Scribner's, 1959), p. 94.

42. Spock, p. 462.

43. Arlene Eisenberg, Heidi E. Murkoff, and Sandee E. Hathaway, *What to Expect the Toddler Years* (New York: Workman, 1994), p. 539.

44. Erica Goode, "Two Experts Do Battle over Potty Training," *New York Times,* January 12, 1999, p. A1. Also see research quoted in Robert R.

Sears, Eleanor E. Maccoby, Harry Levin, *Patterns of Child Rearing* (New York: Harper & Row, 1957), p. 109.

45. Sara Harkness, Charles M. Super, and Constance H. Keefer, "Learning to Be an American Parent," in *Human Motives and Cultural Models,* ed. Roy G. D'Andrade and Claudia Strauss (New York: Cambridge University Press, 1992), pp. 163–178, discuss the tendency of American parents to explain their child's difficult behavior as a result of a "stage." Jacqueline J. Goodnow and W. Andrew Collins, *Development According to Parents* (Hillsdale, N.J.: Erlbaum, 1990), also find that parents see desirable behaviors like friendliness and generosity as part of the child's temperament and consider undesirable behaviors like rudeness and fussiness to be the result of a stage or a difficult situation. In a similar vein, the American Psychological Association says, "Violence is a learned behavior." See "APA Campaign Seeks to Prevent Violence Among Children," *APA Monitor,* vol. 28, June 1997, p. 46

46. Penelope Leach, *Your Baby and Child: From Birth to Five* (New York: Knopf, 1988), p. 325.

47. Leach, p. 318.

48. T. Berry Brazelton, *Toddlers and Parents: A Declaration of Independence* (New York: Dell, 1974), p. 102. Brazelton also views the tantrum as a sign of the young child's "inner turmoil" (p. 20).

49. Leach, pp. 223–24.

50. Alison Clarke-Stewart, "Infant Day Care: Maligned or Malignant?" *American Psychologist,* vol. 44, February 1989, p. 269.

51. Lyn Mikel Brown and Carol Gilligan, *Meeting at the Crossroads: Women's Psychology and Girls' Development* (New York: Ballantine Books, 1993), p. 88.

52. Eisenberg, Murkoff, and Hathaway, *What to Expect the Toddler Years,* p. 130.

53. Spock, p. 424.

54. William Damon, *The Moral Child* (New York: Free Press, 1988), p. 14.

55. Martin L. Hoffman, "Empathy, Its Limitation, and Its Role in Comprehensive Moral Theory," in *Morality, Moral Behavior, and Moral Development,* ed. William M. Kurtines and Jacob L. Gurwitz (New York: Wiley, 1984), p. 290. See also Hoffman, "Empathy, Social Cognition, and Moral Education," in *Approaches to Moral Development: New Research and Emerging Themes,* ed. Andrew Garrod (New York: Teachers College Press, 1993), pp. 151–179.

56. Hoffman, "Empathy, Its Limitation and Its Role," p. 289.

57. Leach, p. 436.

58. William Damon, *Greater Expectations: Overcoming the Culture of Indulgence in America's Homes and Schools* (New York: Free Press, 1995).

59. Arlene Eisenberg, Heidi E. Murkoff, and Sandee E. Hathaway, *What to Expect the First Year* (New York: Workman, 1989), p. 164.

60. Leach, p. 323.

61. Eisenberg, Murkoff, and Hathaway, *What to Expect the Toddler Years,* p. 126.

62. Susan Ludington-Hoe, *How to Have a Smarter Baby* (New York: Rawson Associates, 1985), pp. 5–6.

63. This example and others are in Jean Grasso Fitzpatrick, *Superbaby Syndrome: Escaping the Dangers of Hurrying Your Child* (San Diego: Harcourt Brace Jovanovich, 1988), pp. 5–6.

64. Eisenberg, Murkoff, and Hathaway, *What to Expect the First Year,* p. 160.

65. Sharon Begley, "How to Build a Baby's Brain," *Newsweek* Special Issue: "Your Child," Fall 1998, p. 28.

66. William Caudel, "Tiny Dramas: Vocal Communication Between Mother and Infant in Japanese and American Families," in *Childhood Socialization,* ed. Gerald Handel (New York: Aldine De Gruyler, 1988), p. 67.

67. Estman, pp. 158ff. (see chap. 3, n. 20).

68. See Brian Sutton-Smith, *Toys as Culture* (New York: Gardner Press, 1986).

69. Estman, p. 114.

70. Daniel Glick, "Rooting for Intelligence," *Newsweek* Special Issue: "Your Child," Fall 1998, p. 32.

71. Judith Rich Harris, *The Nurture Assumption: Why Children Turn Out the Way They Do: Parents Matter Less Than You Think and Peers Matter More* (New York: Free Press, 1998), p. 317.

72. Web site: www.iamyourchild.org. Click on the link *Brain Facts.* See also Stanley I. Greenspan with Beryl Lieff Benderly, "How Love Boosts Brainpower," *Parents,* February 1997, pp. 84–90.

73. Julius Segal and Zelda Segal, *Growing Up Smart and Happy* (New York: McGraw-Hill, 1985), p. 37.

74. Kathryn T. Young, "American Conceptions of Infant Development from 1955 to 1984: What the Experts are Telling Parents," *Child Development,* vol. 61, 1990, pp. 21–24.

75. See, for instance, Diane Eyer, *Motherguilt: How Culture Blames Mothers for What's Wrong with Society* (New York: Times Books, 1996), chapter 3.

76. Sandra Blakeslee, "Studies Show Talking with Infants Shapes Basis of Ability to Think," *New York Times,* April 17, 1997, p. D21.

77. Carol Lawson, "Studying Vivaldi and Art in Diapers," *New York Times,* November 2, 1989, p. C1. Harold W. Stevenson and James W. Stigler, *The Learning Gap: Why Our Schools Are Failing and What We Can Learn from Japanese and Chinese Education* (New York: Simon & Schuster, 1992), pp. 78–79, found that American kindergartners and preschoolers are far more likely to be engaging in academic work than are their Japanese and Chinese peers, who are learning to adapt to group life after an indulged infancy.

78. Blakeslee. Interestingly, the same logic was behind Head Start and *Sesame Street* in the late 1960s: proposals for these projects quoted Piaget extensively and lamented that the child's "brain had been ignored, always, by the traditionalists in favor of his emotional and physical development" (Joan Gantz Cooney, quoted in Richard M. Polsky, *Getting to Sesame Street* [New York: Praeger, 1974], p. 9). Also see David Elkind, *Miseducation: Preschoolers at Risk* (New York: Knopf, 1987); Edward Zigler and Susan Muenchow, *Head Start: The Inside Story of America's Most Successful Educational Experiment* (New York: Basic Books, 1992).

79. *Who's Minding Our Preschoolers?* Current Population Reports Series 70, no. 53 (Washington, D.C.: Bureau of the Census, 1996).

80. Tamar Lewin, "The Struggle for Personal Attention in Day Care," *New York Times,* April 27, 1998, p. A1. For a similar critique of day care in Sweden see Rita Liljestrom, "The Public Child, the Commercial Child, and Our Child," in *The Child and Other Cultural Inventions,* pp. 139–40 (see chap. 2, n. 3).

81. Margaret Mead, *Male and Female: A Study of the Sexes in a Changing World* (New York: Morrow, 1949), pp. 118–19. Mead concluded that "there is no place in Samoa for the man or woman capable of great passion, of complicated aesthetic feeling, of deep religious devotion."

82. Eleanor Reynolds, "Waiting to Grow," *Tikkun,* January 11, 1997, pp. 48–49.

83. See Jay Belsky, "A Deconstructionist View," in *Child Care in the 1990's,* ed. Alan Booth (Hillsdale, N.J.: Erlbaum, 1992), pp. 83–94.

84. Quoted in Small, p. 35 (see chap. 2, n. 23).

85. Stephen J. Ceci and Maggie Brick, "The Suggestibility of the Child Witness: A Historical Review," *Psychological Bulletin,* vol. 113, 1993, p. 419. See also Maggie Brick, Stephen J. Ceci, Emmett Francoeur, and Ronald Barr, "I Hardly Cried When I Got My Shot," *Child Development,* vol. 66,

1995, pp. 193–208. Gary L. Wells, John W. Turtle, and C. A. Elizabeth Luftus, "The Perceived Credibility of Child Eyewitnesses: What Happens When They Use Their Own Words," in *Perspectives in Children's Testimony,* ed. Stephen J. Ceci, David F. Ross, and Michael P. Toglia (New York: Springer-Verlag, 1989), p. 30, find that when they are misleadingly questioned by adults (and, to a lesser extent, by older children), even eight-year-olds remain only tenuously attached to their own perceptions. The point isn't so much that young children want to please adults, as some have suggested, but that they expect adults to have access to the truth. See Anne Graffam Walker, *Handbook on Questioning Children: A Linguistic Perspective* (Washington, D.C.: ABA Center on Children and the Law, 1994), p. 37 ("Young children tend to believe that adults know everything, that adults are right about things . . ."). See also the articles in John Doris, ed., *Suggestibility of Children's Recollections,* (Washington, D.C.: American Psychological Association, 1991).

86. Stephen Ceci and Maggie Brick, *Jeopardy in the Courtroom: A Scientific Analysis of Children's Testimony* (Washington D.C.; American Psychological Association, 1995), give the best overview of the important day care abuse cases. See also Paul Eberle and Shirley Eberle, *Abuse of Innocence: The McMartin Preschool Trial* (Buffalo, N.Y.: Prometheus Books, 1993); John Crewsden, *By Silence Betrayed: Sexual Abuse of Children in America* (Boston: Little, Brown, 1988).

87. *Jeopardy in the Courtroom* contains many such examples.

88. Quoted in Richard Wexler, *Wounded Innocents: The Real Victims in the War Against Child Abuse* (Buffalo, N.Y.: Prometheus Books, 1990), p. 150. Wexler notes that in 1936 a committee for the American Bar Association recommended psychiatric examinations in abuse cases because children are so influenced by their "erotic imagination." In 1988, in keeping with the rise of the notion of the competent infant, the ABA committee changed course, arguing that children should be believed because they don't lie. Gary B. Melton, "Children as Partners for Justice: Next Steps for Developmentalists," *Monographs of the Society for Research in Child Development,* vol. 57 (5, Serial No. 229), gives support to their position.

89. The anthropologist Roy D'Andrade estimates that for every scholar studying how children absorb cultural meanings from those around them there are twenty studying individual "cognitive processing questions." See D'Andrade, "The Culture Part of Cognition," *Cognitive Science,* 1981, p. 193.

90. Richard A. Shweder, Manamohan Mahapatra, and Joan G. Miller,

"Culture and Moral Development," in *Cultural Psychology: Essays on Comparative Human Development,* ed. James W. Stigler, Richard A. Shweder, and Gilbert Herdt (New York: Cambridge University Press, 1990), pp. 130–204, find that five-year-old American children already have a "highly developed" idea of personal liberty, an idea more or less unknown to Indian children. William Caudill and Harold Weinstein, "Maternal Care and Infant Behavior in Japan and America," *Psychiatry,* vol. 32, 1969, pp. 12–43, argue that American children are more active and irritable by three or four months, an entirely plausible idea given how differently they are treated in their early weeks.

Chapter 3: Anticultural Education

1. Sol Stern, "My Public School Lesson," *City Journal,* vol. 7, Autumn 1997, pp. 14–29.
2. Howard Gardner, *The Unschooled Mind: How Children Learn and How Schools Should Teach* (New York: Basic Books, 1991), p. 110.
3. John T. Bruer, *Schools for Thought: A Science of Learning in the Classroom* (Cambridge: MIT Press, 1993), p. 2.
4. Sidney Hook, *Out of Step: An Unquiet Life in the Twentieth Century* (New York: Harper & Row, 1987), p. 11.
5. Alfred North Whitehead, "The Rhythmic Claims of Freedom and Discipline," in Whitehead, *The Aims of Education and Other Essays* (New York: Free Press, 1967), p. 33. First published 1929.
6. Quoted in Karen Deigmueller, "A War of Words: Whole Language Under Siege," *Education Week,* March 20, 1996, p. 2.
7. See, for instance, John T. Bruer; Lauren B. Resnick, *Education and Learning to Think* (Washington D.C.: National Academy Press, 1987); Adrian F. Ashma and Robert N. F. Conway, *An Introduction to Cognitive Education: Theory and Applications* (New York: Routledge, 1997); Arthur L. Costa, ed., *Developing Minds: A Resource Book for Teaching Thinking* (Alexandria, Va.: Association for Supervision and Curriculum Development, 1985); Cathy Collings and John N. Mangieri, eds., *Teaching Thinking: An Agenda for the Twenty-first Century* (Hillsdale, N.J.: Erlbaum, 1992); Learner-Centered Principles Work group, *Learner-Centered Psychological Principles: A Framework for School Reform and Redesign* (Washington, D.C.: American Psychological Association, 1997). For a more measured view of natural mathematical abilities, see David C. Geary, "Reflections of Evolution and Culture in Children's Cognition," *American Psychologist,* vol. 50, January 1995, pp. 24–30.

8. Bruer, p. 21.

9. National Council of Teachers of Mathematics, *Curriculum and Evaluation Standards for School Mathematics* (Reston, Va.: National Council of Teachers of Mathematics, 1985), p. 5.

10. Joseph J. Tobin, David Y. H. Wu, and Dana H. Davidson, *Preschool in Three Cultures: Japan, China and the United States* (New Haven, Conn.: Yale University Press, 1989), p. 140.

11. International Reading Association and National Council of Teachers of English, *Standards for the English Language Arts* (International Reading Association and National Council of Teachers of English, 1996), p. 66.

12. Arthur G. Powell, Eleanor Farrar, and David K. Cohen, *Shopping Mall High School: Winners and Losers in the Education Market Place* (Boston: Houghton Mifflin, 1985), p. 39. This philosophy picked up steam in the early seventies. David Nyberg and Kieran Egan, *The Erosion of Education: Socialization and the Schools* (New York: Teachers College Press, 1981), studied forty-three Massachusetts high schools between 1971 and 1976 and found a 50 percent increase in English courses offered as electives, including many on film, television, and science fiction. See also Philip A. Cusick, *The Egalitarian Ideal and the American High School* (New York: Longman Press, 1983), p. 69.

13. Teresa M. Amabile, *Growing Up Creative* (New York: Crown, 1989), pp. 141–42.

14. Gardner, p. 243.

15. Edward B. Fiske, *Smart Schools, Smart Kids* (New York: Simon & Schuster, 1991), p. 123.

16. Anthony DePalma, "Report Cards: Some Say There Must Be a Better Way," *New York Times,* December 9, 1992, p. B13.

17. Vera John-Steiner, *Notebooks of the Mind: Explorations of Thinking* (Albuquerque: University of New Mexico Press, 1985), p. 38.

18. See Geary, who argues that only "strong cultural values that reward mathematical development" and sustained practice will lead children beyond the most basic geometric awareness and that the idea that children happily construct their own knowledge "is largely a reflection of current American cultural beliefs" (p. 32).

19. John Dewey, *School and Society,* ed. Jo Ann Boydston (Carbondale, Ill.: Southern Illinois University Press, 1976), pp. 29–30. First published 1899.

20. My interpretation of Dewey owes much to Robert B. Westbrook, *John Dewey and American Democracy* (Ithaca, N.Y.: Cornell University Press, 1991).

21. According to Richard Hofstadter, *Anti-Intellectualism in American Life* (New York: Vintage, 1963), pp. 359–388, Dewey's ideas began to make mischief with American education almost as soon as they were published.

22. Powell, Farrar, and Cohen.

23. "Taking a Look at a High/Scope Elementary Program," *High/Scope Resource,* Winter 1998, p. 4.

24. George H. Wood, *Schools That Work: America's Most Innovative Public Education Programs* (New York: Dutton, 1992), pp. 155–56.

25. David Perkins, *Smart Schools: From Training Memories to Educating Minds* (New York: Free Press, 1992), p. 61.

26. "Introduction," in *Constructivism in Practice: Designing, Thinking, and Learning in a Digital World,* ed. Yasmin Kafai and Mitchel Resnick (Mahwah, N.J.: Erlbaum, 1996), p. 1.

27. Steve Farkas and Jean Johnson, *Different Drummers: How Teachers of Teachers View Public Education* (New York: Public Agenda, 1997), p. 11.

28. Seymour Papert, *The Children's Machine: Rethinking School in the Age of the Computer* (New York: Basic Books, 1993), p. 67.

29. Lynda Richardson, "Practices of Japanese Business Find a Home in a Brooklyn High School," *New York Times,* December 7, 1994, p. B12.

30. Barry Farber, *Crisis in Education: Stress and Burnout in the American Teacher* (San Francisco: Jossey-Bass, 1991), p. 178.

31. Jerome Bruner, *Acts of Meaning* (Cambridge: Harvard University Press, 1990), p. 12.

32. Dewey, pp. 16–17.

33. Peter F. Drucker, *Managing for the Future: The 1990s and Beyond* (New York: Dutton, 1993), p. 5.

34. Pamela Mendels, "In Colorado Classroom, Students Seek Their Own Olympic Goals," *New York Times,* February 18, 1998, p. B8. Also see both Wood and Fiske. The logical outgrowth of this philosophy is now appearing in math textbooks that refer to brand-name products (like Nike and Oreo) in their word problems. Though critics naturally first assumed that companies had paid to have their product names included, it turns out that textbook writers were merely trying to give students problems reflecting the "real world." Constance L. Hays, "Math Book Salted with Brand Names Raises Alarm," *New York Times,* March 21, 1999, pp. A1, 28.

35. John C. Hill, *The New American School: Breaking the Mold* (Lancaster, Pa.: Technomic, 1992), p. 27.

36. See William Glasser, *Quality Schools: Managing Students Without Coer-*

cion (New York: Perennial Library, 1990) for the most direct presentation of this view and Richardson for an example of a quality school in action. See also Mary B. W. Tabor, "Learning in the Real World of a Boston School," *New York Times,* June 19, 1991, p. 23. Federally mandated "school to work" programs are part of the same phenomenon. See Lynne Cheney, "Limited Horizons," *New York Times,* February 3, 1998, p. A23.

37. Emile Durkheim, *Education and Sociology,* trans. Sherwood D. Fox (Glencoe, Ill.: Free Press, 1956), p. 72.

38. Herbert R. Kohl, *On Teaching* (New York: Schocken Books, 1976), p. 16.

39. Amabile, pp. 4, 135 (see chap. 3, n. 13). See also Robert Schirrmacher, *Art and Creative Development for Young Children* (Albany, N.Y.: Delmar, 1993), p. 52. An even more striking example is Cynde Gregory, *Childmade: Awakening Children to Creative Writing* (New York: Station Hill Press, 1990).

40. Claude Levi-Strauss, "A Belated Word About the Creative Child," in *A View From Afar,* trans. Joachim Neuroschel and Phoebe Hoss (New York: Basic Books, 1985), p. 270.

41. George B. Leonard, "How School Stunts Your Child," in *Children's Liberation,* ed. David Gottlieb (Englewood Cliffs, N.J.: Prentice-Hall, 1973), p. 151.

42. Mihaly Csikszentmihalyi, Kevin Rathunde, and Samuel Whalen, *Talented Teenagers: The Roots of Success and Failure* (New York: Cambridge University Press, 1993), p. 254.

43. John I. Goodlad, *A Place Called School: Prospects for the Future* (New York: McGraw-Hill, 1984), p. 112.

44. For years the assumption was always that children had to be proficient readers before they could receive writing instruction. See E. Jennifer Monoghan and E. Wendy Saul, "A Critical Look at Reading and Writing Instruction," in *The Formation of School Subjects,* ed. Thomas S. Popkewitz (New York: Falmer Press, 1987).

45. Lucy McCormick Culkins, *The Art of Teaching Writing* (Portsmouth, N.H.: Heinemann Educational Books, 1986), pp. 3–5.

46. Quoted in Myra Cohn Livingston, *The Child as Poet: Myth or Reality?* (Boston: Horn Book, 1984), p. 184.

47. Paul Duncum, "The Origins of Self-Expression: A Case of Self-Deception," *Art Education,* vol. 35, September 1982, pp. 32–35. "When I banned Power Rangers as a subject," says a teacher quoted in Peter McLaren and Janet Morris, "Aesthetics of Phallo-Militaristic Justice," in *Kinderculture: The Corporate Construction of Childhood,* ed. Shirley R. Steinberg and Joe L. Kincheloe (Boulder, Colo.: Westview Press,

1997), p. 126, "they had a real problem thinking about other subjects to write about."

48. Theodore Sizer, *Horace's Compromise: The Dilemma of the American High School* (Boston: Houghton Mifflin, 1984), p. 83.

49. Lynda Richardson, "The Street Becomes a Classroom," *New York Times,* October 31, 1993, p. 37.

50. Kathleen J. Roth, "Second Thoughts About Interdisciplinary Studies," *American Educator,* vol. 18, Spring 1994, pp. 44–48.

51. International Reading Association and National Council of Teachers in English, *Standards for the English Language Arts* (International Reading Association and National Council of Teachers in English, 1996), p. 62. For a good example of just how far the search for creativity can go, see Dan Oldenburg, "Revolution in the Classroom," *Washington Post,* August 27, 1996, p. B5, which describes a workshop run by the Center for Artistry in Teaching, in which teachers create, for later classroom use, spatial and geometric concepts in a group dance to the beat of a James Brown tape.

52. Harold W. Stevenson and James W. Stigler, *The Learning Gap: Why Our Schools Are Failing and What We Can Learn from Japanese and Chinese Education* (New York: Simon & Schuster, 1992), p. 187.

53. Stevenson and Stigler, p. 143, and Dirk Johnson, "Many Schools Putting an End to Child's Play," *New York Times,* April 7, 1998, pp. A1, 18.

54. The most thorough and balanced analysis of whole language and the relevant research is Marilyn J. Adams and Maggie Bruck, "Resolving the 'Great Debate,'" *American Educator,* vol. 19, Summer 1995, pp. 7–19; see also Isabel I. Beck and Connie Juel, "The Role of Decoding in Learning to Read," in the same volume. For the California debacle, see Ina Mullis, Jay R. Campbell, and Alan E. Farstrup, *NAEP 1992 Reading Report Card for the Nation and the States* (Washington D.C.: U.S. Department of Education, 1992). And for a more skeptical view, see Nicholas Lemann, "The Reading Wars," *Atlantic Monthly,* November 1997, pp. 128ff. Tutors report seeing many illiterate students from whole language classrooms. See Jane Gross, "Wall Street's Frenetic? Try Eighth Grade," *New York Times,* October 5, 1997, pp. 37–38.

55. Sara G. Tarver and Jane S. Jung, "A Comparison of Mathematics Achievement and Mathematics Attitudes of First and Second Graders Instructed with Either a Discovery-Learning Mathematics Curriculum or a Direct Instruction Curriculum," *Effective School Practices,* vol. 14, Winter 1995, pp. 49–57.

56. William H. Honan, "SAT Scores Decline Even As Grades Rise," *New York Times,* September 2, 1998, p. B8.

57. Ethan Bronner, "U.S. Trails the World in Math and Science," *New York Times,* February 25, 1998, p. B10. H. W. Stevenson, C. Chen, and S. T. Lee, "Mathematics Achievement of Chinese, Japanese, and American Children: Ten Years Later," *Science,* January 1, 1993, pp. 53–58. In addition to comparing unfavorably to Japan with respect to overall scores, the United States also has a higher percentage of students performing at low levels and a lower percentage performing at high levels.

58. William Galston, "The Education Presidency," in Agenda for a Second Term, *New Republic,* November 11, 1996, pp. 29ff.

59. Powell, Farrar, and Cohen, pp. 40, 43 (see chap. 3, n. 12).

60. Cusick, p. 46 (see chap. 3, n. 12).

61. Judy Blume, *Are You There God? It's Me, Margaret* (Englewood Cliffs, N.J.: Bradbury Press, 1970).

62. Laurence Steinberg, *Beyond the Classroom: Why School Reform Has Failed and What Parents Need to Do* (New York: Simon & Schuster, 1996), pp. 19, 62. See also Stevenson and Stigler, p. 66, who report that even though there is more "edutainment" in their schools, American children are less likely to say they like school than are Japanese or Chinese children.

63. "American Freshman," press release, Higher Education Research Institute, Los Angeles, Fall 1995.

64. See Lawrence Diller, *Running on Ritalin* (New York: Bantam, 1998); Carey Goldberg, "For School Nurses, More Than Tending the Sick," *New York Times,* January 28, 1999, p. A20.

65. Cusick describes this dynamic in detail.

66. Arthur Levine, *When Fear and Hope Collide: A Portrait of Today's College Student* (San Francisco: Jossey-Bass, 1998), p. 128–29.

67. Levine, pp. 124ff.

68. Michael Moffatt, *Coming of Age in New Jersey: College and American Culture* (New Brunswick, N.J.: Rutgers University Press, 1995), pp. 276ff.

69. Levine, pp. 115–22. See also William H. Willimon and Thomas H. Naylor, *The Abandoned Generation: Rethinking Higher Education* (Grand Rapids, Mich.: Erdman, 1995).

70. Levine, p. 124, and more generally, p. 116.

71. See, for instance, The Age of Indifference, a Times Mirror survey reported in Alan Deutschman, "The Upbeat Generation," *Fortune,* July 13, 1992, p. 42. See also Cynde Miller, "Marketing to the Disillusioned," *Marketing News,* July 6, 1992, p. 6.

72. Phillip C. Schlechty, *Schools for the Twenty-First Century: Leadership Imperatives for Education Reform* (San Francisco: Jossey-Bass, 1990), p. 42.

73. Robert N. Bellah et al., *Habits of the Heart: Individualism and Commitment in American Life* (New York: Harper & Row, 1985), p. 152.

74. E. D. Hirsch, *The Schools We Need and Why We Don't Have Them* (New York: Doubleday, 1996), p. 27.

75. David Marc, *Bonfire of the Humanities: Television, Subliteracy, and Long-Term Memory Loss* (Syracuse, N.Y.: Syracuse University Press, 1995), p. 120.

76. Jacques Barzun, *Begin Here: The Forgotten Conditions of Learning and Teaching* (Chicago: University of Chicago Press, 1991), p. 44.

77. William W. Wayson, *Up From Excellence: The Impact of the Excellence Movement on Schools* (Bloomington, Ind.: Phi Delta Kappa Educational Foundation, 1988), p. 152.

78. The most prominent exponent of cooperative learning is Robert E. Slavin. See his *Co-operative Learning: Theory, Research and Practice* (Boston: Allyn and Bacon, 1995). See also Deborah Burrett Strother, "Cooperative Learning: Fad or Foundation for Learning?" *Phi Delta Kappan,* vol. 72, October 1990, pp. 158ff.

79. Stern, pp. 24–25.

80. Stevenson and Stigler, p. 219. See also Chuansheng Chen and David H. Uttal, "Cultural Values, Parents' Beliefs, and Children's Achievement in the United States and China," *Human Development,* vol. 31, 1988, pp. 351–58.

81. Public Agenda, *Kids These Days: What Americans Really Think About the Next Generation* (New York: Public Agenda, 1997), p. 33.

82. Judith N. Sklar, *Liberalism Without Illusions* (Chicago: University of Chicago Press, 1996), p. 277.

Chapter 4: The Teening of Childhood

1. The history presented in this chapter is taken from Lynn Spigel, *Make Room for TV: Television and the Family Ideal in Postwar America* (Chicago: University of Chicago Press, 1992); Gerard Jones, *Honey I'm Home: Sitcoms: Selling the American Dream* (New York: Grove Weidenfeld, 1992); William Melody, *Children's Television: The Economics of Exploitation* (New Haven, Conn.: Yale University Press, 1973); Cy Schneider, *Children's Television: The Art, the Business and How It Works* (Chicago: NTC Business Books, 1987). Mark Crispin Miller, "Deride and Conquer," in *Watching Television,* ed. Todd Gitlin

(New York: Pantheon Books, 1986), traces the "long decline of Dad" (pp. 196ff.) and the triumph of the ironic tone discussed later in this chapter.

2. Quoted in Jones, p. 42.

3. Arthur Asa Berger, *The Comic-Stripped American: What Dick Tracy, Blondie, Daddy Warbucks and Charlie Brown Tell Us About Ourselves* (New York: Walker, 1973), p. 103.

4. Spigel, p. 60.

5. The history of toy advertising and Barbie comes from Schneider, pp. 18–26; G. Wayne Miller, *Toy Wars: The Epic Struggle Between G. I. Joe, Barbie, and the Companies That Make Them* (New York: Random House, 1998), p. 67; Gary Cross, *Kids' Stuff: Toys and the Changing World of American Childhood* (Cambridge: Harvard University Press, 1997), chap. 6.

6. Cross, pp. 165–166.

7. Larry McGill, "By the Numbers: What Kids Watch," *Media Studies Journal,* Fall 1994, p. 101. Saturday morning television, though still popular, takes a back seat to the weekday 7:30 to 8:00 P.M. slot, when nearly 33 percent of all children between two and eleven are watching (p. 99).

8. Josh Ozersky, "TV's Anti-Families: Married with Malaise," *Tikkun,* January/February 1991, pp. 11ff., offers the best discussion on the subject and several of my examples come from him. See also Megan Rosenfeld, "Father Knows Squat: TV Parents Used to Be Wise and Stable. Now They're Stupid or Dead," *Washington Post,* November 13, 1994, p. G1. As I write, the latest examples are Fox's *Family Guy,* featuring a father so inept that the family dog raps him on the nose with the newspaper instead of vice versa, and Stewie the Killer Baby, who shoots at his mother with high-tech weapons hidden in his tuna fish.

9. Quoted in Ozersky, p. 11.

10. Anne MacLeod, *American Childhood: Essays on Children's Literature of the Nineteenth and Twentieth Century* (Athens, Ga.: University of Georgia Press, 1994), pp. 200, 207–8.

11. Deborah Haitzig, *Why Are You So Mean to Me?* (New York: Random House/Children's Television Workshop, 1986); Lynne Jonell, *Mommy, Go Away!* (New York: Putnam, 1997); Rodman Philbrick, *Freak the Mighty* (Blue Sky Press, 1993); Michael Dorris, *The Window* (New York: Hyperion Books for Children, 1997); Brock Coles, *The Facts Speak for Themselves* (Arden, N.C.: Front Street, 1997). See also Sara Mosle, "The Outlook's Bleak," *New York Times Magazine,* August 2, 1998, p. 34.

12. Schneider, p. 2. Assertions about the competence and "sophistication" of the child viewer are commonplace among people in the media and advertising as well as among academics. See, for instance, Milton Chen, "Six Myths About Television and Children," *Media Studies Journal,* Fall 1994, pp. 105–114; Daniel R. Anderson, "Looking at Television: Action or Reaction," in *Children's Understanding of Television: Research on Attention and Comprehension,* ed. Jennings Bryant and Daniel R. Anderson (New York: Academic Press, 1983); Brian M. Young, *Television Advertising and Children* (New York: Oxford University Press, 1990).

13. Quoted in Eric Schmuckler, "In 'Rugrats' Babies Know Best," *New York Times,* Arts and Leisure, August 3, 1998, p. 32.

14. According to Ellen Winner, *The Point of Words: Children's Understanding of Metaphor and Irony* (Cambridge: Harvard University Press, 1988), children under six or seven don't understand irony.

15. Bruno Bettelheim, *The Uses of Enchantment: The Meaning and Importance of Fairy Tales* (New York: Vintage Books, 1989), p. 166.

16. Jon Scieszka, *Frog Prince, Continued* (New York: Viking, 1991).

17. See Joan Gantz Cooney, "Foreword," of Gerald S. Lesser, *Lessons from Sesame Street* (New York: Vintage, 1974).

18. In an essay in *In Front of the Children: Screen Entertainment and Young Audiences,* ed. Cary Bazalgette and David Buckingham (London: British Film Institute, 1995), p. 124, for instance, Jack Zipes argues that these adaptations allow children to "gain a sense of assembling and reassembling the frames of their lives for themselves." See also Zipes, *Happily Ever After: Fairy Tales, Children and the Culture* (New York: Routledge, 1997); Maria Tatar, *Off with Their Heads: Fairy Tales and the Culture of Childhood* (Princeton, N.J.: Princeton University Press, 1992).

19. This quote is taken from Douglas Rushkoff, *Media Virus! Hidden Agendas in Popular Culture,* rev. ed. (New York: Ballantine, 1996), p. 111. Rushkoff also quotes one of *The Simpsons* writers about the show's thesis: "There's nothing to believe in anymore . . ." (p. 114).

20. Alison Lurie, *Don't Tell the Grown-Ups: Why Kids Love the Books They Do* (Boston: Little, Brown, 1990).

21. Ellen Seiter, *Sold Separately: Parents and Children in the Consumer Culture* (New Brunswick, N.J.: Rutgers University Press, 1993), notes this same theme (in chap. 4), and several of my examples come from there. Seiter, like other academics today writing in the Ariès tradition, believes Kid Kulture can "express a resistance to the middle-class culture

of parenting . . . that may be very healthy indeed," (p. 232). In other words, she finds ads genuinely subversive.

22. Example from Selina S. Guber and Jon Berry, *Marketing to and Through Kids* (New York: McGraw-Hill, 1993), p. 133.

23. Patricia Winters, "Pepsi Harkens Back to Youth," *Advertising Age,* January 25, 1993, p. 3.

24. Seiter (p. 130) quotes research, comparing boys' toy ads from the fifties and those of today, which finds that the adult male voice-over or on-camera spokesman has almost entirely disappeared.

25. Charles McGrath, "Giving Saturday Morning Some Slack," *New York Times Magazine,* November 9, 1997, p. 54.

26. Seiter, p. 121.

27. John E. Coons, "Intellectual Liberty and the Schools," *Notre Dame Journal of Law, Ethics, and Public Policy,* vol. 1, 1985, p. 503.

28. These examples are from Guber and Berry, pp. 33, 100–101.

29. "News/Trends - Kidpower," *Fortune,* March 30, 1987, pp. 9–10.

30. Guber and Berry, pp. 27, 78.

31. James McNeal, "Growing Up in the Market," *American Demographics,* October 1992, p. 47.

32. Figure cited in Lisa Bannon, "As Children Become More Sophisticated, Marketers Think Older," *Wall Street Journal,* October 13, 1998, p. A1. McNeal says that aggregate spending on or for children between ages four and twelve doubled every decade in the 1960s, 1970s, and 1980s. In the 1990s the children's market picked up more steam: between 1990 and 1997, it had already tripled.

33. Jane Weaver, "Girl Scout Campaign: Shedding Old Image for Media Cool," *Adweek,* September 11, 1989, p. 11.

34. Quoted in Bernard Weinraub, "Who's Lining Up at Box Office? Lots and Lots of Girls," *New York Times,* Arts Section, February 23, 1998, p. 1.

35. Bannon, p. A8; Michele Willens, "Young and in a Niche That Movies Neglect," *New York Times,* Arts and Leisure Section, June 14, 1998, pp. 13, 14.

36. Quoted in Weinraub, p. 4.

37. Bannon, pp. A1, 8.

38. The number of magazines for children almost doubled between 1986 and 1991. S. K. List, "The Right Place to Find Children," *American Demographics,* February 1992, pp. 44–47.

39. Toy Industry Factbook at www.toy-tma.com/PUBLICATIONS/factbook98/economics.html.

40. Bannon, p. A1.

41. Laura Klepacki, "Courting the 'Tweenie' Boppers," *WWD,* February 27, 1998, p. 10; Becky Ebenkamp, "Packaging: Sara Lee Repackages Youthful Underwear to Better Draw Juniors," *Brandweek,* January 5, 1998, p. 36.

42. James McNeal and Chyon-Hwa Yeh, "Born to Shop," *American Demographics,* June 1993, p. 37.

43. Carrie Telegardin, "Growing Up Southern: The Kids Take Over," *Atlanta Journal-Constitution,* June 7, 1993, p. E1. According to Telegardin, "America's new housewife [is] the housekid."

44. Quoted in Toy Industry Factbook. See also "Generation Y," *Business Week,* February 15, 1999, pp. 80–88, for how this generation is changing the marketplace.

45. The psychologist Marilyn Bradford found that preschoolers ask for an average of 3.4 toys for Christmas and receive 11.6. Cited in Gary Cross, "Too Many Toys," *New York Times,* November 24, 1995, p. 35.

46. Lisa Gubernick and Marla Matzer, "Babies as Dolls," *Forbes,* February 27, 1995, p. 78.

47. Patricia A. Adler and Peter Adler, *Peer Power: Preadolescent Culture and Identity* (New Brunswick, N.J.: Rutgers University Press, 1998), p. 55. Tellingly, by 1991 shoes and clothing were the fastest-growing categories among children up to age twelve and accounted for 13 percent of their spending, up from an unmeasurably small amount in 1988, according to Susan Antilla, "'I Want' Now Gets," *New York Times,* Education Life, April 4, 1993, p. 17. See also Carol Pogash, "The Clothing Boom in the Land of the Little People," *Los Angeles Times,* August 29, 1995, p. 22.

48. Interview by the author, July 1998.

49. Judith Waldrop, "The Tween Scene," *American Demographics,* September 1992, p. 4.

50. Hannah Arendt, "Crisis in Education," *Partisan Review,* Fall 1958, p. 500.

51. Quoted in Guber and Berry, p. 84. See also Claire Collins, "Fighting the Holiday Advertising Blitz," *New York Times,* December 1, 1994, p. C4; Matt Murray, "Hey Kids! Marketers Want Your Help!" *Wall Street Journal,* May 6, 1997, pp. B1, 8; Antilla, p. 17; Steven A. Holmes, "Shoppers! Deciding? Just Ask Your Child," *New York Times,* Week in Review, January 8, 1995, p. 4; Becky Ebenkamp, Mike Beirne, and Christine Bittar, "Products for the Sophisticated Little Nipper," *Brandweek,* February 22, 1999, pp. 1, 53.

52. See Don Oldenberg, "Consummate Consumer: Children's Business:

America's 90 Billion Plus Youth Market," *Washington Post*, July 6, 1995, p. C5.

53. Deborah Stead, "Classrooms and Commercialism," *New York Times*, Education Life, January 5, 1997, p. 30.

54. Quoted in Michael F. Jacobson and Laurie Ann Mazur, *Marketing Madness: A Survival Guide for a Consumer Society* (New York: Westview Press, 1995), p. 21. See also Carrie Goerne, "Marketers Try to Get More Creative at Reaching Teens," *Marketing News*, August 5, 1991, pp. 2, 6; Judann Dagnoli, "Consumer's Union Hits Kids Advertising," *Advertising Age*, July 23, 1990, p. 4.

55. Quoted in Lawrie Mifflin, "Critics Assail PBS over Plan for Toys Aimed at Toddlers," *New York Times*, April 20, 1998, p. A17.

56. Quoted in Oldenberg, p. C5. Mary Ellen Podmolik, "Kids' Clothing Boom," *Chicago Sun Times*, Financial Section, August 21, 1994, p. 1, quotes McNeal to the effect that 10 percent of a two-year-old's vocabulary is made up of brand names.

Chapter 5: Fourteen-Year-Old Women and Juvenile Men

1. The story of the Emancipation of Minors Act comes from Carol Sanger and Eleanor Willemsen, "Minor Changes: Emancipating Children in Modern Times," *University of Michigan Journal of Law Reform*, vol. 25, 1992, pp. 239–350. The quote from the president of Youth Advocates Inc. appears on p. 254. Michael J. Dale, *Representing the Child Client*, publication 584 by Matthew Bender and Co., updated September 1998, section 3.05[2], says that before 1970 the few emancipation statutes that were on the books focused on the property rights of minors. After that time, a number of states passed laws that had more to do with minors' ability "to pursue their own 'lifestyle.'" Along with Connecticut, California has the most comprehensive statute, allowing kids as young as fourteen to apply and to do so without parental consent.

2. Martha Minow, "The Public Duties of Families and Children," in *From Children to Citizens*, vol. 2, ed. Francis X. Hartman (New York: Springer-Verlag, 1987), p. 9.

3. This is Mary Ann Glendon's important point in *The Transformation of Family Law: State, Law, and Family in the United States and Europe* (Chicago: University of Chicago Press, 1989).

4. *In re Gault*, 387 U.S. 1 (1967).

5. *In re Gault*, 387 U.S. 13, 34–57.

6. Julian W. Mack, "The Chancery Procedure in the Juvenile Court," in *The Child, the Clinic, and the Court* (New Republic, 1925; reprint, New York: Johnson Reprint, 1970), p. 310.

7. Quoted in Robert M. Mennel, *Thorns and Thistles: Juvenile Delinquents in the United States* (Hanover, N.H.: University Press of New England, 1973), p. 135.

8. *In re Gault,* 387 U.S. 28.

9. Mack, pp. 315–16.

10. Christopher Lasch, "Hillary Clinton, Child Saver," *Harper's Magazine,* October 1992, p. 76.

11. Quoted in Thomas J. Bernard, *The Cycle of Juvenile Justice* (New York: Oxford University Press, 1992), p. 64.

12. *McKeiver v. Pennsylvania,* 403 U.S. 550 (1971). Indeed, although in several cases around this time (e.g., *Kent v. United States,* 383 U.S. 541 [1966] and *In re Winship,* 397 U.S. 358 [1970]) the Court condemned the paternalism of the juvenile court and expanded procedural safeguards, it drew the line at requiring jury trials for minors in *McKeiver,* affirming, in Justice Brennan's concurrence, that the juvenile court shows "the community's sympathy and concern for the young" (403 U.S. 555). A later decision, *Schall v. Martin,* 476 U.S. 253, handed down in 1984 went even further, allowing juveniles to be preventively detained.

13. Gary B. Melton, "Psycholegal Issues in Juveniles' Competency to Waive Their Rights," *Journal of Clinical Child Psychology,* Winter 1981, pp. 60–61. The most significant research comes from Thomas Grisso, *Juvenile Waiver of Rights: Legal and Psychological Competence* (New York: Plenum, 1981); Vance L. Cowden and Geoffrey R. McKee, "Competency to Stand Trial in Juvenile Delinquency Proceedings: Cognitive Maturity and the Attorney-Client Relationship," *Journal of Family Law,* vol. 33, 1994–5, pp. 629–60. Joseph Adelson confirms this picture of the younger adolescent's inability to grasp the logic of political rights in "The Political Imagination of Adolescent" in his *Inventing Adolescence: The Political Psychology of Everyday Schooling* (New Brunswick, N.J.: Transaction, 1986).

14. *Fare v. Michael C.,* 442 U.S. 706 (1979).

15. *Fare v. Michael C.,* 442 U.S. 710, 711.

16. *Fare v. Michael C.,* 442 U.S. 732, 733.

17. "Boy's Murder Confession Tossed Aside," *Washington Post,* May 8, 1998, p. A25. See also Pam Belluck, "Lawyers Struggle in Defense of Children in Deadly Crimes," *New York Times,* August 17, 1998, p. A1.

18. Alex Kotlowitz, "The Unprotected," *New Yorker,* February 8, 1999, pp. 42–53.

19. Edward Humes, *No Matter How Loud I Shout* (New York: Simon & Schuster, 1996), describes a year in the life of the Los Angeles juvenile court and points out the irony of lawyers (for what is supposed to be a family court) sometimes telling kids not to talk to their parents even about things that "will profoundly affect a child's future" (p. 211).

20. Grisso, pp. 150–80.

21. Eloise L. Snyder, "Impact of Court Hearing on the Child," *Crime and Delinquency,* April 1971, pp. 182–83.

22. Public Agenda, *Kids These Days: What Americans Really Think About the Next Generation* (New York: Public Agenda, 1997), pp. 19, 24.

23. Gary B. Melton, "Children's Concepts of Their Rights," *Journal of Clinical Child Psychology,* Fall 1980, pp. 186–90.

24. Grisso.

25. Ira M. Schwartz, *(In)justice for Juveniles: Rethinking the Best Interests of the Child* (Lexington, Mass.: Heath, 1989), p. 160; Gary B. Melton, "Taking Gault Seriously: Towards a New Juvenile Court," *Nebraska Law Review,* vol. 68, 1989, pp. 172ff. Melton's argument is a good example of the incoherence of the post-*Gault* system. On the one hand, he believes, in line with *Gault,* that juveniles are more "competent . . . than the law historically has presumed"; on the other, their youth necessitates a "Super Court" to protect them. As it is, many critics have pointed out the confusion among lawyers for juveniles. Are they merely lawyers or also social workers? Do they do everything they can to get their clients off, or do they think about the child's best interest? See Anthony Platt, Howard Schecter, and Phyllis Tiffany, "In Defense of Youth: A Case Study of the Public Defender in Juvenile Court," in *Children of Ishmael: Critical Perspectives on Juvenile Justice,* ed. Barry Krisberg and James Austin (Palo Alto, Calif.: Mayfield, 1978).

26. This has been the logic from the time of *Gault,* when Justice Fortas quoted social science to prove that children under the present system would learn the lesson of injustice.

27. Humes, pp. 52, 93.

28. Ian Fisher, "Gun Decision Raises Furor in the Schools," *New York Times,* September 19, 1996, pp. B1, 7.

29. Humes, p. 26.

30. George's story is told throughout Humes.

31. See John de Iullio and Beth Z. Palubinsky, "How Philadelphia Salvages Teen Criminals," *City Journal,* Summer 1997, pp. 28–40. See also

Francis A. J. Ianni, *The Search for Structure: A Report on American Youth Today* (New York: Free Press, 1989), p. 189, for a description of a community committee to deal with minor infractions in one suburban town.

32. Humes. See, in particular, pp. 178, 230–37.

33. Quoted in Peter Prescott, *The Child Savers: Juvenile Justice Observed* (New York: Knopf, 1981), p. 169.

34. David Matza, *Delinquency and Drift* (New York: Wiley, 1964).

35. *In re Gault,* 387 U.S. 80.

36. *Thompson v. Oklahoma,* 487 U.S. 815 (1988).

37. Gregory Bassham, "Rethinking the Emerging Jurisprudence of Juvenile Death," *Notre Dame Journal of Law, Ethics and Public Policy,* vol. 5, 1991, p. 493. See also Victor L. Streib, "Perspectives on the Juvenile Death Penalty in the 1990's," in *Child, Parent and State: Law and Policy Reader,* ed. Randall Humm (Philadelphia: Temple University Press, 1994).

38. Strictly speaking, *Eisenstadt v. Baird,* which was decided in 1972 and which allowed physicians to give minors contraception without parental approval, was the first step in this direction. See Joan Jacobs Brumberg, *The Body Project* (New York: Random House, 1997), pp. 171ff. For the best discussion of the Court's challenge to the traditional assumption that parents are best able to consider their children's interests and of the dramatic transfer of supervision over the minor from parents to doctors and experts, see Margaret O'Brien Steinfels, "Ethical and Legal Issues in Teenage Pregnancy," in *Teenage Pregnancy in a Family Context,* ed. Theodora Ooms (Philadelphia: Temple University Press, 1981); Steinfels, "Children's Rights, Parental Rights, Family Privacy, and Family Autonomy," in *Who Speaks for the Child? The Problem of Proxy Consent,* ed. Willard Gaylin and Ruth Macklin (New York: Plenum Press, 1982).

39. *Planned Parenthood of Missouri v. Danforth,* 428 U.S. 74. (1976).

40. *Thornburgh et al. v. American College of Obstetricians Gynecologists et al.,* 106 S.Ct. 2169 (1986). The *amicus* brief is reprinted in *American Psychologist,* January 1987, pp. 77–78. See also Gary B. Melton and Nancy Felipe Russo, "Adolescent Abortion: Psychological Perspectives on Public Policy," in the same volume, pp. 69–76, and Bruce Ambuel and Julian Rappaport, "Developmental Trends in Adolescents' Psychological and Legal Competence to Consent to Abortion," *Law and Human Behavior,* vol. 16, 1992, pp. 129–54. Several articles have raised the important question of whether the usual cognitive terms in which this discussion has been confined (does the minor understand the terms of the choice facing

her? What is her reasoning?) are too narrow. Laurence Steinberg and Elizabeth Cauffman, in *Law and Human Behavior,* vol. 20, 1996, pp. 249–72, point out that there is little research on adolescent "sensation seeking" or "moodiness" and that most of what research has been done is in an artificial laboratory environment. See also Elizabeth S. Scott, N. Dickon Repucci, and Jennifer L. Woolard, "Evaluating Adolescent Decision-Making in Legal Contexts," *Law and Human Behavior,* vol. 19, 1995, pp. 221–44; William Gardner, David Scherer, and Myra Tester, "Asserting Scientific Authority: Cognitive Development and Adolescent Legal Rights," *American Psychologist,* June 1989, pp. 895–902, and the letters in response, vol. 45, pp. 1171–1173.

41. Concern for parents' feelings and fear of disappointing them are the most frequently cited reason in several studies, for example, Freddie Clary, "Minor Women Obtaining Abortions: A Study of Parental Notification in a Metropolitan Area," *American Journal of Public Health,* vol. 76, 1982, pp. 283–85. Stanley K. Henshaw and Kathryn Kost, "Parental Involvement in Minors' Abortion Decisions," *Family Planning Perspectives,* September/October 1992, pp. 200, 203. Henshow and Kost found girls who avoided notifying their parents were more likely to be white and from intact families. Ianni, in a study comparing inner-city, suburban, and rural communities, found that suburban girls found it much more difficult to go to their parents if they were pregnant than did inner-city girls, simply because their condition was so out of keeping with their family's and community's expectations (pp. 80–82).

42. Robert W. Blum, Michael D. Resnick, and Tricia A. Stark, "The Impact of a Parental Notification Law on Adolescent Decision-Making," *American Journal of Public Health,* May 1987, pp. 619–20. Incidentally, though it was widely claimed that the Minnesota parental notice law increased the birth rate among minors, it appears that this rise was attributable to a growing racial minority in Minneapolis that was more prone to teen motherhood. See James L. Rogers and Amy M. Miller, "Inner-City Birth Rates Following Enactment of the Minnesota Parental Notification Law," *Law and Human Behavior,* vol. 17, 1993, pp. 27–42.

43. Henshaw and Kost, pp. 196–213.

44. Henshaw and Kost found that girls cited parental insistence on abortion as the second most common consequence to parents knowing about their pregnancy. Parents whose daughters avoided telling them about their pregnancy were more than twice as likely to insist on an abortion as were those whose daughters had volunteered the informa-

tion. It seems likely, Henshaw and Kost concluded, that a good number of girls avoid telling their parents because they believe they will be forced to abort. Boyfriends and friends were far more likely to try to talk girls, particularly the younger ones, into continuing the pregnancy (pp. 204–5). As for the issue of parental violence, the number of girls truly in danger is likely to be extremely small: Henshaw and Kost cited 6 percent who feared it, a number that may well be subject to exaggeration, given kids' tendency to dramatize. It's a fair guess that a parent who might harm a girl for getting pregnant might also harm her for, say, getting suspended from school or being picked up by the police. Yet no one has ever suggested there should be judicial bypass in these instances.

45. Robert H. Mnookin, "Bellotti v. Baird: A Hard Case," in *In the Interest of Children: Advocacy, Law Reform, and Public Policy,* ed. Robert H. Mnookin (New York: Freeman, 1985). Tamar Lewin, "Parental Consent to Abortion: How Enforcement Can Vary," *New York Times,* May 28, 1992, p. A1, cited the figure between 1981 and 1991. A five-year study in Minnesota, cited in Linnet Myers, "Pregnant Teens Face Parents—Emotions Strong over Requiring Notice Before Abortion," *Chicago Tribune,* July 5, 1990, p. 1, found a similar rubber-stamping of petitions. Incidentally, Mnookin's article is a highly informative study of the politics behind *Bellotti v. Baird;* one notable fact is that while experts and the minor on behalf of whom the case was brought were allowed to testify, the girls' parents were not, though their daughter had claimed that her father would kill her boyfriend if she told him about her pregnancy. Virginia G. Cartoof and Lorraine V. Klerman, "Parental Consent for Abortion: Impact of the Massachussetts Law," *American Journal of Public Health,* vol. 78, 1986, pp. 397–400, also found that as many as one in three pregnant minors crossed state lines in order to avoid parental notification requirements; their conclusion—that since such laws are failing to promote family unity and parent–child communication, they should be overturned—ignores the broader problem of a society that so frequently tells parents they have nothing to offer their children.

46. See Lewin, p. A1.

47. Ianni, p. 86.

48. Robert W. Blum and Peggy Mann Rinehart, "Connections That Make the Difference," based on findings from the National Longitudinal Study on Adolescent Health (Bethesda, Md.: c/o Burness Communications, 1997).

49. Mihalyi Csikszentmihalyi, Kevin Rathunde, and Samuel Whalen, *Talented Teenagers: The Roots of Success and Failure* (New York: Cambridge University Press, 1993), pp. 154ff.

50. This was the finding in the sample studied by Henshaw and Kost, p. 198.

51. In response to the argument that if nineteen-year-olds are old enough to be drafted to fight in Southeast Asia, they are old enough to buy a beer, most states in the early 1970s lowered the age at which minors could buy alcoholic beverages from twenty-one to eighteen. There followed a significant rise in drunk driving accidents, and gradually, with incentives from the federal government, every state reverted to twenty-one.

52. In 1976 in *Ingraham et al. v. Wright*, 430 U.S. 651, the Supreme Court upheld the constitutionality of the "moderate use of physical force" in schools, denying that it constituted cruel and unusual punishment. Some states have passed their own laws banning corporal punishment; in others, local districts prohibit it.

53. *Tinker v. Des Moines School District*, 393 U.S. 506, 511 (1969).

54. *Goss v. Lopez*, 419 U.S. 565 (1975).

55. *Goss v. Lopez*, 419 U.S. 584.

56. Franklin E. Zimring and Rayman L. Solomon, "*Goss v. Lopez:* The Principle of the Thing," in *In the Interest of Children: Advocacy, Law Reform, and Public Policy*, ed. Robert H. Mnookin (New York: Freeman, 1985), cite other factors responsible for the changing atmosphere in the schools at the time, including racial tension, Vietnam, television and its impact on students, desegregation, and the increases in federal funding for public schools.

57. Gerald Grant, *The World We Created at Hamilton High* (Cambridge: Harvard University Press, 1988), pp. 106–7. See also Grant, "Children's Rights and Adult Confusions," *Public Interest*, Fall 1982, pp. 87–98.

58. Grant, pp. 53–54.

59. One such case, involving a medical student who sued her university when she was dismissed for her poor academic work without a due process hearing, reached the Supreme Court before it was rejected. It's worth noting that three Justices—Marshall, Blackmun and Brennan—argued in a partial dissent that in general there should be due process in academic as in disciplinary matters. *Board of Curators v. Horowitz*, 435 U.S. 78 (1978).

60. Teacher burnout is extraordinarily high in this country; 40 to 50 percent give up on the profession in the first five years, and most cite stu-

dent discipline as their biggest source of stress. See Barry Farber, *Crisis in Education: Stress and Burnout in the American Teacher* (San Francisco: Jossey-Bass, 1991).

61. Philip A. Cusick, *The Egalitarian Ideal and the American High School* (New York: Longman, 1983), p. 60; Grant, pp. 67–70.

62. See Adam Marcus, "How Liberals Put Teachers in the Line of Fire," *Washington Monthly,* June 1994, p. 19.

63. Cited in John Judis, "TRB," *New Republic,* October 20, 1997, p. 45.

64. Jackson Toby, "Crime in the American Public Schools," *Public Interest,* Winter 1980, p. 30.

65. *Bethel School District v. Fraser,* 478 U.S. 675 (1986).

66. *Bethel School District v. Fraser,* 478 U.S. 680.

67. *Bethel School District v. Fraser,* 478 U.S. 676. Justice Stevens' dissent to this decision is a fine example of adult uncertainty in the face of child empowerment. Matthew Fraser, he wrote, is obviously respected by his peers and is better at determining what might be offensive to them "than is a group of judges who are at least two generations and 3,000 miles away from the scene of the crime" (p. 692).

68. *New Jersey v. T.L.O.,* 469 U.S. 348 (1985), and *Hazelwood School District v. Kulmeier,* 484 U.S. 260 (1988), were probably the most important of these cases. *T.L.O.* allows teachers to search students' property and *Hazelwood* permits educators to supervise the content of "school-sponsored expressive activities" (in other words, to censor school newspapers). But, interestingly, after *Hazelwood* a number of states passed laws giving back to students the guarantee of free speech rights the Supreme Court had taken away.

69. James Dao, "School Rightly Curbed Student Speech, State's Highest Court Rules," *New York Times,* December 3, 1997, p. B5.

70. 393 U.S. 525.

71. John T. McQuiston, "Magazines Found Too Adult for School," *New York Times,* February 13, 1998, p. B5.

72. Cited in Elaine Yaffe, "Expensive, Illegal, and Wrong: Sexual Harassment in Our Schools," *Phi Delta Kappan,* vol. 77, November 1995, p. K8.

73. Patricia Hersch, *A Tribe Apart: A Journey into the Heart of American Adolescence* (New York: Fawcett Columbine, 1998), p. 65.

74. Laurence Steinberg, *Beyond the Classroom: Why School Reform Has Failed and What Parents Need to Do* (New York: Simon & Schuster, 1996), pp. 11–12.

75. Frank Bruni, "Student's Violent Prose Pits Free Speech Against Safety," *New York Times,* May 8, 1998, p. A10. In another 1997 case, a fifteen-

year-old student from Statesboro, Georgia, who had a Web site on which he proposed shooting the school principal and kidnapping his seven-year-old daughter and which included instructions for making bombs and committing suicide, was arrested and charged with making terroristic threats against the principal of his high school. One of the student's lawyers argued that the students "were just expressing the kind of dislike of authority that every generation feels." Whether or not "every generation" dislikes authority, the law, beginning with *Gault,* has encouraged this generation to do so. See Tamar Lewin, "Schools Challenge Students' Internet Talk," *New York Times,* March 3, 1998, p. A16.

76. Yaffe, p. K8.

77. Don Terry and Frank Bruni, "Lethal Fantasies of a Fifteen-Year-Old Became a Reality," *New York Times,* May 24, 1998, p. A14; Jodi Wilgoren and Dirk Johnson, "Sketch of Killers: Contradictions and Confusion," *New York Times,* April 23, 1999, p. A21.

78. Cited in Marcus, p. 16 (see chap. 5, n. 62).

79. Grant, p. 57.

80. Gerald Grant, "The Character of Education and the Education of Character," *Daedalus,* Summer 1981, p. 141.

81. "Hostile Hallways," conducted by Harris/Scholastic Associates and commissioned by the American Association of University Women, 1993. In the study, interestingly enough, 66 percent of boys and 52 percent of girls who had been harassed also admitted to harassing others.

82. Yaffe, p. K3.

83. Cited in Ruth Shalit, "Romper Room," *New Republic,* March 29, 1993, p. 16. See also John Leland, "A Kiss Isn't Just a Kiss," *Newsweek,* October 21, 1996, pp. 71–72.

84. Adam Nossiter, "Six-Year-Old's Sex Crime: Innocent Peck on the Cheek," *New York Times,* September 27, 1996, p. A14.

85. Tamar Lewin, "Kissing Cases Highlight Schools' Fears of Liability for Sexual Harassment," *New York Times,* October 22, 1996, p. A22.

Chapter 6: Sex and the Anticultural Teenager

1. Eric Konigsberg, "Sex Ed," *Spin,* June 1998, pp. 99, 104.

2. Conversation between author and Bryanna Hocking, editor of *The Guide: A Little Beige Book for Today's Miss G.* and a student at Georgetown.

3. Lillian B. Rubin, *Erotic Wars: What Happened to the Sexual Revolution?* (New York: Harper Perennial, 1990), p. 72.

4. Quoted in Sharon Thompson, *Going All the Way: Teenage Girls' Tales of Sex and Romance* (New York: Hill & Wang, 1995), p. 73.

5. Interview by the author, July 21, 1998.

6. For a discussion of oral sex and teens, see Tamar Lewin, "Teen-Agers Alter Sexual Practices, Thinking Risks Will Be Avoided," *New York Times,* April 5, 1997, p. 8. On anal sex, see the survey in Leland Elliott and Cynthia Brantley, *Sex on Campus* (New York: Random House, 1997), pp. 138–39, which concludes that somewhere around a fifth of sexually experienced undergraduates have had anal sex.

7. Sherril Jaffe, *Ground Rules: What I Learned My Daughter's Fifteenth Year* (New York: Kodansha International, 1997), p. 179.

8. Carol Lawson, "A Bedtime Story That's Different," *New York Times,* April 4, 1991, pp. C1, 8; Stephen Buckley and Debbi Wilgoren, "Young and Experienced," *Washington Post,* April 24, 1994, p. A1. It appears to be mostly the parents of boys who allow these arrangements.

9. Planned Parenthood of Bergen County, Inc., *Bodies, Birth and Babies: Sexuality Education in Early Childhood Programs,* Center for Family Life Education (Bergen County, N.J.: 1989), p. 17. For a heated critique of the "new religion of sexuality" see Stephen Heath, *The Sexual Fix* (New York: Schocken Books, 1982).

10. Niels H. Lauersen and Eileen Stukane, *You're in Charge: A Teenage Girl's Guide to Sex and Her Body* (New York: FawcettColumbine, 1993), p. 160.

11. Quoted in Barbara Dafoe Whitehead, "The Failure of Sex Education," *Atlantic Monthly,* October, 1994, p. 57.

12. Lynn Leight, *Raising Sexually Healthy Children: A Loving Guide for Parents, Teachers, and Caregivers* (New York: Rawson Associates, 1988), p. 9.

13. Naomi Wolf, *Promiscuities: The Secret Struggle for Womanhood* (New York: Random House, 1997), pp. 27, 28. The feminist literature subscribing to this view is extensive. See especially Sharon Thompson; Michelle Fine, "Sexuality, Schooling and Adolescent Females: The Missing Discourse of Desire," *Harvard Education Review,* vol. 58, February 1988, pp. 29–53; Kristin Luker, *Dubious Conceptions: The Politics of Teenage Pregnancy* (Cambridge: Harvard University Press, 1996); Constance A. Nathanson, *Dangerous Passage: The Social Control of Sexuality in Women's Adolescence,* (Philadelphia: Temple University Press, 1991); and Deborah L. Tolman, "Daring to Desire: Culture and the Bodies of Adolescent Girls," in *Sexual Cultures and the Construction of Adolescent Identities,* ed. Janice M. Irvine (Philadelphia: Temple University Press, 1994).

14. Mary Pipher, *Reviving Ophelia: Saving the Selves of American Girls* (New York: Ballantine, 1994), p. 39.

15. Barbara Sprung, *Learning About Family Life: Resources for Learning and Teaching* (New Brunswick, N.J.: Rutgers University Press, 1992), p. 55.

16. William Yarber, "Sex Education and Government Censors," *USA Today,* July 29, 1992, p. 7A. Yarber was writing as chairman of the SIECUS task force on school curricula.

17. Douglas Kirby, *Sexuality Education: An Evaluation of Programs and Their Effects: An Executive Summary* (Santa Cruz, Calif.: ETR Associates, 1984), p. 10. For a more recent statement, see "How to Discuss Sex Without Blushing," *APA Monitor,* vol. 26, November 1995, p. 38.

18. Sprung, p. 55.

19. "Analysis of a Phobia in a Five Year Old Boy" (vol. 10, pp. 3ff.), and "Civilization and Its Discontents" (vol. 21, pp. 59ff.), in Sigmund Freud, *The Standard Edition of the Complete Psychological Works of Sigmund Freud,* trans. James Strachey (London: Hogarth Press, 1955–64).

20. Rubin, pp. 81–84, and Jamie Victoria Ward and Jill McLean Taylor, "Sexuality Education for Immigrant and Minority Students," in *Sexual Cultures and the Construction of Adolescent Identities*, p. 61, are among the few who mention the very obvious point that kids are as likely, if not more likely, to be uneasy when talking with each other about sex as when talking to their parents about it.

21. In 1996 Congress passed a bill providing funds for states if they used "abstinence only" programs. All fifty states applied, though it appears that many are using these programs not in schools but in private and community organizations. See the following articles in the *New York Times:* Abby Goodnough, "Sex Classes Get 4 Million in Federal Aid," January 27, 1998, p. B6; "Sex Education That Teaches Abstinence Wins Support," July 23, 1997, p. A19; Tamar Lewin, "States Slow to Take Aid to Teach Sexual Abstinence," May 8, 1997, pp. A1, 22.

22. *The Teenager's Bill of Rights,* Division of AIDS Program Services, New York City Department of Health, 1991.

23. Kirby, p. 11.

24. Ruth Bell, *Changing Bodies, Changing Lives* (New York: Random House, 1987), p. 115.

25. Alan Guttmacher Institute, *Teenage Pregnancy: The Problem That Hasn't Gone Away* (New York: Guttmacher Institute, 1981).

26. Pipher, p. 255.

27. Search Institute, *Human Sexuality: Values and Choices* (Minneapolis: Search Institute, 1986).

28. Quoted in Joseph Berger, "Proposed AIDS Curriculum Stirs Heated Debate," *New York Times,* June 17, 1992, p. B3.

29. Cited in William Kilpatrick, *Why Johnny Can't Tell Right from Wrong* (New York: Simon & Schuster, 1992), pp. 56–57. "Just Say Know: An Educator's Guide to Helping Young People Make Informed Decisions," from Planned Parenthood of Utah, suggests that students in each other's arms recall the seven steps of the decision-making process, including the following: "Define the problem. Consider all the alternatives. Consider the consequences of each alternative. Consider family and personal values."

30. Quoted in Philip J. Hilts, "Blunt Style on Teen Sex and Health," *New York Times,* September 14, 1993, p. C1.

31. Colleen Kelly Mast, *Sex Respect* (Bradely, Ill.: Respect, 1990).

32. Bell, p. 75.

33. Quoted in Bernice Hirabayashi, "Schools Focus on Sexual Abstinence," *Los Angeles Times,* Sunday Home Edition, October 4, 1992, p. J1. See also Patrick Welsh, "Newt Is Right . . . and So Is Jocelyn: The Safest Sex: Kids Know What Elders Meant," *Washington Post,* December 18, 1994, p. C1.

34. Lauersen and Stukane, p. 160 (see chap. 6, n. 10).

35. Kilpatrick, p. 66. See also Katie Roiphe's description of a Parsippany, New Jersey, class on masturbation in *Last Night in Paradise: Sex and Morals at the Century's End* (Boston: Little, Brown, 1997), pp. 152–162.

36. Alan Guttmacher Institute, *Sex and America's Teenagers* (New York: Guttmacher Institute, 1994), p. 19. Comparable data for men is not available.

37. Ibid., p. 24.

38. Wendy Shalit, "Sex Ed's Dead End," *City Journal,* Spring 1998, pp. 55–56. See also Shalit's *A Return to Modesty* (New York: Free Press, 1999). For research on the importance of the peer group in sexual initiation and the sensitivity of girls to its signals, see Herant Katchadourian, "Sexuality," in *At the Threshold: The Developing Adolescent,* ed. S. Shirley Feldman and Glen R. Elliott (Cambridge: Harvard University Press, 1993), p. 340.

39. See Kay S. Hymowitz, "The Teen Mommy Track," *City Journal,* Autumn 1994, pp. 19–31.

40. Rubin, p. 68.

41. Patricia Hersch, *A Tribe Apart: A Journey into the Heart of American Adolescence* (New York: Fawcett Columbine, 1998), p. 156.

42. Lou Harris and Associates, *America's Teens Speak: Sex, Myths, TV and Birth Control: The Planned Parenthood Poll,* 1986; EDK Associates for *Seventeen* and the Ms. Foundation for Women, *Teenagers Under Pressure,* 1996.

43. These findings are reported and confirmed in Joyce Abma, Anne Driscoll, and Kristin Moore, "Young Women's Degree of Control over First Intercourse: An Exploratory Analysis," *Family Planning Perspectives,* vol. 30, January/February 1998, pp. 12–18.

44. Robert W. Blum and Peggy Mann Rinehart, *Reducing the Risk: Connections That Make a Difference in the Lives of Youth,* Based on Findings from the National Longitudinal Study on Adolescent Health (Bethesda, Md.: Add Health Project c/o Burness Communications, 1997), p. 20. Arland D. Thornton and D. Camburn, "The Influence of the Family on Premarital Sexual Attitudes," *Demography,* vol. 24, 1987, pp. 323–40. For a summary of the research on the subject, see Brent C. Miller, *Families Matter: A Research Synthesis of Family Influences on Adolescent Pregnancy* (Washington, D.C.: National Campaign to Prevent Teen Pregnancy, 1998).

45. See Katchadourian, p. 342. Also see LaWanda Raviola and Andrew L. Cherry Jr., *Social Bonds and Teenage Pregnancy* (Westport, Conn.: Praeger, 1992).

46. Arland D. Thornton and D. Camburn, "Religious Participation and Adolescent Sexual Behavior," *Journal of Marriage and the Family,* vol. 51, 1989, pp. 611–53; M. L. O'Connor, "Religion Plays a Growing Role in White Teenagers' Sexual Decision-Making," *Family Planning Perspectives,* vol. 30, November/December 1998, p. 295.

47. Connie S. Chan, "Asian-American Adolescents: Issues in the Expression of Sexuality," in *Sexual Cultures: The Construction of Adolescent Identities,* p. 92 (see chap. 6, n. 13).

48. Brent C. Miller and Kristin A. Moore, "Adolescent Sexual Behavior, Pregnancy, and Parenting: Research Through the 80's," *Journal of Marriage and the Family,* vol. 52, November 1990, pp. 1028–29.

49. Quoted in Whitehead, p. 64 (see chap. 6, n. 11).

50. Quoted in Grace Palladino, *Teenagers: An American History* (New York: Basic Books, 1996), p. 253.

51. Hymowitz, p. 26.

52. David Elkind, "Understanding the Young Adolescent," *Adolescence,* Spring 1978, p. 127.

53. Rubin, p. 78.

54. The 1998 National Survey of Family Growth reported a decline in sexual activity among teenaged boys and girls and a rise in contraceptive use. See Tamar Lewin, "Youth Pregnancy Rate Falls, Report Says," *New York Times,* October 15, 1998, p. A27.

55. National Campaign to Prevent Teen Pregnancy, *Whatever Happened to Childhood?* (Washington, D.C.: National Campaign, 1997).

56. Mihaly Csikszentmihalyi, Kevin Rathunde, and Samuel Whalen, *Talented Teenagers: The Roots of Success and Failure* (New York: Cambridge University Press, 1993), pp. 246–47.

57. Frank Furstenburg, "As the Pendulum Swings," *Family Relations,* vol. 40, April 1991, p. 134.

58. The most frequently cited scholarship detailing European adolescents' greater access to birth control remains Elise F. Jones et al., *Teenage Pregnancy in Industrialized Countries* (New Haven, Conn.: Yale University Press, 1986).

59. Laurence Wylie, "Youth in France and the United States," in *The Challenge of Youth,* ed. Erik H. Erikson (New York: Doubleday, 1965), p. 292.

60. Denise B. Kandel and Gerald S. Lesser, *Youth in Two Worlds* (San Francisco: Jossey-Bass, 1972).

61. Quoted in Peggy Orenstein, *Schoolgirls: Young Women, Self-Esteem, and the Confidence Gap* (New York: Anchor Books, 1994), p. 54.

62. Pipher, p. 205.

63. Dorothy Baruch, *New Ways in Sex Education: A Guide for Parents and Teachers* (New York: McGraw-Hill, 1959), p. 57.

64. Ann Swidler, "Love and Adulthood in American Culture," reprinted in *Individualism and Commitment in American Life: Readings on the Themes of Habits of the Heart* (New York: Harper & Row, 1987), p. 115. Love is far more important to Westerners as a basis for marriage than it is to people in other parts of the world. See Robert Levine, Suguru Sato, Tsukasa Hashimoto, Jyoti Verma, "Love and Marriage in Eleven Cultures," *Journal of Cross-Cultural Psychology,* vol. 26, September 1995, pp. 554–70. Also Nicholas D. Kristof, "So Who Needs Love! In Japan, Married Couples Survive Without It," *New York Times,* February 11, 1996, pp. 1, 12.

65. "Abstinence education" also fails to take this change in emotional climate into account. Focusing only on prohibiting intercourse without a broad vision of the meaning of sex leads to unintended consequences. It now appears that adolescents, and some very young adolescents at

that, are avoiding sexual intercourse and simply turning to oral sex instead: Mark A. Shuster, Robert M. Bell, and David E. Kanouse, "The Sexual Practices of Adolescent Virgins: Genital Sexual Activities of High School Students Who Have Never Had Vaginal Intercourse," *American Journal of Public Health,* vol. 86, 1996, pp. 1570–76; Ralph Gardner Jr., "Babes in the Woods," *New York Magazine,* April 28, 1997, p. 56.

66. Christopher Lasch, *Women and the Common Life* (New York: Norton, 1997), p. 34.

67. For a different reading of the same phenomenon, see Vivian Gornick, *The End of the Novel of Love* (Boston: Beacon Press, 1997).

68. Sheri Tepper, *The Perils of Puberty* (Denver: Rocky Mountain Planned Parenthood, 1974), p. 15.

69. Ward and Taylor, p. 64 (see chap. 6, n. 20).

70. Pipher, p. 210.

71. Michael Schulman, *Bringing Up a Moral Child* (Reading, Mass.: Addison-Wesley, 1985), p. 290.

72. Ward and Taylor, p. 61.

73. Hersch, p. 286 (see chap. 6, n. 41).

74. Despite the increase in their sexual freedom, high school girls are reporting strikingly lower levels of happiness than they were twenty years ago. See tabulations of Monitoring the Future data by Norval Glenn, reported in Barbara Dafoe Whitehead, "The Girls of Gen X," *American Enterprise,* January/February 1998, p. 55.

75. Wolf, p. 124 (see chap. 6, n. 13).

76. Rubin, p. 73.

77. Rubin, p. 84.

78. Pipher, p. 247.

79. See Hymowitz (chap. 6, n. 39) and Francis A. J. Ianni, *The Search for Structure: A Report on Youth Today* (New York: Free Press, 1989), pp. 80ff.

80. Orenstein, pp. 120ff.

81. "Hostile Hallways," a Lou Harris poll commissioned by the American Association of University Women, 1993.

82. Arthur Levine, *When Hope and Fear Collide: A Portrait of Today's College Student* (San Francisco: Jossey-Bass, 1998), p. 93. See also Anne Matthews, *Bright College Years: Inside the American Campus Today* (New York: Simon & Schuster, 1997), pp. 88ff. In this spirit Connecticut College president Claire Guadiani proposed in 1996 transforming Valentine's Day ("It's just so focused on personal relations") into a celebration of community service ("to let our neighbors know we love

them"). "A Question for Claire Gaudiani," *New York Times Magazine,* February 11, 1996, p. 15.

83. David Denby, *Great Books: My Adventures with Homer, Rousseau, Woolf and Other Indestructible Writers of the Western World* (New York: Simon & Schuster, 1996), p. 405.

84. Konigsberg, p. 105 (see chap. 6, n. 1).

85. Roiphe, p. 93 (see chap. 6, n. 35).

86. Mark Oppenheimer, "Sex and Man at Yale," *Playboy,* November, 1998, p. 161.

87. Levine, p. 111.

88. Trip Gabriel, "Pack Dating: For a Good Time, Call a Crowd," *New York Times,* Education Life, January 5, 1997, pp. 22, 23.

89. Study from Harvard School of Public Health, cited in Gabriel, p. 38. Although heavy drinking has risen among both sexes in recent decades, the most striking increase has come from women. Since the mid-1970s, their rates have tripled and now nearly equal those of men. Brooke A. Masters, "Women Drinking Like Men, College Alcohol Study Finds," *Washington Post,* June 8, 1994, p. A1.

90. Levine, p. 106. Levine found that only 49 percent of his sexually active subjects said they always used a condom, whether sober or not (p. 112). Matthews cites similar findings (p. 89).

91. Paul Amato and Alan Booth, *A Generation at Risk: Growing Up in an Era of Family Upheaval* (Cambridge: Harvard University Press, 1997), pp. 118–19.

92. Konigsberg, p. 100.

93. Gabriel, p. 22.

94. Roiphe, p. 27.

95. Quoted in "Perspective," *Chicago Tribune,* March 1, 1994, p. 19. For an overview of college sexual harassment codes, see Alan Charles Kors and Harvey A. Silvergate, *Shadow University: The Betrayal of Liberty on America's Campuses* (New York: Free Press, 1998), pp. 92–96, 154–55.

96. Roiphe, p. 188.

Chapter 7: Postmodern Postadolescence

1. Elizabeth Wurtzel, *Prozac Nation* (New York: Riverhead Books, 1994), p. 341.

2. Marlis Buchmann, *The Script of Life in Modern Society: Entry into Adulthood in a Changing World* (Chicago: University of Chicago, 1989) is the most extensive study of postadolescence as it first appeared. See

also Thomas Held, "Institutionalization and Deinstitutionalization of the Life Course," *Human Development,* vol. 29 (1986), pp. 157–70.

3. The United States Department of Census reports 58 percent of 22-to-24-year-olds, 30 percent of 25-to-29-year-olds, and 23 percent of 30-to-34-year-olds living with their parents. See also "Feathered Nest/Gilded Cage," *Demography,* August 1992; Marcia Mogelonsky, "The Rocky Road to Adulthood," *American Demographics,* May 1996; Susan Litwin, *The Postponed Generation: Why America's Grown-Up Kids Are Growing Up Later* (New York: Morrow, 1986). For the view that postadolescence is almost entirely a product of economics, see David Lipsky and Alexander Abrams, *Late Bloomers: Coming of Age in Today's America: The Right Place at the Wrong Time* (New York: Times Books, 1994).

4. Department of Education, *The Digest of Education Statistics* (Washington, D.C.: GPO, 1995). The figure on graduation rates is from American College Testing (ACT), 1996.

5. "Marital Status and Living Arrangements," *Current Population Reports,* P20-514, U.S. Bureau of the Census, Washington, D.C., 1998.

6. Quoted in Mogelonsky, p. 28.

7. Katie Roiphe, "A Grandmother's Biological Clock," *New York Times Magazine,* February 9, 1998, p. 80.

8. Cynde Miller, "Marketing to the Disillusioned," *Marketing News,* July 6, 1992, p. 7.

9. Alexander Astin et al., *The American Freshman: Thirty Year Trends* (Los Angeles: Higher Education Research Institute, 1997), pp. 28–29.

10. Ibid., p. 28.

11. The Age of Indifference, cited in Alan Deutschman, "The Upbeat Generation," *Fortune,* July 13, 1992, p. 42.

12. Katie Roiphe, *Last Night in Paradise* (Boston: Little, Brown, 1996), pp. 30–31.

13. Roiphe, *Paradise,* p. 141.

14. Barbara Dafoe Whitehead and David Popenoe, *Why Wed? Young Adults Talk About Sex, Love and First Unions* (New Brunswick, N.J.: National Marriage Project, 1998).

15. David Popenoe and Barbara Dafoe Whitehead, *Should We Live Together? What Young Adults Need to Know About Cohabitation Before Marriage* (New Brunswick, N.J.: National Marriage Project, 1999).

16. Lipsky and Abrams, p. 146.

17. Candace Bushnell, *Sex in the City* (New York: Atlantic Monthly Press, 1996), p. 2.

18. Barbara Dafoe Whitehead, "The Girls of Gen X," *The American Enterprise,* January/February 1998, p. 58.

19. Bushnell, p. 5.

20. The history outlined in the following paragraph follows Gerard Jones, *Honey I'm Home! Sitcoms: Selling the American Dream* (New York: Grove Weidenfeld, 1992), pp. 184ff and chap. 14.

21. Quoted in Jones, p. 201

22. Quoted in Gerri Hirshey, "David Schwimmer," *GQ,* March 1996, p. 234.

23. Erik H. Erikson, *Childhood and Society,* 2nd ed. (New York: Norton, 1962), p. 267.

24. Laurel Kendall, *Getting Married in Korea: Of Gender, Morality and Modernity* (Berkeley: University of California Press, 1996), p. 7. Elsewhere the author remarks that when female anthropologists ask women in more traditional societies, "Why do you marry?" their subjects find the question laughable. "The question for them is like asking, 'Why do you get older?'"

25. Michael Mitterauer, *A History of Youth* (Cambridge, Eng.: Blackwell, 1993), p. 79. The only exceptions to the rule that marriage equals adulthood are the cultures, such as in parts of India, where the married person remains a child to his parents or in-laws.

26. Mitterauer, pp. 79, 165.

27. Elaine Tyler May, *Barren in a Promised Land: Childless Americans and the Pursuit of Happiness* (New York: Basic Books, 1995). Witches, who were sometimes accused of causing stillbirths and miscarriages, have almost always been childless older women; their uncertain status evidently made them seem dangerous.

28. Kendall, p. 7

29. Clifford Geertz and Hildred Geertz, *Kinship in Bali* (Chicago: University of Chicago Press, 1975), p. 90.

30. Lawrence Stone, *The Family, Sex, and Marriage in England 1500–1800* (New York: Harper & Row, 1979), p. 44; Peter Laslett, *The World We Have Lost: England Before the Industrial Age* (New York: Scribner's, 1965), pp. 82–83.

31. Even when living far from home, youth were expected to contribute some of their pay to their families and were supposed to help out in case of injury, layoffs, and death. See John Modell, Frank F. Furstenberg Jr., and Theodore Hershberg, "Social Change and Transitions to Adulthood in Historical Perspective," *Journal of Family History I,* vol. 1, 1976, pp. 29–30; John R. Gillis, *Youth and History: Tradition and*

Change in European Age Relations, 1770–Present (New York: Academic Press, 1981). Also see Mitterauer, pp. 162ff.

32. Norval D. Glenn, *Closed Hearts, Closed Minds: The Textbook Story of Marriage* (New York: Institute for American Values, 1997), p. 3.

33. See Lipsky and Abrams, chap. 3; their discussion of this theme is similar to mine.

34. This information came from an interview with Stephanie Ventura, demographer at the National Center for Health Statistics, March 23, 1999.

35. Gail Sheehy, *Passages: Predictable Crises of Adult Life* (New York: Dutton, 1976), pp. 21, 251.

36. Robert Jay Lifton, *The Protean Self: Human Resilience in an Age of Fragmentation* (New York: Basic Books, 1993), p. 1.

37. Barbara Dafoe Whitehead, *The Divorce Culture* (New York: Knopf, 1997), p. 90.

38. Joseph Epstein, "My 1950's," *Commentary,* September 1993, p. 39.

39. Quoted in Barbara Ehrenreich, *The Hearts of Men: American Dreams and the Flight From Commitment* (New York: Anchor, 1984), p. 17.

40. Quoted in Hilary De Vries, "Peter Pan for the New-Age 90's," *New York Times,* Arts and Leisure Section, December 8, 1991, p. 13.

41. John Bradshaw, *Homecoming: Reclaiming and Championing Your Inner Child* (New York: Bantam Books, 1990), p. 92.

42. Ellen Bass and Laura Davis, *Courage to Heal: A Guide for Women Survivors of Child Sexual Abuse* (New York: Harper & Row, 1988), p. 113.

43. Douglas Rushkoff, *Playing the Future: How Kids' Culture Can Teach Us to Thrive in an Age of Chaos* (New York: Harper Collins, 1996), p. 105.

44. Seymour Papert, *The Children's Machine: Rethinking School in the Age of the Computer* (New York: Basic Books, 1993), p. 33.

45. Peter F. Drucker, *The Age of Discontinuity: Guidelines to Our Changing Society* (New York: Harper & Row, 1968).

46. Rosabeth Moss Kanter, *When Giants Learn to Dance: Mastering the Challenge of Strategy, Management, and Careers in the 1990s* (New York: Simon & Schuster, 1989), p. 365.

47. Figure from Richard Belous, "The Contingent Economy," National Policy Association, 1998, quoted in Carl T. Camden, "Free Agents by Choice," *New Democrat,* March/April 1998, p. 16.

48. Quoted in "Special Strategies for Continuing Education," *New York Times,* Special Advertising Supplement, April 24, 1996. The University of Phoenix is an institution entirely geared toward working

adults. See Ethan Bronner, "University for Working Adults Shatters Mold," *New York Times,* October 15, 1997, pp. A1, B8.

49. Sam Roberts, *Who We Are: A Portrait of America Based on the Latest U.S. Census* (New York: Times Books, 1993) p. 227; Department of Education, National Center for Education Statistics, *Digest of Education Statistics, 1996,* NCES96-133 (Washington D.C.: GPO, 1996).

50. Kanter, p. 361.

51. Drucker, p. 305.

52. Quoted in Thomas Frank, *The Conquest of Cool* (Chicago: University of Chicago Press, 1997), p. 120. The following material on advertising in the early sixties comes from Frank, chaps. 1, 6.

53. Thomas Doherty, *Teenagers and Teenpics: The Juvenilization of the Movies* (Boston: Unwin Hyman, 1988).

54. Quoted in Karen de Witt, "Burning at Both Ends, Boomers Turn 50," *New York Times,* November 13, 1966, p. C3.

55. Judith Martin, *You Make Me Feel So Old,* Working Paper #54 (New York: Institute for American Values, 1997).

56. Mary Hatwood Futrell, "Public Schools and Four-Year-Olds," *American Psychologist,* vol. 42, March 1987, p. 251.

57. Quoted in Sylvia Anne Hewlett, *Breaking the Bough: The Cost of Neglecting Our Children* (New York: Basic Books, 1991), p. 186.

Conclusion: Refilling the Nest

1. Alan Wolfe, *One Nation, After All* (New York: Viking, 1998), p. 116.

2. Dale Russakoff, "On Children's TV: An Unusual New Character: Cool Parents; Shows Tap into a Longing for Adult Company," *Washington Post,* December 13, 1998, p. A1.

3. Katie Roiphe, "Campus Climate Control" *New York Times,* March 5, 1999, p. A21.

4. Ethan Bronner, "In a Revolution of Rules, Campuses Go Full Circle," *New York Times,* March 3, 1999, pp. A1, 15.

5. Stephan Helman, principal of the George Fischer Middle School in Carmel, New York. Interview with the author, July 1998.

6. See Daniel Goleman, *Emotional Intelligence* (New York: Bantam, 1995).

7. S. Shirley Feldman and Doreen A. Rosenthal, "Culture Makes a Difference . . . or Does It?" *Adolescence in Context: The Interplay of Family, School, Peers and Work in Adjustment,* ed. Rainer K. Silbereisen and Eberhard Todt (New York: Springer-Verlag, 1994), p. 105.

8. Cited in Nick Ravo, "Nation's Index of Well-Being Is at Lowest in 25 Years," *New York Times,* October 14, 1996, p. A11. Incidentally, the conventional wisdom that Japanese teenagers are highly stressed and commit suicide at high rates can be put to rest; American teens are worse off in both respects. David Crystal et al., "Psychological Maladjustment and Academic Achievement: A Cross-Cultural Study of Japanese, Chinese, and American High School Students," *Child Development,* vol. 65, 1994, pp. 738–53.

9. Arthur Levine, *When Hope and Fear Collide: A Portrait of Today's College Student* (San Francisco: Jossey-Bass, 1998), p. 95.

10. Levine, pp. 95, 96.

11. Elizabeth Wurtzel, "The Void That Even the Safest College Can't Fill," *New York Times,* March 13, 1999, p. A21.

12. Norval D. Glenn, "Values, Attitudes, and the State of American Marriage," *Promises to Keep: Decline and Renewal of Marriage in America,* ed. David Popenoe, Jean Bethke Elshtain, and David Blankenhorn (Lanham, Md.: Roman Littlefield, 1996), pp. 15–33.

13. See, for instance, the books and Web sites of James Dobson and John Rosemond, two of the most popular of the new disciplinarians.

Index